Studies in Miscue Analysis:
An Annotated Bibliography

Joel Brown
University of Arizona
Tucson, Arizona

Kenneth S. Goodman
University of Arizona
Tucson, Arizona

Ann M. Marek
Nevada Department of Education
Carson City, Nevada

INTERNATIONAL
**Reading
Association**

800 Barksdale Road, PO Box 8139
Newark, Delaware 19714-8139, USA

Director of Publications   Joan M. Irwin
Assistant Director of Publications   Wendy Lapham Russ
Senior Editor   Christian A. Kempers
Associate Editor   Matthew W. Baker
Assistant Editor   Janet S. Parrack
Editorial Assistant   Cynthia C. Sawaya
Production Department Manager   Iona Sauscermen
Graphic Design Coordinator   Boni Nash
Design Consultant   Larry F. Husfelt
Desktop Publishing Supervisor   Wendy A. Mazur
Desktop Publisher   Anette Schütz-Ruff
Desktop Publisher   Cheryl J. Strum
Production Services Editor   David K. Roberts

Library of Congress Cataloging in Publication Data
    Studies in miscue analysis: An annotated bibliography/Joel Brown, Kenneth S. Goodman, Ann M. Marek, editors.
        p.   cm.
    Includes indexes.
    1. Miscue analysis—Bibliography.   I. Brown, Joel.   II. Goodman, Kenneth S. III. Marek, Ann M
Z5818.L3S88   1996
[LB1050.33]
016.4284—dc20   96-24993
ISBN 0-87207-238-X

CONTENTS

ABBREVIATIONS:

The following abbreviations are used to classify documents in this bibliography:

ED   Educational Resources Information Center (ERIC) number for documents on microfiche.

EJ   Current Index to Journals in Education number refers to published articles that have abstracts in the ERIC database.

UMI   University microfilm.

PREFACE

M Y RESEARCH on the reading process did not start out as an analysis of reading miscues. In 1962, I set out to see if I could study reading as a language process using what little knowledge of linguistics I had at the time. My design was simple, if naive. I decided that I would have young readers read whole texts, comparable to those that they might encounter in school. Had I known more about linguistics I would have realized how complex natural language texts are and how difficult it would be to analyze a child's reading of even a short text.

The texts I chose were from a basal reader series edited by Emmett Betts. I chose them because Betts was one of the leading reading authorities of the time and because they were a series not used in the school where I was working. I wanted the stories to be unfamiliar to my young readers. By choosing selections from pre-primer to eighth grade books in this series, I had a sequence of stories that an authoritative group had determined to be of increasing reading difficulty. Since I used stories wide apart from one another in the series I felt I was justified in my assumption of increasing difficulty, though even then I had questions about readability formulas and controlled vocabulary in basals.

The procedure I used then, with a few refinements over the years, is similar to most current miscue research. It is the analysis that has become increasingly sophisticated and complex. I had each pupil read a complete selection from the original book, orally and privately, with only a research associate or me present. I tape recorded the reading while I marked down on a typescript everything that *I was aware* the reader did or said. I have highlighted *I was aware* because I soon realized that I needed to listen to the tape carefully to be fully aware of everything the reader did or said. And over the years, as I (and others) became more knowledgeable about the reading process, we became more aware of the complex things our readers were doing. After the reading, the reader was asked to retell the story. In time our sophistication in eliciting a retelling also became more effective.

There really was an "Aha!" moment of discovery with miscue analysis. It happened within the first naive analysis of the first subject of the first pilot study (funded only with seed money; $200 from Wayne State University). I suppose I had expected that, in their oral reading, my young subjects would give me some indications of their linguistic knowledge of the English language in their reading. But I had not expected that the evidence I was looking for would be richly abundant in their reading errors and not nearly so evident when they read accurately. "Aha!" I said (or more colorful words to that effect). Just as young children learning to speak show their growing control over the grammar of their language by their "errors," such as "I taked it" or "Me wanna dink," readers use the same process for producing their errors as they do for their accurate reading. By comparing their observed oral responses to the text with the expected responses that would appear accurate to a listener I had a continuous window on their reading. I could see the process of reading at work!

But now I had a problem. I was aware of a body of earlier research that had been done on reading errors. However, unlike my research that started as exploration of reading as a language process, this error research was motivated by the notion that if common reading errors could be catalogued, then they could be eliminated through drill and practice until the readers became accurate. Error was thus defined as bad reading to be eradicated, and good reading was defined as accurate.

But even these first few miscues showed the readers' linguistic strength. When a pre-primer reader substituted "ride" for "run" after omitting "run" the first two times it occurred, that showed possible use of grammatical knowledge. When another reader read "the" instead of "a" the reader showed awareness of the need for a determiner in a common noun phrase. Another reader read "train" for "toy." The errors my first subjects were making showed they were using their knowledge of language to make sense of the printed text.

But if I continued to use the term "error," teachers and other researchers might continue to think of them as simply wrong rather than resulting from the language strengths of the learners. In deciding to call them miscues, I did not coin the word "miscue." I had already begun to talk about the cue systems of language. If language provides cues that readers use, then why not call these unexpected responses "miscues." It was a term I knew was in use in the theater. And it had the advantage that it implied cue use rather than random error. Every so often in our search for early precursors of miscue analysis we find references to awareness by others who have studied reading before miscue analysis began. Here is an example:

> In introspective-retrospective case studies and in models, reading is represented as a dynamic, complex process in which the reader is actively engaged in a search for meaning. Moreover, the success of this search depends to a considerable degree upon the selection of appropriate language clues. This selection process, particularly as described in the studies of Swain (1953) and Jenkinson (1957), is remarkably similar to the "psycholinguistic guessing game" postulated by Goodman (1970), even to Swain's use of the term "miscue" (p. 188) to describe an incorrect response in the reader's search for meaning. (W. John Harker in the Twenty-third Yearbook of the National Reading Conference, 1974, pp. 93)

The first article I published in which I used the term miscue was "A linguistic study of cues and miscues in reading" (Oct. 1965). Out of that work grew two assumptions that still underlie miscue analysis.

- Miscues are never random
- Unexpected responses result from the same process as expected responses

A simple definition of a miscue also emerged.

> A miscue is a point in reading where the expected response (ER) and the observed response (OR) are not the same: ER ≠ OR.

My research for the next decade or so (1965–1978) and that of my associates focused on exploration of the reading process. In the course of that research, we looked at readers of varying proficiency, in varying texts, and in various populations. Our goal was a better understanding of the reading process, a more complete theory of reading, and a taxonomy of miscue analysis appropriate to all readers (Goodman 1969). Miscue analysis has always been the basis for the transactional view of reading I developed, and in turn the model of reading makes the understanding of the miscues possible. One problem with attempts to develop simple forms of miscue analysis is that they are often made without an underlying theory of the reading process.

As miscue analysis became more commonly understood, it was then used with second language readers of English, with readers of other languages, and with special populations. My own research involved black and white speakers of several dialects in the Detroit area. This expanded to a study of readers of stable rural dialects.

During the course of several major miscue studies with my colleagues, I developed a large database of several hundred readers reading one or more texts. That made possible a series of studies that focused on particular phenomena in or across populations. It also made it possible to do studies of how texts influence miscue patterns by looking at the same text read by many readers.

Yetta Goodman and Carolyn Burke developed the Reading Miscue Inventory (1972) to make it possible to use miscue analysis in teacher education, in clinical settings, and in classrooms as a means of revaluing the reading process. Subsequently, many research studies have used the RMI rather than the more complete taxonomy. Dorothy Watson joined them in 1987 to produce an expanded and updated version of the RMI that offered alternative procedures for different uses of miscue analysis.

In the early years of miscue analysis research, the method had to be defended frequently because it did not use the experimental, hypothecated, quantitative designs popular among reading researchers. We referred to the research as qualitative since it focused in depth on the quality of miscues rather than simply on their number. Informal reading inventories, in contrast with miscue analysis, count errors in simple paragraphs but do not get into the complexity of the miscues. But miscue analysis produces large quantities of data. In the miscue taxonomy, 28 questions are answered about each miscue and each question has a range of data possibilities. Contingency tables can be constructed comparing the coding of each pair of variables. And coefficients of concordance can be used to test the significance of the relationships. Because miscue analysis produces so much data, it is common to study small numbers of subjects: 3 to 10. It produces in-depth views of small numbers of readers compared to the shallow information that experimental studies with large numbers of subjects but few data points produce.

Over time the research uses of miscue analysis have shifted from support and refinement of the model of reading to incidental use of miscue analysis as an established procedure for close examination of reading while studying other issues. In this expanded use of miscue analysis in research, diagnosis, evaluation, teacher education, and classroom practice, miscue analysis has taken on many forms and has been used by people with varying levels of knowledge and specific courses in miscue analysis. There is no way that my colleagues or I could have controlled what is done in the name of miscue analysis nor would we have wanted to do so. Knowledge and ideas cannot be patented, and copyright cannot protect them from misunderstanding and misuse.

One force that has surely shaped the use of miscue analysis in research studies is the dissertation process. Often the doctoral student works with a committee unfamiliar with miscue analysis and with psycholinguistic views of reading. Committee members may push the researcher to use too many subjects and inappropriate designs and statistical analysis.

For a variety of reasons, there is a renewed interest in miscue analysis at this time. One reason may be the number of knowledgeable teachers and administrators looking for authentic assessment tools. Whole language teachers want to look at their pupils reading in real texts rather than tests. Reading specialists are also looking for sophisticated ways of looking positively at the strengths as well as the needs of readers.

One purpose of compiling this annotated bibliography is to make it possible for educators, researchers, and others to access the many published books and articles and unpublished ERIC documents and dissertations that deal with or use miscue analysis. We hope that the bibliography will contribute to the quality of use of miscue analysis as people become aware of what other reading educators are doing.

The future of miscue analysis

I believe that as more teachers come to think of themselves as kid-watchers, there will be a great expansion of uses of informal forms of miscue analysis by classroom teachers in reading conferences with their pupils and in casual ongoing observation.

It may be that the most important research with miscue analysis lies ahead. Though we, as a profession, have a good basic understanding of how people make sense through written language, as readers and writers, there is much yet to be learned. Particularly, it is possible to look more completely at how meaning is constructed in reading using concepts from reader response theory, from Halliday's systemic linguistics, and from Piaget and Vygotsky. We need to know more about how readers handle different genre, and we need to know more about reading in the world's languages, both alphabetic and nonalphabetic.

The phenomenon of miscue making is not confined to reading. But oral reading offers a unique opportunity to study language processing because of the continuous window it offers for comparison of expected and observed responses. I believe that those interested in psycholinguistic and sociolinguistic processes, in disruption of language in aphasia and brain damage, and in human learning will find miscue analysis a powerful tool.

How the bibliography is organized

The main, annotated body of this bibliography is organized chronologically. Harold Herber in his historical chapter in the fourth edition of *Theoretical Models and Processes of Reading*

(1994) talks about the rolling history of much professional literature. Few articles cite authorities older than 10 years, and almost no citations are over 20 years old. We thought it was important in organizing an inclusive miscue analysis bibliography to present the literature in the order in which it was published. That will help users of the bibliography put things in historical context.

An author index and a subject index are also provided. Within each subject in the subject index, entries are alphabetic by author's name. Users may want to go first to the subject heading and then find the full entries in the chronological list.

Though our intent has been to be inclusive, we also exercised some judgment to avoid redundancy and to avoid inclusion of superficial, uninformed, or grossly inappropriate material. We would not claim, however, that we have not somehow missed anything that should have been included. We intend to continuously update this bibliography, so please help us to be inclusive and up-to-date by sending us nominations that were missed or that have been published since this book was published.

Ken Goodman

PART 1

1898–1964

1898–1939

IREDELL, HARRIET (1898, December). Eleanor learns to read. *Education, 19*(4), 233–238.

> An early description and comment on how children learn to read in the same way they learn to talk—without formal instruction. Reprinted October 1987 in *Language Arts, 59*(7), 668–671.

THORNDIKE, EDWARD L. (1917, June). Reading as reasoning: A study of mistakes in paragraph reading. *Journal of Educational Psychology, 8*(6), 323–332.

> Reprinted in 1971 in *Reading Research Quarterly, 6*(4), 425–434, with accompanying commentary. This early article advocates reading for meaning.

MONROE, MARION (1928, October). Methods for diagnosis and treatment of cases of reading disability. *Genetic Psychology Monographs, 4*(4–5), 334–456.

> Classic study in reading; includes error counts and analysis used to distinguish "retarded" and "normal" readers.

PITKIN, WALTER BROUGHTON (1929). *The art of rapid reading: A book for people who want to read faster and more accurately.* New York: McGraw-Hill.

> An early speed reading book; includes the quote: "In a sense, then, all reading is a guessing game. If you guess the general subject matter and the drift of the writer's remarks, you readily fit the right meaning to the right marks on the page. And if you cannot guess it, then you are lost" (p. 38).

PAYNE, CASSIE SPENCER (1930, October). The classification of errors in oral reading. *Elementary School Journal, 31*(2), 142–146.

> An early study of oral reading errors, using words in isolation as well as in context.

MONROE, MARION (1932). *Children who cannot read: The analysis of reading disabilities and the use of diagnostic tests in the instruction of retarded readers.* Chicago, IL: University of Chicago Press.

> An early attempt to qualitatively study oral reading errors that looks at letter and word level errors.

DAVIDSON, HELEN P. (1934). A study of reversals in young children. *Journal of Genetic Psychology, 45*(1), 452–464.

> Finds that the number of word reversals made by young children varies inversely with mental age and that some children recognize words presented upside down.

REED, H.B. (1938, September). Meaning as a factor in learning. *Journal of Educational Psychology, 29*(6), 419–430.

> Raises questions about the interpretation of behavioristic research, because results differ when meaningful materials are used. Reprinted in the same journal in December 1992, 84(4), 395–399.

1940–1964

MADDEN, MABLE, & PRATT, MARGORIE (1941, April). An oral reading survey as a teaching aid. *Elementary English Review, 18*(4), 122–126, 159.

> An early study of the reading errors of 1,154 third to ninth graders. The author's mix of comprehension and word accuracy concerns produce a set of contradictory instructional suggestions.

ARTLEY, A. STERL (1943, February). Teaching word-meaning through context. *Elementary English Review, 20*(2), 68–74.

> An early study of contextual factors in reading from typographical to structural to inference to background experience.

MCCULLOUGH, CONSTANCE M. (1943, April). Learning to use context clues. *Elementary English Review, 20*(4), 140–143.

> A concurrent study to Artley's that examines the contextual aspects of written language in learning new words. This example of early cloze procedure looks at guessing words from similes and synonyms through background experience of the reader.

MORGAN, C.L., & BAILEY, WILBERT L. (1943, December). The effect of context on learning a vocabulary. *Journal of Educational Psychology, 34*(9), 561–565.

> An experimental study using artificial words to assess the effects of context on dictionary use, translation time, or recall.

SEIBERT, LOUISE C. (1945, April). A study on the practice of guessing word meanings from context. *Modern Language Journal, 29*(4), 296–322.

> French language students are given Spanish word lists and passages and are assessed for how they translate unknown words. Translation categories are: known, etymologically defined, contextually defined, incorrect, and omitted. For context alone it is found 31% to 71% can be obtained by inference from the context.

SHANNON, CLAUDE E. (1951). Prediction and entropy of printed English. *Bell System Technical Journal, 30,* 50–64.

> Describes an advance in mathematical assessment of language predictability. At the letter level a 50% predictability of the following letter had previously been found for English. In a new study using a 100 letter string, to include phrase and sentence level influences, the new finding is that for a speaker of a language the predictability of the following letter is 75%.

SWAIN, EMELIZA. (1953). *Conscious thought processes used in the interpretation of reading materials.* Unpublished doctoral dissertation, University of Chicago, Chicago, IL.

> A study of college freshmen that finds readers' central focus to be on meaning interpretation.

CHOMSKY, NOAM (1959, January). Review of Skinner's verbal behavior. *Language, 35*(1), 26–58.

> A critique of the behaviorist interpretation of verbal behavior that occludes the active contributions of the language user. Chomsky says, "The study of the actual observed ability of a speaker to distinguish sentences from non-sentences, detect ambiguities, etc., apparently forces us to the conclusion that this grammar is of an extremely complex and abstract character, and that the young child has succeeded in carrying out what from the formal point of view, at least, seems to be a remarkable type of theory construction" (pp. 57).

FREUD, SIGMUND. (1960). Misreadings and slips of the pen. In J. Strachey (Ed. and Trans.), The standard edition of the complete psychological works of Sigmund Freud (Vol. 6, pp. 106–133). London: Hogarth Press. (Original work published 1916)

> A survey of personal and collected examples of miscues. Special emphasis is placed on semantics and background experiences. The notion of a pathology is undermined through Freud's own comments, such as "In this case the disturbing thought can scarcely be called an objectionable one."

WEAVER, WENDELL W. (1962). The predictability of omission in reading and listening. In E.P. Bliesmer & R.C. Staiger (Eds.), *Problems, programs, and projects in college-adult reading* (Eleventh Yearbook of the National Reading Conference, pp. 148–153). Milwaukee, WI: National Reading Conference.

> Discusses redundancy in language and covers views on the separateness of syntactic and semantic information.

GOODMAN, KENNETH S. (1964, April). The linguistics of reading. *Elementary School Journal*, 64(8), 355–361.

> Discusses how linguistics has been interpreted and misinterpreted for educators and classroom practice. Contributions and important generalizations are listed.

PART 2

1965–1969

1965

BURKE, CAROLYN L. (1965). *A study of some initial reading errors in experience chart and textbook reading made by children with deviant dialects*. Unpublished master's thesis, Wayne State University, Detroit, MI.

> An early examination of the use of the Goodman taxonomy in different classroom contexts.

GOODMAN, KENNETH S. (1965, October). A linguistic study of cues and miscues in reading. *Elementary English*, 42(6), 639–643.

> An early miscue study in which the author looks at reading of words in and out of context, finding that even first graders can read many words in context that they cannot recognize on lists.

GOODMAN, KENNETH S. (1965, December). Dialect barriers to reading comprehension. *Elementary English*, 42(8), 853–860.

> Discusses dialect relationship to reading.

1966

CLAY, MARIE M. (1966). *Emergent reading behavior*. Unpublished doctoral dissertation, University of Auckland, Auckland, New Zealand.

> Systematic analysis of the errors of 5-year-old readers analyzing semantic and syntactic acceptability and correction strategies among other phenomena.

GOODMAN, KENNETH S. (1966). A psycholinguistic view of reading comprehension. In G.B. Schick & M.M. May (Eds.), *New frontiers in college-adult reading*. (Fifteenth Yearbook of the

National Reading Conference, pp. 188–196). Milwaukee, WI: National Reading Conference.

An early overview of the Goodman Model of Reading.

1967

CLAY, MARIE M. (1967). The reading behavior of five year old children: A research project. *New Zealand Journal of Educational Studies*, 2, 11–31.

Reports the same study as her 1966 report.

GOODMAN, KENNETH S. (1967a). Reading: A psycholinguistic guessing game. *Journal of the Reading Specialist*, 6(4), 126–135.

Discusses the selective process of reading and the use of miscues in reading analysis.

GOODMAN, KENNETH S. (1967b). Word perception: Linguistic bases. *Education*, 87(9), 539–543.

A discussion of the historical and modern notions of "word," with explanation of the problems of limiting reading to a word level.

GOODMAN, YETTA M. (1967). *A psycholinguistic description of observed oral reading phenomena in selected young beginning readers*. Unpublished doctoral dissertation, Wayne State University, Detroit, MI. (UMI No. AAC 68-9961)

The author uses miscue analysis to trace the reading development in six young beginning readers over an 11-month period and generates hypotheses for future research.

1968

CLAY, MARIE M. (1968). A syntactic analysis of reading errors. *Journal of Verbal Learning and Verbal Behavior*, 7(2), 434–438.

The analysis of 100 children's (age 5) reading substitutions shows evidence of self-correction behavior guided by syntactic rather than phoneme-grapheme relationships.

CURTIS, WILLIAM J. (1968). *An analysis of the relationship of illustration and text in picture story books as indicated by the oral responses of young children.* Unpublished doctoral dissertation, Wayne State University, Detroit, MI. (UMI No. AAC 69-14665)

Compares the retelling with and without picture books to determine what the readers use as cues.

GOODMAN, KENNETH S. (1968). The psycholinguistic nature of the reading process. In K.S. Goodman (Ed.), *The psycholinguistic nature of the reading process*, (pp. 13–28). Detroit, MI: Wayne State University Press.

Discusses proficiency in the reading process and how the cuing systems interact during reading.

GOODMAN, KENNETH S. (1968, April). Linguistic insights which teachers may apply. *Education*, *88*(4), 313–316.

An early statement of linguistic knowledge needed by teachers.

GOODMAN, KENNETH S., & BURKE, CAROLYN L. (1968, March). *Study of children's behavior while reading orally* (Final Report, Project No. S 425). Washington, DC: U.S. Department of Health, Education, and Welfare, Office of Education. (ED 021 698)

First funded miscue study.

WEBER, ROSE MARIE (1968, Fall). The study of oral reading errors: A survey of the literature. *Reading Research Quarterly*, *4*(1), 96–119.

Reviews how miscues are analyzed in more than 30 early research studies.

1969

ALLEN, P. DAVID (1969). *A psycholinguistic analysis of the substitution of miscues of selected oral readers in grades 2, 4, and 6 and the relationships of these miscues to the reading process, a descriptive study.* Unpublished doctoral dissertation, Wayne State University, Detroit, MI. (UMI No. AAC 70-03414)

> Recommends syntactically and semantically acceptable miscues not be corrected by teachers; oral reading should be kept to a minimum; and reading material should be real language.

BURKE, CAROLYN L. (1969). *A psycholinguistic description of grammatical restructurings in the oral reading of a selected group of middle school children.* Unpublished doctoral dissertation, Wayne State University, Detroit, MI. (UMI No. AAC 70-3416)

> Concludes that the use of the transformational grammar concept of deep and surface structures (with consideration for interrelationship between meaning and structure) offers a sound basis for analysis of miscues.

CLAY, MARIE M. (1969, February). Reading errors and self-correction behavior. *British Journal of Educational Psychology, 39*(1), 47–56.

> An exploration of self-corrections in 5-year-old children links information processing strategies developed by children to intuitive rather than logical thinking.

GOODMAN, KENNETH S. (1969a). Analysis of oral reading miscues: Applied psycholinguistics. *Reading Research Quarterly, 5*(1), 9–30.

> Presents the theoretical argument that reading must be considered a psycholinguistic process. The article also analyzes oral reading phenomena.

GOODMAN, KENNETH S. (1969b). Words and morphemes in reading. In K.S. Goodman & J.S. Fleming, *Psycholinguistics and the teaching of reading* (pp. 25–33). Newark, DE: International Reading Association. (ED 074 446)

> Discusses the relationship of words to meaning.

GOODMAN, KENNETH S. (1969c). A psycholinguistic approach to reading: Implications for the mentally retarded. *Journal on the Education of Backward Children, 16*, 85–90.

> A discussion of reading and intelligence in an Australian journal.

GOODMAN, KENNETH S. (1969d). What's new in curriculum. *Nation's Schools, 84*(2), 38–40.

> A look at four views influencing curriculum development. Notes the beginning of change in basal materials.

GOODMAN, KENNETH S. (1969, April). Linguistics in a relevant curriculum. *Education, 89*(4), 303–306.

> Discusses the necessary linguistic base for a curriculum relevant to all language learners.

GOODMAN, KENNETH S. (1969, October). Let's dump the uptight model in English. *Elementary School Journal, 70*(1), 1–13.

> A discussion of dialect and language use with an analysis of dialect attitudes and suggestions for teachers.

GOODMAN, KENNETH S. (1969, December). On valuing diversity in language. *Childhood Education, 46*(3), 123–126.

> Argues that linguistic diversity in children's language should be cherished.

GOODMAN, KENNETH S., & BURKE, CAROLYN L. (1969, June). *A study of oral reading miscues that result in grammatical retransformations* (Final Report, Project No. 7-E-219). Washington, DC: U.S. Department of Health, Education, and Welfare, U.S. Department Education. (ED 039 101)

> Oral reading miscues of 18 proficient readers in grades 2, 4, and 6 are divided into those that do not change syntactic structure and those that do.

GOODMAN, KENNETH S., & FLEMING, JAMES T. (EDS.). (1969). *Psycholinguistics and the teaching of reading.* Newark, DE: International Reading Association. (ED 074 446)

> Includes Paul Kolers' "Reading is only Incidentally Visual" and work by Robert C. Calfee, Kenneth S. Goodman, Robert B. Ruddell, Robert Shuy, and others.

GOODMAN, YETTA M., ALLEN, PAUL DAVID, BURKE, CAROLYN L., & MARTELLOCK, HELEN (1969, April). *Studies of reading miscues*. Paper presented at the International Reading Association Annual Convention, Kansas City, MO. (ED 033 831)
> An early account of miscue analysis as each author reports on the findings of his or her research.

GOODMAN, YETTA M., & BURKE, CAROLYN L. (1969). Do they read what they speak? *Grade Teacher, 86*(7), 144, 146–148, 150.
> Indicates how linguistic principles can be applied to analysis of reading miscues and what insights this can give a teacher about the strengths and weaknesses of a specific reader.

IRWIN, JOAN M. (1969). *An analysis of the miscues in the oral reading of Indian children in selected grades*. Unpublished master's thesis, University of Calgary, Calgary, AB.
> Finds some variation in phoneme-grapheme and phoneme-morpheme relationships for 25 readers across grades 2, 4, and 6. Lack of self-correction suggests the use of single cuing systems in their reading.

IRWIN, JOAN M. (1969, April). *An analysis of miscues in the oral reading of Canadian Indian children*. Paper presented at the 14th Annual Convention of the International Reading Association, Kansas City, MO. (ED 033 828)
> Discusses the miscues of 75 students, grades 2, 4, and 6, who read science materials.

KOZACHUCK, JEAN KARABIN (1969). *A study of the miscues of a selected number of children reading orally and an analysis of the significance in the area of syntax*. Unpublished master's thesis, Wayne State University, Detroit, MI.
> A study of five fourth grade readers' knowledge of grammar and their reading.

MOIR, LEO HUGHES (1969). *A linguistic analysis of certain stylistic elements of selected works of literature for children and their relationship to readability*. Unpublished doctoral dissertation, Wayne State University, Detroit, MI. (UMI No. AAC 70-03433)

Presents the responses of sixth graders to 10 cloze tests analyzed according to modified RMI and other literary factors. Results are correlated to cloze scores and conclusions are drawn about determined reading levels.

NURSS, JOANNE R. (1969, March). Oral reading errors and reading comprehension. *The Reading Teacher*, 22(6), 523–527.
A study of the reading of 108 second graders that finds the number of errors related to syntactic complexity regardless of vocabulary knowledge.

PART 3

1970–1974

1970

BURKE, CAROLYN L., & GOODMAN, KENNETH S. (1970, January). When a child reads: A psycholinguistic analysis. *Elementary English*, 47(1), 121–129.

> Illustrates through the detailed analysis of a fourth grade child's oral reading miscues how such analysis can reveal the reading process at work.

CARLSON, KENNETH L. (1970). *A psycholinguistic description of selected fourth grade children reading a variety of contextual material.* Unpublished doctoral dissertation, Wayne State University, Detroit, MI. (UMI No. AAC 71-17243)

> Miscue analysis is used to study fourth graders' reading basal reader, science, and social studies material. Data support the theory that reading is a psycholinguistic process.

DELAWTER, JAYNE A. (1970). *Oral reading errors of second grade children exposed to two different reading approaches.* Unpublished doctoral dissertation, Teachers College at Columbia University, New York, NY. (UMI No. AAC 71-1097)

> Focuses on the relationship of oral reading errors to two instructional approaches considered to be at opposite ends of a continuum of reading approaches.

GOODMAN, KENNETH S. (1970a). Behind the eye: What happens in reading. In K.S. Goodman & O. Niles (Eds.), *Reading: Process and program* (pp. 3–38). Urbana, IL: National Council of Teachers of English. (ED 072 431 or ED 045 664)

> Discusses language in both oral and written forms, perception, the reading process, and objectives of the reading program.

GOODMAN, KENNETH S. (1970b). Comprehension-centered reading. In M.P. Douglas (Ed.), *Reading and school life* (Thirty-fourth Yearbook of the Claremont Reading Conference, Vol. 34, pp. 125–135). Claremont, CA: Claremont College Curriculum Laboratory.

> Discusses the focus on comprehension in reading.

GOODMAN, KENNETH S. (1970c). Dialect rejection and reading: A response. *Reading Research Quarterly*, 5(4), 600–603.

> Explains why Rystrom's (1970, same issue) hypotheses about dialect interference are untenable due to the implicit assumptions that (1) different means deficient, and (2) reading is matching phonemes with graphemes.

GOODMAN, KENNETH S. (1970d). Psycholinguistics in reading. *Innovations in the elementary school: The report of a national seminar sponsored by the Institute for Development of Educational Activities*, (pp. 22–23). Dayton, OH: Institute for Development of Educational Activities (Kettering Foundation).

> A description of a reader, summarizing what miscue research has revealed about the reading process.

GOODMAN, KENNETH S. (1970, Spring). Psycholinguistic universals in the reading process. *Journal of Typographic Research*, 4, 103–110. (EJ025029)

> Discusses the strategies and cuing systems used in the reading process as well as characteristics of visual activity and suggests the need for more research in different languages and orthographies. Reprinted in P. Pimsleur & T. Quinn (1971). *Psychology of second language learning*. London: Cambridge University Press.

GOODMAN, KENNETH S., & NILES, OLIVE S. (EDS.). (1970). *Reading: Process and program*. Champaign, IL: National Council of Teachers of English, Commission on the English Curriculum. (ED 072 431)

> Contains a chapter by K.S. Goodman discussing the psycholinguistic process as well as a discussion by Niles of application of these concepts in a school situation.

GOODMAN, YETTA M. (1970, February). Using children's miscues for new teaching strategies. *The Reading Teacher, 23*(5), 455–459.

> Introduces the concepts of building strategy lessons from children's miscues.

LEVIN, HARRY, & KAPLAN, ELEANOR L. (1970). Grammatical structure and reading. In H. Levin & J.P. Williams (Eds.), *Basic studies on reading*, (pp. 119–133). New York: Basic Books.

> A discussion of how readers' eye-movements suggest they are processing units of meaning larger than a word. Discusses confirming and disconfirming and the tentativeness involved in this reading strategy.

PAGE, WILLIAM D. (1970a). Environmental context: Key to a broader spectrum on the word recognition scene. *The Michigan Reading Journal, 4,* 17–20.

> Discusses the influence of environmental context to broaden the concept of word recognition.

PAGE, WILLIAM D. (1970b). *A psycholinguistic description of patterns of miscues generated by a proficient reader in second grade, an average reader in fourth grade, and an average reader in sixth grade encountering ten basal reader selections ranging from pre-primer to sixth grade.* Unpublished doctoral dissertation, Wayne State University, Detroit, MI. (UMI No. AAC 71-17296)

> The theory that reading is a psycholinguistic guessing game is extended to a position that reading is a case of knowledge acquisition or knowledge construction.

RYSTROM, RICHARD C. (1970). Dialect training and reading: A further look. *Reading Research Quarterly, 5*(4), 581–595.

> In a study to determine interference of black dialect with reading, four groups of first graders are given various instruction. No relation between dialect and reading achievement is found.

WEBER, ROSE MARIE (1970). First graders' use of grammatical context in reading. In H. Levin & J.P. Williams (Eds.), *Basic studies on reading* (pp. 147–163). New York: Basic Books.

> This study looks at reading errors with low graphic similarity and at self-corrections to better understand readers' use of contextual information in reading.

WEBER, ROSE MARIE (1970, Spring). A linguistic analysis of first grade reading errors. *Reading Research Quarterly*, 5(3), 427–451.

> This analysis of information readers use in identifying words compares errors of the weaker readers to those of the stronger.

1971

COOMBER, JAMES ELWOOD (1971). *A psycholinguistic analysis of oral reading errors made by good, average, and poor readers.* Unpublished doctoral dissertation, University of Wisconsin, Madison. (UMI No. AAC 72-18972)

> Examines the extent to which good, average, and poor third graders depend on two main types of reading cues—graphic features and context—in making substitution miscues.

DAVEY, BETH (1971). *A psycholinguistic investigation of cognitive styles and oral reading strategies in achieving and underachieving 4th grade boys.* Unpublished doctoral dissertation, Case Western Reserve University, Cleveland, OH. (UMI No. AAC 72-6282.

> Results suggest that cognitive styles are implicated in reading underachievement, as reflected through unsuccessful and inefficient hypotheses-testing strategies in oral reading.

GOODMAN, KENNETH S. (1971a). Children's language and experience: A place to begin. In H.M. Robinson (Ed.), *Coordinating reading instruction* (pp. 46–52). Glenview, IL: Scott, Foresman.

> Argues for the use of children's natural language in learning to read. Outlines steps for using their experience stories as part of the curriculum.

GOODMAN, KENNETH S. (1971b). The search called reading. In H.M. Robinson (Ed.), *Coordinating reading instruction*, (pp. 10–14). Glenview, IL: Scott, Foresman.

> A restatement of the psycholinguistic guessing game.

GOODMAN, KENNETH S., & MENOSKY, DOROTHY (1971, March). Unlocking the program: Two viewpoints. *Instructor*, 80(7), 44–46.

Argues for the natural language competence of readers and the importance of the information they generate and strategies they use in reading.

GOODMAN, YETTA M. (1971). *Longitudinal study of children's oral reading behavior* (Final Report, Project No. 9-E-062). Washington, DC: U.S. Department of Health, Education, and Welfare, Office of Education. (ED 058 008)

Six children are taped reading orally at eight regular intervals during their second and third year of reading instruction to analyze their oral reading miscues and reading development.

GUTKNECHT, BRUCE ARTHUR (1971). *A psycholinguistic analysis of the oral reading behavior of selected children identified as perceptually handicapped.* Unpublished doctoral dissertation, Wayne State University, Detroit, MI. (UMI No. AAC 72-14563)

The study suggests that the classification of perceptually handicapped be carefully examined and that reading programs be adopted that enable the child to use syntactic and semantic strategies along with graphophonic strategies.

HITTLEMAN, DANIEL R. (1971). *The readability of subject matter material rewritten on the basis of students' oral reading miscues.* Unpublished doctoral dissertation, Hofstra University, Hempstead, NY. (UMI No. AAC 72-10847)

Attempts to determine whether text revised on the basis of students' miscues has greater readability than the original text. Several implications for future research are suggested.

KLING, MARTIN, DAVIS, FREDERICK B., & GEYER, JOHN J. (1971). *The literature of research in reading with emphasis on models* (Final Report). Washington, DC: Office of Education, National Center for Educational Research and Development, U.S. Department of Health, Education, and Welfare. (ED 059 023)

A review of models on reading. The Goodman model is included.

MARTELLOCK, HELEN ANNA (1971). *A psycholinguistic description of the oral and written language of a selected group of middle school children.* Unpublished doctoral dissertation, Wayne State University, Detroit, MI. (ED 067 634, UMI No. AAC 72-14598)

Miscue analysis indicates that the subjects are making semantic and syntactic changes to clarify the text of a basal story.

MENOSKY, DOROTHY M. (1971). *A psycholinguistic analysis of oral reading miscues generated during the reading of varying portions of text by selecting readers from grades 2, 4, 6, and 8.* Unpublished doctoral dissertation, Wayne State University, Detroit, MI. (ED 067 618, UMI No. AAC 72-14600)

> Presents a detailed analysis and comparison of the reading strategies used by 18 research subjects. The study notes positive change in miscues as readers progress further in longer texts.

OHAVER, ALLAN ROY (1971). *A comparison study of semantic and syntactic cuing by low reading performance college freshmen.* Unpublished doctoral dissertation, New Mexico State University, Las Cruces. (UMI No. AAC 71-28050)

> Compares two groups of college freshmen (one testing high on comprehension and low on vocabulary, and one scoring low on comprehension and high on vocabulary on a standardized test). Reading sentences, semigrammatical sentences, and word strings, the study finds the higher comprehension group makes more miscues and uses semantics and syntax, while the high vocabulary group relies on syntax.

PAGE, WILLIAM D. (1971). A linguistic appraisal of isolated word recognition testing. *The Michigan Reading Journal*, 5(2), 28–35.

> Appraises tests of word recognition by linguistic criteria.

ROBISON, SYBIL LEWIS (1971). *A study of lingua-orthographic dialectical miscues.* Unpublished doctoral dissertation, Auburn University, Auburn, AL. (UMI No. AAC 72-11283)

> Looks at the spelling ability of 104 children in relationship to oral dialectical miscues.

SMITH, FRANK, & GOODMAN, KENNETH S. (1971). On the psycholinguistic method of teaching reading. *Elementary School Journal*, 71(4), 177–181. (EJ030547)

> An appraisal of the term "psycholinguistic" respective to its possible abuse in the form of reading programs and instructional materials.

ZUCK, LOUIS V., & GOODMAN, YETTA M. (1971). *Social class and regional dialects: Their relationship to reading* (An annotated bibliography) (3rd ed.). Newark, DE: International Reading Association. (ED 071 058 [3rd. ed.]. Also see ED 055 755)

> Addresses research, implications for teachers, second language learning, and social dialect issues related to reading.

1972

ALLEN, P. DAVID (1972). What teachers of reading should know about the writing system. In R. Hodges & E.H. Rudorf, *Language and learning to read: What teachers should know about language*, (pp. 87–99). Boston, MA: Houghton Mifflin. (ED 264 586)

> Examines common misconceptions about written language and presents what is known about the English writing system, including a discussion of implications.

ALLEN, P. DAVID (1972, February). Cue systems available during the reading process: A psycholinguistic viewpoint. *Elementary School Journal, 72*(5), 258–264.

> A brief summary with examples of the child's use of the three cuing systems.

BURKE, CAROLYN L. (1972). The language process: Systems or systematic? In R. Hodges, & E.H. Rudorf (Eds.), *Language and learning to read: What teachers should know about language*, (pp. 24–30). Boston, MA: Houghton Mifflin. (ED 264 586)

> Discusses the vital interaction of the cuing systems.

GOODMAN, KENNETH S. (1972). The reading process: Theory and practice. In R. Hodges & E.H. Rudorf (Eds.), *Language and learning to read: What teachers should know about language*, (pp. 143–159). Boston, MA: Houghton Mifflin. (ED 264 586)

> Discusses language and the necessary attention of the reader on meaning; situations leading to miscues; units of processing in reading; and effective strategies of the proficient reader.

GOODMAN, KENNETH S. (1972, January). Oral language miscues. *Viewpoints: Bulletin of the School of Education*, 48(1), 13–28.

> Argues that teachers must rid themselves of ethnocentric evaluations of children's speech.

GOODMAN, KENNETH S. (1972, March). Reading: The key is in children's language. *The Reading Teacher*, 25(6), 505–508. (EJ053270)

> Discusses why solutions to the teaching and learning problems lie in the children themselves. Supporting what children know and focusing on comprehension rather than fragmenting language resources for learners supports the reading process.

GOODMAN, KENNETH S. (1972, December). Orthography in a theory of reading instruction. *Elementary English*, 49(8), 1254–1261.

> Discusses the assumptions of orthographically weighted instructional practices and shows examples of how such practices may be counter-productive to the decisions readers must make to read efficiently.

GOODMAN, YETTA M. (1972). Qualitative reading miscue analysis for teacher training. In R. Hodges & E.H. Rudorf (Eds.), *Language and learning to read: What teachers should know about language*, (pp. 160–166). Boston, MA: Houghton Mifflin. (ED 264 586)

> General, introductory remarks regarding miscue analysis and its application in a classroom setting.

GOODMAN, YETTA M. (1972, October). Reading diagnosis—qualitative or quantitative? *Reading Teacher*, 26(1), 32–37.

> Differentiation of qualitative miscue analysis and quantitative error count—emphasizes strengths and weaknesses of readers.

GOODMAN, YETTA M., & BURKE, CAROLYN L. (1972). *Reading miscue inventory manual: Procedure for diagnosis and evaluation*. New York: Macmillan.

> This is the original form of the Reading Miscue Inventory, now out of print.

HODGES, RICHARD, & RUDORF, E. HUGH (EDS.). (1972). *Language and learning to read: What teachers should know about language.* Lanham, MD: University Press of America. (ED 264 586)

> A collection of essays about language and reading that shows that effective reading instruction is based on an understanding of what language is and an understanding of the way children use it.

JENSEN, LOUISE J. (1972). *A psycholinguistic analysis of the oral reading behavior of selected proficient, average and weak readers reading the same material.* Unpublished doctoral dissertation, Michigan State University, East Lansing. (ED 079 669, UMI No. AAC 73-5408)

> The data suggest an instructional model directed toward meaning rather than the processing of visual information. The weak readers overuse graphophonic skills to the detriment of meaning.

KOT, CAROL A. (1972). *An analysis of the reading miscue inventories of an inefficient reader over a six year period.* Specialist of education thesis, Wayne State University, Detroit, MI.

> Finds that the quality not the quantity of miscues evidences readers' development. Semantic acceptability of miscues improves but the readers' own criteria only develops to a grammatical level.

LIPTON, AARON (1972, May). Miscalling while reading aloud: A point of view. *The Reading Teacher, 25*(8), 759–762.

> Examines the semantic dimension of what children do when they read. Suggests a meaning focus for teachers as well as students.

OHAVER, ALLAN ROY (1972). A comparison study of semantic and syntactic cuing by low reading performance college freshman. In F. Greene (Ed.), *Investigations relating to mature reading* (Twenty-first Yearbook of the National Reading Conference, pp. 110–118). Milwaukee, WI: National Reading Conference. (ED 059 836, December, 1971)

> Thirty college students read 150 expressions of three types: sentences, semi-grammatical strings (semantically anomalous), and ungrammatical strings. Higher comprehension subjects have more miscues than the higher vocabulary group. Syntactic and semantic use do not differ.

ROMATOWSKI, JANE A. (1972). *A psycholinguistic description of miscues generated by selected bilingual subjects during the oral reading of instructional reading material as presented in Polish readers and in English basal readers.* Unpublished doctoral dissertation, Wayne State University, Detroit, MI. (UMI No. AAC 73-12586)

> Among other conclusions, the Goodman Taxonomy of Reading Miscues is effective, with slight modification, in dealing with miscues generated during the reading of a Polish story.

ROUSCH, PETER DESMOND (1972). *A psycholinguistic investigation into the relationship between prior conceptual knowledge, oral reading miscues, silent reading and post-reading performance.* Unpublished doctoral dissertation, Wayne State University, Detroit, MI. (UMI No. AAC 73-12588)

> Complex interrelationships are found among prior knowledge, oral reading, retelling, and cloze performance, for 72 average fourth graders.

SIMS, RUDINE (1972). *A psycholinguistic description of miscues generated by selected young readers during oral reading of text material in black dialect and standard English.* Unpublished doctoral dissertation, Wayne State University, Detroit, MI. (UMI No. AAC 72-28487)

> Finds no evidence to support the development of dialect specific readers for wide-scale use in beginning reading instruction with speakers of black dialect.

UPSHUR, JOHN A. (1972, March). *A search for new reading tests.* Speech presented at the 6th Annual Teachers of English to Speakers of Other Languages Convention, Washington, DC. (ED 061 805)

> Discusses the shortcomings of tests, suggesting cloze procedure, eye-movement studies, and miscue analysis to help refine the understanding of reading.

VOGEL, SUSAN ANN (1972). *An investigation of syntactic abilities in normal and dyslexic children.* Unpublished doctoral dissertation, Northwestern University, Evanston, IL. (UMI No. AAC 72-32599)

Findings corroborate the importance of syntactic ability in the reading process and confirm Goodman's psycholinguistic model of reading.

YOUNG, FREDA MCKINNEY (1972). *An analysis of the miscues of selected Mexican-American readers made when reading from their fifth grade instructional up to their frustration level.* Unpublished specialist in education thesis, New Mexico State University, Las Cruces.

> Thirty bilingual readers reveal an overuse of graphophonic cues at the expense of syntactic and semantic cues in reading.

1973

ANASTASIOW, NICHOLAS J., & STAYROCK, NICHOLAS G. (1973). Miscue language patterns of mildly retarded and non-retarded students. *American Journal of Mental Deficiency*, 77(4), 431–434.

> Study of miscue patterns in mildly retarded and normal children.

BRODY, DEBORAH P. (1973). *A psycholinguistic comparison of oral reading behavior of proficient and remedial readers.* Unpublished master's thesis, Rutgers University, New Brunswick, NJ. (ED 085 659)

> Uses the RMI to compare strategies of good and poor fourth grade readers to determine whether the RMI can delineate qualitative differences between the groups.

BUCK, CATHERINE (1973). Miscues of non-native speakers of English. In K.S. Goodman (Ed.), *Miscue analysis: Applications to reading instruction* (pp. 91–96). Urbana, IL: National Council of Teachers of English. (ED 080 973)

> Uses insights from miscue analysis to comment about learning to read English as a foreign language. Discusses implications for teachers.

BURKE, CAROLYN L. (1973). Preparing elementary teachers to teach reading. In K.S. Goodman (Ed.), *Miscue analysis: Applica-*

tions to reading instruction (pp. 15–29). Urbana, IL: National Council of Teachers of English. (ED 080 973)

> Outlines a way to adapt miscue research procedures to an instructional program in reading for undergraduate teachers.

DeLawter, Jayne A. (1973). The module and the miscue. In K.S. Goodman (Ed.), *Miscue analysis: Applications to reading instruction* (pp. 44–48). Urbana, IL: National Council of Teachers of English. (ED 080 973)

> Explains how miscue analysis can be taught in a modularized language-reading program at the university level.

Gates, Vicki (1973). Organizing a seventh grade reading class based on psycholinguistic insights. In K.S. Goodman (Ed.), *Miscue analysis: Applications to reading instruction* (pp. 40–43). Urbana, IL: National Council of Teachers of English. (ED 080 973)

> Describes the objectives and organization of a remedial reading class for seventh graders.

Goodman, Kenneth S. (1973a). Miscues: Windows on the reading process. In K.S. Goodman (Ed.), *Miscue analysis: Applications to reading instruction*, (pp. 3–14). Urbana, IL: National Council of Teachers of English. (ED 080 973)

> An introductory presentation for the book, this discusses the analysis of miscues, procedures used, and the methodological implications of miscue analysis.

Goodman, Kenneth S. (1973b). The thirteenth easy way to make learning to read difficult: A reaction to Gleitman and Rozin. *Reading Research Quarterly*, 8(4), 484–493.

> Argues against a contention by Gleitman and Rozin that children should be taught to read English as a syllabary.

Goodman, Kenneth S. (Ed.). (1973c). *Miscue analysis: Applications to reading instruction*. Urbana, IL: National Council of Teachers of English. (ED 080 973)

> Series of essays about what we learn from children about reading and how to apply that knowledge.

GOODMAN, KENNETH S., & BUCK, CATHERINE (1973, October). Dialect barriers to reading comprehension revisited. *The Reading Teacher*, 27(1), 6–12. (EJ084342)
> Uses miscue analysis to challenge some widely held beliefs about dialect.

GOODMAN, KENNETH S., & BURKE, CAROLYN L. (1973, April). *Theoretically based studies of patterns of miscues in oral reading performance* (Final Report). Washington, DC: U.S. Department of Health, Education, and Welfare, Office of Education. (ED 079 708)
> Examines the reading process of 94 subjects ranging in proficiency from low second grade to high tenth grade.

GOODMAN, YETTA M. (1973). Miscue analysis for in-service reading teachers. In K.S. Goodman (Ed.), *Miscue analysis: Applications to reading instruction*, (pp. 49–64). Urbana, IL: National Council of Teachers of English. (ED 080 973)
> Discusses the use of miscue analysis to help teachers revalue reading.

HITTLEMAN, DANIEL R. (1973, May). Seeking a psycholinguistic definition of readability. *The Reading Teacher*, 26(8), 783–789.
> Discusses inadequacies of readability formulas and the cloze technique.

HITTLEMAN, DANIEL R., & ROBINSON, H. ALAN (1973). *Readability of high school text passages before and after revision* (Final Report, Project No. I-B-025). National Center for Educational Research and Development. Flushing, NY. (ED 075 794)
> Studies text revision based on miscues in science, social studies, and English. The report states that miscue analysis can be used to make text easier but it creates so many other problems that it is not recommended.

HOLLANDER, SHEILA K. (1973). *Strategies of selected 6th graders reading and working verbal arithmetic problems*. Unpublished doctoral dissertation, Hofstra University, Hempstead, NY. (UMI No. AAC 74-7896)
> Modifies RMI for use in the study of reading and solving mathematical problems.

HOOD, JOYCE E., KENDALL, JANET R., & ROETTGER, DORIS M. (1973, February). *An analysis of oral reading behavior for reflective and impulsive beginning readers*. Paper presented at the Annual Meeting of the American Educational Research Association, New Orleans, LA. (ED 078 376)

> Of 79 first graders, the author finds that reflective readers make fewer miscues and self-correct more substitution miscues when semantically or syntactically inappropriate.

KAPLAN, ELAINE M. (1973). *An analysis of oral reading miscues of selected 4th grade boys identified as having high or low manifest anxiety*. Unpublished doctoral dissertation, Hofstra University, Hempstead, NY. (UMI No. AAC 74-19455)

> The most frequent type of miscues for all subjects is substitution with heavy dependence on graphophonic cues. High anxiety subjects correct significantly more syntactically and semantically acceptable substitution miscues.

KOLCZYNSKI, RICHARD GERALD (1973). *A psycholinguistic analysis of oral reading miscues in selected passages from science, social studies, mathematics, and literature*. Unpublished doctoral dissertation, The Ohio State University, Columbus. (UMI No. AAC 74-10989)

> Discusses 20 average or above average sixth grade readers' miscues in relation to questions five through nine of the RMI; patterns of comprehension and grammatical relationships are also analyzed. Regardless of the content of the reading material, readers make similar use of syntactic and semantic cues in order to gain meaning.

LIU, STELLA S.F. (1973). *An investigation of oral reading miscues made by nonstandard dialect speaking black children*. Unpublished doctoral dissertation, University of California, Berkeley. *Reading Research Quarterly* (1975–1976), 11(2), 193–197 for abstract.

> Regarding miscues as cues to linguistic competence, this study of dialect influence in reading finds dialect texts are not advantageous to standard English texts.

LUDWIG, JAY B., & STALKER, JAMES C. (1973). Miscue analysis and the training of junior and senior high school English teachers. In K.S. Goodman (Ed.), *Miscue analysis: Applications to reading instruction*, (pp. 30–39). Urbana, IL: National Council of Teachers of English. (ED 080 973)

> Describes the use of miscue analysis in a course designed to make prospective English teachers more knowledgeable about the reading process.

MCKINNEY, O. DAVENE (1973). *Linguistic concepts and reading miscues.* Unpublished education specialist's thesis, Wayne State University, Detroit, MI.

> A miscue analysis of one 10- and one 12-year-old dialect speaking reader, each two years behind grade level.

NIERATKA, ERNEST B. (1973a). *Miscue analysis: A needed diagnostic dimension for non-traditional students.* (ED 215 301)

> States that miscue analysis is more appropriate than standardized tests for measuring the strengths and weaknesses of nontraditional students.

NIERATKA, ERNEST B. (1973b). Using miscue analysis to advise content area teachers. In K.S. Goodman (Ed.), *Miscue analysis: Applications to reading instruction*, (pp. 97–99). Urbana, IL: National Council of Teachers of English. (ED 080 973)

> Describes the use of miscue analysis data in helping content area teachers understand the strengths and weaknesses of their students.

NIERATKA, SUZANNE (1973). Miscue analysis in a special education resource room. In K.S. Goodman (Ed.), *Miscue analysis: Applications to reading instruction*, (pp. 100–102). Urbana, IL: National Council of Teachers of English. (ED 080 973)

> Shows how miscue analysis can be used in the evaluation and curriculum planning for students in special programs.

PAGE, WILLIAM D. (1973). Clinical uses of miscue research. In K.S. Goodman (Ed.), *Miscue analysis: Applications to reading instruction* (pp. 65–76). Urbana, IL: National Council of Teachers of English. (ED 080 973)

> Discusses the contributions of miscue analysis research to clinical practice.

PAGE, WILLIAM D. (1973, March). Observing oral reading: A language-bound process. *Illinois Reading Council Journal, 1*(1), 17–18.

> Discusses language base to the observation of oral reading.

SMITH, FRANK (ED.). (1973a). *Psycholinguistics and reading.* New York: Holt, Rinehart and Winston. (ED 071 031)

> George Miller, Paul Kolers, Carol Chomsky, Kenneth Goodman and others explore the issues and findings of psycholinguistic research and its implications for teaching.

SMITH, FRANK (1973b). Twelve easy ways to make learning to read difficult (and one difficult way to make it easy). In F. Smith (Ed.), *Psycholinguistics and Reading* (pp. 183–196). New York: Holt, Rinehart and Winston.

> Discusses 12 classroom teaching practices that inappropriately complicate reading and suggests one practice that supports a reader's growth. See Goodman, K.S. (1973b).

SMITH, LAURA A., & LINDBERG, MARGARET (1973). Building instructional materials. In K.S. Goodman (Ed.), *Miscue analysis: Applications to reading instruction* (pp. 77–90). Urbana, IL: National Council of Teachers of English. (ED 080 973)

> Outlines procedures that can be used by authors, publishers, and teachers in designing or evaluating reading material.

THORNTON, MERVIN F. (1973). *A psycholinguistic description of purposive oral reading and its effect on comprehension for subjects with different reading backgrounds.* Unpublished doctoral dissertation, Wayne State University, Detroit, MI. (ED 092 864, UMI No. AAC 73-31787)

> Finds that when a specific purpose is set for reading, an interference phenomenon appears to reduce the efficiency of the reading process.

WATSON, DOROTHY J. (1973a). Helping the reader: From miscue analysis to strategy lessons. In K.S. Goodman (Ed.), *Miscue analysis: Applications to reading instruction* (pp. 103–115). Urbana, IL: National Council of Teachers of English. (ED 080 973)

Demonstrates how to design strategy lessons based on readers' miscue patterns.

WATSON, DOROTHY J. (1973b). *A psycholinguistic description of the oral reading miscues generated by selected readers prior to and following exposure to a saturated book program.* Unpublished doctoral dissertation, Wayne State University, Detroit, MI. (ED 092 863, UMI No. AAC 73-31791)

All subjects become more proficient readers as a result of the saturated book program.

WINKELJOHANN, ROSEMARY (1973). Introduction. In K.S. Goodman (Ed.), *Miscue Analysis: Applications to Reading Instruction* (pp. 1–2). Urbana, IL: National Council of Teachers of English. (ED 080 973)

Discusses the growth of work then being done in miscue analysis.

YOUNG, KELVIN K.K. (1973). *An analysis of oral reading miscues of Hawaiian Islands dialect speakers in grades one through six.* Unpublished doctoral dissertation, Syracuse University, Syracuse, NY. (UMI No. AAC 75-14040)

Studies 10 dialect speakers from each of grades 1 through 6 and finds Hawaiian Islands dialect does not appear to influence greatly the oral reading of these subjects. Notes that the use of context clues appears to increase across succeeding grade levels.

1974

ANDERSON, DOROTHY JEAN (1974). *A psycholinguistic description of the oral reading miscues of selected first-grade students participating in a supplemental language based program.* Unpublished doctoral dissertation, Virginia Polytechnic Institute and State University, Blacksburg. (UMI No. AAC 74-23796)

Uses miscue analysis to study beginning readers in a language program.

BOARD, PETER E. (1974). *A descriptive analysis of the oral reading behavior of a selected group of disabled readers.* Unpublished master's thesis, University of Toronto, Toronto, ON.

Twenty learning disabled students, ages 8–16, are shown to use strategies similar to proficient readers but with emphasis on the graphophonic level. Suggests more instructional emphasis on syntactic and semantic level.

CARDER, MARY ELIZABETH (1974). *A comparison of oral reading miscues of poor readers assigned to learning disability classes with those assigned to remedial reading classes.* Unpublished doctoral dissertation, University of Northern Colorado, Greeley. (UMI No. AAC 75-11081)

> Readers similar in reading level, grade, and intelligence, but identified as learning disabled vs. remedial readers are compared using the RMI with no differences found.

COSENS, GRACE VELINA (1974). *The effect of deletion produced structures on word identification and comprehension of beginning readers.* Unpublished doctoral dissertation, University of Alberta, Edmonton.

> Examination of cloze procedure finds that the short frequency sentences present in most introductory reading material are difficult for beginning readers to comprehend.

DULAY, HEIDI C., & BURT, MARINA K. (1974). You can't learn without goofing. In J.C. Richards (Ed.), *Error analysis: Perspectives on second language acquisition* (pp. 95–123). London: Longman.

> Finds over-generalization in processing strategies, not interference of language structures, accounts for the errors made by second language learners.

GOODMAN, KENNETH S. (1974, November). Reading: You can get back to Kansas anytime you're ready, Dorothy. *English Journal,* 63(8), 62–64. (EJ109121)

> Suggests that children need to be encouraged to use their linguistic knowledge when reading.

GOODMAN, YETTA M. (1974, November). I never read such a long story before. *English Journal,* 63(8), 65–71. (EJ109122)

> Teachers are encouraged to let the students read, encourage guessing and predicting, and focus students on meaning.

GOODMAN, YETTA M., & SIMS, RUDINE (1974). Whose dialect for beginning readers? *Elementary English*, *51*(6), 837–841.

> Suggests an examination of coping behaviors rather than special dialect readers might prove more realistic for insights into reading problems.

GREENE, BARBARA H. (1974). *A psycholinguistic analysis of the multiple attempts produced in oral reading by selected readers upon the single appearance of an item.* Unpublished doctoral dissertation, Wayne State University, Detroit, MI. (UMI No. AAC 75-13323)

> Examines multiple miscues for developmental trends by age and proficiency as revealed by the reading strategies employed by various groups in their repeated attempts at lexical items.

HAYDEN, JOHN BLAIR (1974). *Psycholinguistic analysis of oral reading of three selected groups of seventh grade students.* Unpublished doctoral dissertation, University of Southern California, Los Angeles. (UMI No. AAC 74-11688)

> Finds that low, average, and high readers resort to the same reading strategies when reading orally a selection approximately one grade level above their reading grade level.

HOFFNER, DOROTHEA R. (1974). *A psycholinguistic analysis of oral reading miscues by junior college students.* Unpublished master's thesis, Rutgers University, New Brunswick, NJ. (ED 086 964)

> Uses miscue analysis to examine the oral reading behavior of five college students. Results are compared to eighth and tenth grade readers.

HUTSON, BARBARA A., & NILES, JEROME A. (1974). Parallel analysis of oral language and reading miscues. In P.L. Nacke (Ed.), *Interaction: Research and practice for college-adult reading* (Twenty-third Yearbook of the National Reading Conference, pp. 232). Clemson, SC: National Reading Conference. (ED 094 324, 1973)

> Seventy-five children in grades 1–3 are presented reading and attempting auditory cloze tasks at three levels of difficulty. Although the main effects for grade and complexity are not significant, the interaction of grade by complexity is significant. For responses that are both semantically and syntactically appropriate, there is a significant effect for task, with a higher mean for the cloze task. Complexity is significant with a decrease from the easiest to most difficult passage.

LITTLE, LARRY J. (1974). *A study of the relationship between syntactic development and oral reading substitution miscues of average and disabled third grade readers.* Unpublished doctoral dissertation, University of Kansas, Lawrence. (UMI No. AAC 75-06139)

> Fifteen average and 15 disabled third grade readers' miscues are compared using the RMI in analyzing the reading of 50 sentences. Each substitution miscue is analyzed with regard to semantic and syntactic acceptability. Analysis of the data reveals no relationship between syntactic language development and oral substitution miscues of average or disabled readers.

MCKENZIE, MOIRA GWENDOLINE (1974). *The range of operative structures underlying the behaviors of young readers and non-readers engaged in reading and writing activities.* Unpublished doctoral dissertation, The Ohio State University, Columbus. (UMI No. AAC 75-7511393)

> Miscue analysis is used in this exploratory study of what tacit (Polanyi) resources are naturally available to a beginning reader. Attention is given to how these resources relate to instructional activity.

PAGE, WILLIAM D. (1974). Are we beginning to understand oral reading? *Reading World, 13*(3), 161–170.

> Defines altercues (any oral reading deviation), supercues (meaningful altercues), and pseudocues (meaningless altercues).

PAGE, WILLIAM D. (1974, September). The author and the reader in writing and reading. *Research in the Teaching of English, 8*(2), 170–183.

> Theoretical view of the roles of readers and writers in the two processes.

RIGG, PATRICIA STEVENS (1974). *A psycholinguistic analysis of the oral reading miscues generated by speakers of rural black dialect compared to the miscues of speakers of an urban black dialect.* Unpublished doctoral dissertation, Wayne State University, Detroit, MI. (UMI No. AAC 75-13378)

> Results show widely varying individual proficiency in reading with no relationship between an individual's reading proficiency and his or her own dialect.

RODE, SARA S. (1974–1975). Development of phrase and clause boundary reading in children. *Reading Research Quarterly*, *10*(1), 124–142. (EJ107224)

> Studies the effects of syntactic structure on the eye-voice span using children at three developmental levels.

SMITH, BRENDA VOGEL (1974). *A descriptive study of the effectiveness of reading strategy lessons as indicated by the 'Reading Miscue Inventory' profiles of selected below average readers*. Unpublished doctoral dissertation, Virginia Polytechnic Institute and State University, Blacksburg. (UMI No. AAC 75-03468)

> Looks at instruction of 10 below average fifth graders in reading strategies and compares the instructed group to an uninstructed group. Also compares RMI assessment of "initial, mid, final and all codable miscues" to find no significant differences.

TORTELLI, JAMES PETER (1974). *A psycholinguistic description of the effects of strategy lessons upon the oral reading behavior of 12 below-average readers of different linguistic backgrounds, grades four, five and six*. Unpublished doctoral dissertation, Wayne State University, Detroit, MI. (UMI No. AAC 74-29872)

> Concludes that basing reading instruction on the ways readers use their own dialect helps them acquire meaning from the printed language.

WILLIAMSON, LEON E., & YOUNG, FREDA (1974, July). The IRI and RMI diagnostic concepts should be synthesized. *Journal of Reading Behavior*, *6*(2), 183–194. (EJ105662)

> Argues that Reading Miscue Inventory concepts should be utilized within the boundary set by Informal Reading Inventory procedures.

PART 4

1975–1979

1975

BROWN, VIRGINIA (1975, December). Programs, materials and techniques: Reading miscue analysis. *Journal of Learning Disabilities, 8*(10), 605–611. (EJ132579)
> Reviews the RMI in relation to the learning disabled.

BURKE, CAROLYN L. (1975). Oral reading analysis: A view of the reading process. In W.D. Page (Ed.), *Help for the reading teacher: New directions in research* (pp. 23–33). Urbana, IL: ERIC/CRCS. (ED 101 322)
> Discusses the reading process as seen through miscue analysis.

CARLSON, KENNETH L. (1975). A different look at reading in the content areas. In W.D. Page (Ed.), *Help for the reading teacher: New directions in research* (pp. 52–59). Urbana, IL: ERIC/CRCS. (ED 101 322)
> Looks at the differences in miscues produced by reading different content materials.

DeLAWTER, JAYNE A. (1975). The relationship of beginning reading instruction and miscue patterns. In W.D. Page (Ed.), *Help for the reading teacher: New directions in research* (pp. 42–51). Urbana, IL: ERIC/CRCS. (ED 101 322)
> Looks at patterns of miscues in children who have received different kinds of reading instruction.

GLENN, HUGH W. (1975). Miscue analysis: Some diagnostic and instructional implications. In R. Sugimoto (Ed.), *College learning skills: Today and tomorrow.* (Proceedings of the 8th Annual Conference of the Western College Association, pp. 93–99). Whittier, CA: Western College Association.
> Introduction to miscue concepts and their instructional implications.

GOODMAN, KENNETH S. (1975, February). Influences of the visual peripheral field in reading. *Research in the Teaching of English*, 9(2), 210–222. (EJ135871)

> States that the influence of cues in the visual peripheral field is not a random one.

GOODMAN, YETTA M. (1975). Reading strategy lessons: Expanding reading effectiveness. In W.D. Page (Ed.), *Help for the reading teacher: New directions in research* (pp. 34–41). Urbana, IL: ERIC/CRCS. (ED 101 322)

> Develops a concept of readers' strategies.

GUTKNECHT, BRUCE ARTHUR (1975). How the handicapped are handicapped in reading. *Florida Reading Quarterly*, 11(3), 17–19.

> Based on author's original research, stresses the need of graphophonic, syntactic, and semantic reading instructional strategies, especially for less able readers.

HITTLEMAN, DANIEL R., & ROBINSON, H. ALAN (1975, December). Readability of high school text passages before and after revision. *Journal of Reading Behavior*, 7(4), 369–382.

> This study looks at text revision based on miscues in three areas: science, social studies, and English. Points out that miscue analysis can be used to make text easier as measured by cloze, but can also create many other problems. (See ED 075 794, 1973)

HOOD, JOYCE (1975–1976). Qualitative analysis of oral reading errors: The inter-judge reliability of scores. *Reading Research Quarterly*, 11(4), 577–598. (EJ144586)

> Detailed analysis of inter-judge reliability in scoring the RMI.

HOOD, JOYCE E., & KENDALL, JANET R. (1975). A qualitative analysis of oral reading errors of reflective and impulsive second graders: A follow-up study. *Journal of Reading Behavior*, 7(3), 269–281. (EJ130758. Also see ED 092 880)

> Uses oral reading analysis to describe the strategies and miscues of reflective and impulsive second graders.

JACKSON, EVELYN WEICHERT (1975). *Teachers' responses to the miscues made by low-average and average readers in five second-grade classrooms: A descriptive study*. Unpublished doctoral dissertation, Southern Illinois University, Carbondale. (UMI No. AAC 78-13552)

> Audiotaping and questionnaires show five response categories. Nearly half of all clues given a reader involve phonics; most of the rest involve structural analysis. It is suggested that teachers encourage a reader to use more background knowledge and more context clues. Teachers should also take more time to let readers self-correct.

JACKSON, SHEILA M. (1975). *An evaluation of oral reading miscues in second grade subjects*. Unpublished doctoral dissertation, University of South Carolina, Conway. (UMI No. AAC 76-16624)

> One hundred twenty-eight students are examined through a modified version of Gray's oral reading test, the Gates-MacGinitie reading test, and the Goodman taxonomy.

JOHNS, JERRY L. (1975). Strategies for oral reading behavior. *Language Arts*, 52(8), 1104–1107. (EJ136018)

> Intends to help teachers understand oral reading behavior and how miscues can be used to design minilessons.

JOHNSON, KENNETH R. (1975, April). Black dialect shift in oral reading. *Journal of Reading*, 18(7), 535–540.

> Illustrates examples of dialect-related miscues typically made by speakers of black dialect.

LAMBERG, WALTER J. (1975). *Accuracy in measuring oral reading in English by a student with a Spanish language background*. Unpublished; ERIC document only. (ED 128 767)

> Shows how teachers who trained with miscue inventory use informal assessment of reading miscues of students' who have Spanish influence. Shows how teachers recognize Spanish influence and utilize assessment instruments appropriately.

LOPEZ, SARAH JANE HUDELSON (1975). *The use of context by native Spanish speaking Mexican American children when they read in Spanish*. Unpublished doctoral dissertation, University of Texas, Austin. (UMI No. AAC 75-24904)

> Concludes that young Spanish speakers reading in Spanish use other than strictly phonics skills—specifically, contextual clues. They also use their language background to anticipate and predict while reading.

MILLER, BONNIE L. (1975). *A kindergartner learns to read for meaning*. Unpublished; ERIC document only (ED 228 620)

> Details a case study of six weeks spent with a five-year-old who has an excellent understanding of sound/symbol relationships but does not know how to read for meaning.

MILLER, JOHN W. (1975). An interdisciplinary view of reading as a qualitative process. *Reading Improvement, 10*(2), 40–45. (EJ095950)

> Discusses the basic precepts of the Reading Miscue Inventory as an evaluation of oral reading.

MILLER, JOHN W. (1975, June). Disruptive effect: A phenomenon in oral reading. *Reading Horizons, 15*(4), 198–207. (EJ120786)

> Suggests that a higher incidence of miscues is associated with close proximity to unknown words.

NEY, JAMES W. (1975). *A comparison of reading miscues and writing miscues*. Tempe, AZ: Arizona State University. (ED 161 009)

> Results from the comparison of reading and writing miscues suggest that reading and writing should not be kept apart in instruction.

NEY, JAMES W., & LEYBA, RACHEL (1975). *Miscue analysis in writing*. Tempe, AZ: Arizona State University. (ED 161 078)

> Analysis of miscues made in writing reveals individual differences in language processing and the possibility of two or three different styles of processing written linguistic forms.

PAGE, WILLIAM D. (1975a). The reading process: Its evaluation through miscues. *Educating Children: Early and Middle Years, 20*(2), 17–21.

> Interprets the findings of miscue analysis into a series of principles for teachers to consider when evaluating the reading process.

PAGE, WILLIAM D. (ED.). (1975b). *Help for the reading teacher: New directions in research*. Urbana, IL: ERIC Clearinghouse on Reading and Communication Skills. (ED 101 322)

> This collection of essays is designed to bridge the gap between teachers and research on such topics as the cloze procedure, readability formulas, miscue analysis, reading strategies, informal reading inventories, and content area reading.

PAGE, WILLIAM D. (1975, December). The post oral reading cloze test: New link between oral reading and comprehension. *Journal of Reading Behavior*, 7(4), 383–389.

> Demonstrates that post oral-reading cloze tests are strongly predictive of silent reading cloze tests.

PAGE, WILLIAM D., & BARR, REBECCA C. (1975). Use of informal reading inventories. In W.D. Page (Ed.), *Help for the reading teacher: New directions in research* (pp. 101–110). Urbana, IL: ERIC/CRCS. (ED 101 322)

> Suggests ways to improve informal reading inventories based on insights from research.

PAGE, WILLIAM D., & CARLSON, KENNETH L. (1975). The process of observing oral reading scores. *Reading Horizons*, 15(3), 147–150.

> A study of how reading specialists view oral reading and what they consider to be errors.

PIPER, CAROL JEAN (1975). *A measure of the effectiveness of instructional strategies based on psycholinguistic principles of teaching reading when applied to a program to aid seventh and eighth grade underachievers*. Unpublished doctoral dissertation, Wayne State University, Detroit, MI. (ED 114 813, UMI No. AAC 75-25296)

> Findings suggest that reading strategy lessons based on psycholinguistic principles and focused on meaning can only enhance reading development.

READENCE, JOHN EDWARD (1975). *A psycholinguistic analysis of the oral reading miscues of impulsive and reflective third grade children*. Unpublished doctoral dissertation, Arizona State University, Tempe. (UMI No. AAC 75-27087)

> Analysis of 41 third graders shows a statistically significant relationship between impulsive, mixed impulsive-reflective, and reflective readers with regards to their use of the linguistic cue systems.

ROY, JOY KYLE (1975). *The application of remedial reading techniques, including miscue analysis, to high school students in remedial classes: An exploration study.* Unpublished doctoral dissertation, University of North Carolina, Chapel Hill. (ED 131 404, UMI No. AAC 76-20071)

> Investigates the usefulness of miscue analysis as a teaching organizer for diagnostic and evaluative remedial reading instruction.

STEINRUCK, YVONNE SIU (1975). *The effects of instruction in miscue analysis on teachers' perceptions of the reading process and on their instruction in reading.* Unpublished doctoral dissertation, University of Toledo, Toledo, OH. (ED 120 701,UMI No. AAC 76-08365)

> Studies 20 inservice teachers' reading knowledge and instruction practices before and after an intensive course in miscue analysis.

STENROOS, CAROL J. (1975). *A psycholinguistic description of selected gifted readers relating prior conceptual knowledge to the concept density of varied contextual materials.* Unpublished doctoral dissertation, Wayne State University, Detroit, MI. (UMI No. AAC 76-11004)

> A primary implication of this study is that gifted students need programs designed to expand their experiences and their thinking potential with activities other than reading.

THOMAS, KEITH JOHN (1975). *Syntactic/semantic acceptability and semantic similarity of oral reading errors as functions of variation in attained comprehension.* Unpublished doctoral dissertation, University of Arizona, Tucson. (UMI No. AAC 75-17826)

> Syntactic and semantic acceptability of word recognition errors is shown to be related to comprehension.

VOGEL, SUSAN ANN (1975). *Syntactic abilities in normal and dyslexic children.* Baltimore, MD: University Park Press. (ED 120 720)

> Examination of the syntactic abilities of normal and dyslexic readers confirms the Goodman model. The study also explores syntactic abilities as a potential screening tool.

WOFFORD, BARBARA ANN (1975). *Using reading miscue analysis to investigate publishers' suggested readability levels for elementary science textbooks: A comparison study.* Unpublished doctoral dissertation, Virginia Polytechnic Institute and State University, Blacksburg. (UMI No. AAC 75-23721)

> Miscue analysis data reveals flaws in grade level designations provided by science textbooks. Understanding content may be dependent upon organization, concept and vocabulary load, or author's style.

1976

ALLEN, EDWARD D. (1976, December). Miscue analysis: A new tool for diagnosing oral reading proficiency in foreign languages. *Foreign Language Annals*, 9(6), 563–567. (EJ150305)

> Study of the miscues of 30 third-year French students in high school.

ALLEN, P. DAVID (1976a). An afterward and a look forward. In P.D. Allen & D. Watson (Eds.), *Findings of research in miscue analysis: Classroom implications* (pp. 152–153). Urbana, IL: ERIC and National Council of Teachers of English. (ED 128 762)

> Reviews the miscue research conducted between 1965 and 1974.

ALLEN, P. DAVID (1976b). Implications for reading instruction. In P.D. Allen & D. Watson (Eds.), *Findings of research in miscue analysis: Classroom implications*, (pp. 107–112). Urbana, IL: ERIC and National Council of Teachers of English. (ED 128 762)

> States generalizations about the reading process that have been derived from miscue analysis research.

ALLEN, P. DAVID (1976c). The miscue research studies. In P.D. Allen & D. Watson (Eds.), *Findings of research in miscue analy-*

sis: Classroom implications (pp. 3–10). Urbana, IL: ERIC and National Council of Teachers of English. (ED 128 762)

> A reflection on research trends in the field of language study and reading as a context for the development of miscue analysis.

ALLEN, P. DAVID (1976d). Some general implications concerning specific taxonomy categories. In P.D. Allen & D. Watson (Eds.), *Findings of research in miscue analysis: Classroom implications* (pp. 70–75). Urbana, IL: ERIC and National Council of Teachers of English. (ED 128 762)

> Discusses the miscue analysis categories of correction, graphic and phonemic proximity, intonation, and semantic word relationships.

ALLEN, P. DAVID, & WATSON, DOROTHY J. (EDS.). (1976). *Findings of research in miscue analysis: Classroom implications*. Urbana, IL: National Council of Teachers of English. (ED 128 762)

> Provides background for the miscue research studies, describes the Goodman taxonomy, and contains essays on reading instruction, strategies, and implications.

ANDREWS, NANCY CUNNINGHAM (1976). *Six case studies in learning to read*. Unpublished doctoral dissertation, Indiana University, Bloomington. (ED 140 247, UMI No. AAC 77-03274)

> Miscue analysis is used to describe the individual strategies developed by six first grade children over a seven month period.

AU, KATHRYN HU-PEI (1976). *An analysis of oral reading errors and its implications for improvement of reading instruction* (Tech. Rep. No. 50). Honolulu, HI: Kamehameha Early Education Project. (ED 159 590)

> The oral reading errors of 15 second graders are analyzed to find out if strategies used by good and poor readers can be differentiated.

BEAN, THOMAS WILLIAM (1976). *An analysis of the oral reading miscues of Hawaiian Islands dialect speakers in grades four, five, and six*. Unpublished doctoral dissertation, Arizona State University, Tempe. (ED 133 710, UMI No. AAC 76-26805)

> Compares the oral reading strategies of 50 students who are speakers of Hawaiian dialect.

BEAN, THOMAS WILLIAM (1976, July). *Recent psycholinguistic research in reading and Hawaiian Islands dialect.* Paper presented at the 4th Annual Meeting of the International Reading Association Far East Regional Conference, Honolulu, HI. (ED 137 770)

> The conclusions of previous dialect miscue research in Hawaiian Islands dialect are described and two recent miscue studies involving Hawaiian populations are summarized. The paper includes instructional implications.

BEEBE, MONA JANE (1976a). Case studies of grade level effects on children's miscues and reading comprehension. *Canadian Journal of Education, 1*(2), 51–61.

> Examines the interactions of grades two and four pupils with reading materials, using the RMI for the analysis. The focus is on the discovery of differences in interaction between grade levels and the determination of the extent to which different miscues affect comprehension.

BEEBE, MONA JANE (1976b). *The effects of substitution miscues on the reading performance of selected grade four boys,* Unpublished master's thesis, Memorial University of Newfoundland, St. John's.

> Studies substitutions of fourth grade boys and the effects on their reading.

BRANDT, DOREY (1976). *Young children's responses to environmental printed stimuli as it is related to beginning reading experiences.* Unpublished master's thesis, University of California, Berkeley.

> Looks at the environmental awareness of print in 25 kindergartners when they enter school. The study finds the children respond to print as meaningful and suggests enriched print experience in classrooms.

BRAZEE, PHYLLIS ELLEN (1976). *A qualitative and quantitative description of eighth grade students' oral reading in both narrative and expository materials.* Unpublished doctoral dissertation, University of Northern Colorado, Greeley. (ED 131 408, UMI No. AAC 76-23166)

> Describes the strategies used by eighth graders reading expository and narrative materials.

BURKE, CAROLYN L. (1976a). Reading miscue research: A theoretical position. In P.D. Allen & D. Watson (Eds.), *Findings of research in miscue analysis: Classroom implications* (pp. 10–23). Urbana, IL: ERIC and National Council of Teachers of English. (ED 128 762)

> Presents miscue analysis and its theoretical base. Discusses author-reader relationships and provides examples of how miscues illustrate the reading process. The article also introduces the taxonomy questions.

BURKE, CAROLYN L. (1976b). The three cue systems: #2—syntactic. In P.D. Allen & D. Watson (Eds.), *Findings of research in miscue analysis: Classroom implications* (pp. 79–88). Urbana, IL: ERIC and National Council of Teachers of English. (ED 128 762)

> Explains how readers use the syntactic cuing system.

BURKE, ELIZABETH (1976, November). A developmental study of children's reading strategies. *Educational Review, 29*(1), 30–46. (EJ156365)

> Looks at children's miscues across age and finds that miscues are generally of a higher quality in older children. Use of semantics shows the greatest improvements.

CAMBOURNE, BRIAN (1976–1977). Getting to Goodman: An analysis of the Goodman model of reading with some suggestions for evaluation. *Reading Research Quarterly, 12*(4), 605–636. (EJ165775)

> Reviews the development of the Goodman reading model and suggests approaches to evaluating the model.

COOPER, CHARLES R., & PETROSKY, ANTHONY R. (1976, December). A psycholinguistic view of the fluent reading process. *Journal of Reading, 20*(3), 184–207.

> Describes the psycholinguistic model, lists reading strategies derived from the model, and outlines a secondary school reading course utilizing the strategies.

CUNNINGHAM, PATRICIA M. (1976–1977). Teachers' correction responses to Black-dialect miscues which are non-meaning-changing. *Reading Research Quarterly, 12*(4), 637–653. (EJ165777)

Presents findings from questionnaires asking graduate students whether they would correct certain miscues, and whether they thought the miscues were made by black or white readers.

DANK, MARION E. (1976). *A study of the relationship of miscues to the mode of formal reading instruction received by selected second graders.* Unpublished doctoral dissertation, University of Massachusetts, Amherst. (ED 126 431, UMI No. AAC 76-14676)

Finds definite relationships between the kind of instruction received and the kinds of miscues made by second graders.

DESANTI, ROGER JOSEPH (1976). *The older reader: An investigation of the reading strategies, habits and interests of four persons sixty years of age or older.* Unpublished doctoral dissertation, Indiana University, Bloomington. (ED 141 778, UMI No. AAC 77-03285)

Concludes that the ability to comprehend does not insure comprehension, and exposition allows use of language skills more effectively than narration.

EWOLDT, CAROLYN (1976). *Miscue analysis of the reading of third grade follow through and non-follow through children in Wichita, Kansas.* Tucson, AZ: Arizona Center for Educational Research and Development. (ED 136 219)

Provides data on the effectiveness of the Tucson Early Education Model, a reading instruction program that advocates the language experience approach.

GLENN, JUNE CAROL (1976). *A psycholinguistic analysis of the effect of silent and oral reading on the comprehension and oral reading miscues of average fourth-grade readers.* Unpublished doctoral dissertation, University of Southern California, Los Angeles.

Thirty-nine fourth graders are studied. Results show silent reading does not influence oral reading comprehension. It is noted that use of graphophonic information is not directly related to comprehension as measured by a post reading cloze test.

GOODMAN, KENNETH S. (1976a). Miscue analysis: Theory and reality in reading. In J.E. Merritt (Ed.), *New horizons in reading*

(Proceedings of the 5th International Reading Association World Congress on Reading, Vienna, 1974, pp. 15–26). Newark, DE: International Reading Association. (ED 116 182)

> Provides a miscue taxonomy and explains why psycholinguistics is a base for the study of reading; examines five subjects and their miscues to distinguish efficient and effective readers.

GOODMAN, KENNETH S. (1976b). What we know about reading. In P.D. Allen & D. Watson (Eds.), *Findings of research in miscue analysis: Classroom implications* (pp. 57–70). Urbana, IL: ERIC and National Council of Teachers of English. (ED 128 762)

> A summary of knowledge of the reading process.

GOODMAN, KENNETH S. (1976–1977). From the strawman to the tin woodman: A response to Mosenthal. *Reading Research Quarterly*, *12*(4), 575–585. (EJ165771)

> Responds to Mosenthal's critique of Goodman's work. See *Reading Research Quarterly*, *12*(1).

GOODMAN, YETTA M. (1976a). Developing reading proficiency. In P.D. Allen & D. Watson (Eds.), *Findings of research in miscue analysis: Classroom implications* (pp. 113–128). Urbana, IL: ERIC and National Council of Teachers of English. (ED 128 762)

> Miscue analysis applies to developing proficiency.

GOODMAN, YETTA M. (1976b). Miscues, errors, and reading comprehension. In J.E. Merritt (Ed.), *New horizons in reading* (Proceedings of the 5th International Reading Association World Congress on Reading, Vienna, 1974, pp. 86–93). Newark, DE: International Reading Association.

> Discusses a simpler form of miscue analysis dealing with only the most significant questions.

GOODMAN, YETTA M. (1976c). Strategies for comprehension. In P.D. Allen & D. Watson (Eds.), *Findings of research in miscue analysis: Classroom implications* (pp. 94–102). Urbana, IL: ERIC and National Council of Teachers of English. (ED 128 762)

> Discusses building comprehension strategies on miscue patterns.

GOODMAN, YETTA M., & BURKE, CAROLYN L. (1976). Reading: Language and psycholinguistic bases. In P. Lamb & R. Arnolds (Eds.), *Reading: Foundations and instructional strategies* (pp. 93–120). Belmont, CA: Wadsworth.
> A psycholinguistic view of reading instruction.

GREENE, BARBARA H., & WATSON, MARIANNE (1976, February). Psycho-what? *English Journal, 65*(2), 39–44.
> Describes the experiences of several teachers studying psycholinguistic theory for the first time.

GUTKNECHT, BRUCE ARTHUR (1976a). Intonation. In P.D. Allen & D. Watson (Eds.), *Findings of research in miscue analysis: Classroom implications* (pp. 44–45). Urbana, IL: ERIC and National Council of Teachers of English. (ED 128 762)
> Explains the coding of intonation in miscue analysis.

GUTKNECHT, BRUCE ARTHUR (1976b). Learning disabilities. In P.D. Allen & D. Watson (Eds.), *Findings of research in miscue analysis: Classroom implications* (pp. 136–139). Urbana, IL: ERIC and National Council of Teachers of English. (ED 128 762)
> Describes research that shows only slight differences between the oral reading of children identified as perceptually handicapped and the oral reading of children in regular classrooms.

HARRIS, ANNE GILLELAND (1976). Graphic and phonemic proximity. In P.D. Allen & D. Watson (Eds.), *Findings of research in miscue analysis: Classroom implications*, (pp. 30–33). Urbana, IL: ERIC and National Council of Teachers of English. (ED 128 762)
> Explains the coding of graphic and phonemic proximity in miscue analysis.

HODES, PHYLLIS (1976). *A psycholinguistic study of reading miscues of Yiddish-English bilingual children.* Unpublished doctoral dissertation, Wayne State University, Detroit, MI. (UMI No. AAC 76-26141)
> Study of six 7- and 8-year-olds using English and Yiddish materials shows the RMI to be completely useful with a language having a different alphabetical and directional system.

HUCK, CHARLOTTE S. (1976, November). *Beginnings and becomings.* Paper presented at the 66th Annual Meeting of the National Council of Teachers of English, Chicago, IL. (ED 136 256)
> Cites miscue analysis as one research method that concentrates on the process of children's learning rather than on the end product of testing.

JENSEN, LOUISE J. (1976). Dialect. In P.D. Allen & D. Watson (Eds.), *Findings of research in miscue analysis: Classroom implications* (pp. 28–30). Urbana, IL: ERIC and National Council of Teachers of English. (ED 128 762)
> Explains the coding of dialect in miscue analysis.

KAUFMAN, MAURICE (1976, October). The oral reading sample in reading diagnosis. *Reading World, 16*(1), 39–47. (EJ144638)
> Discusses the oral reading errors made by one child to illustrate how a diagnosis is made (principally for instructional needs in word recognition).

LIPSET, CORINE B. (1976). *The nature of regressions in oral reading and their relationship to three measures of comprehension.* Unpublished doctoral dissertation, Hofstra University, Hempstead, NY. (ED 136 198, UMI No. AAC 76-24396)
> Results are interpreted to indicate that regressions in oral reading are not indicative of readers' inability to comprehend, and they may be beneficial to reading.

MARTELLOCK, HELEN ANNA (1976). Correction. In P.D. Allen & D. Watson (Eds.), *Findings of research in miscue analysis: Classroom implications,* (pp. 27–28). Urbana, IL: ERIC and National Council of Teachers of English. (ED 128 762)
> Describes the coding of correction in miscue analysis.

MASON, JANA, M. (1976, June). Over-generalization in learning to read. *Journal of Reading Behavior, 8*(2), 173–182. (EJ150112)
> An acquisition model of decoding explains the kinds of miscues children make when reading.

MENOSKY, DOROTHY M. (1976a). Modes and materials. In P.D. Allen & D. Watson (Eds.), *Findings of research in miscue analy-*

sis: Classroom implications (pp. 102–107). Urbana, IL: ERIC and National Council of Teachers of English. (ED 128 762)

> Suggests guidelines for the selection of reading material for the classroom.

MENOSKY, DOROTHY M. (1976b). The three cue systems: #1—graphophonic. In P.D. Allen & D. Watson (Eds.), *Findings of research in miscue analysis: Classroom implications* (pp. 75–79). Urbana, IL: ERIC and National Council of Teachers of English. (ED 128 762)

> Explains how readers use the graphophonic cuing system.

MILLER, JOHN W., & ISAKSON, RICHARD L. (1976, April). *The effect of syntactic and semantic violation on high and low reading comprehenders.* Paper presented at the Annual Meeting of the American Educational Research Association, San Francisco, CA. (ED 123 591)

> The reading comprehension and the perception of syntactic and semantic errors are compared for 48 fourth graders. Analysis reveals that high comprehenders show greater sensitivity to semantic and syntactic violations than do low comprehenders.

MITCHELL, CAROL (1976, August). *A psycholinguistic analysis of oral reading errors of children with learning disabilities.* Paper presented at the 3rd International Scientific Conference of the International Federation of Learning Disabilities, Montreal, PQ. (ED 135 129)

> Findings suggest the possibility of using analysis of oral reading errors as a diagnostic tool for learning disabled students.

MONTORO, CATHERINE BUCK (1976). Syntactic acceptability, syntactic change and transformations. In P.D. Allen & D. Watson (Eds.), *Findings of research in miscue analysis: Classroom implications* (pp. 34–37). Urbana, IL: ERIC and National Council of Teachers of English. (ED 128 762)

> Describes coding for syntactic acceptability, syntactic change, and transformations in miscue analysis.

MOSENTHAL, PETER (1976–1977). Bridge principles in an abridged reply to Goodman. *Reading Research Quarterly*, *12*(4), 586–603. (EJ165773)

> Responds to Goodman's criticism of his critique of Goodman's work.

NEY, JAMES W. (1976). *Sentence combining and reading*. Arizona State University, Tempe. Unpublished; ERIC document only. (ED 161 080)

> Uses miscue analysis to examine two modes of sentence combining instruction, individualized and group. No differences are found.

NORTON, DONNA E. (1976). *A comparison of the oral reading errors of high and low ability 1st and 3rd graders taught by two approaches—synthetic phonic and analytic-eclectic*. Unpublished doctoral dissertation, University of Wisconsin, Madison. (ED 136 191, UMI No. AAC 76-20681)

> Results from an analysis of a reading miscue inventory used with each student indicate that miscue patterns are directly related to reading approaches. (Also see ED 145 393).

PAGE, WILLIAM D. (1976a). Miscue research and diagnosis. In P.D. Allen & D. Watson (Eds.), *Findings of research in miscue analysis: Classroom implications* (pp. 139–146). Urbana, IL: ERIC and National Council of Teachers of English. (ED 128 762)

> Presents long-range implications of miscue research for clinical practice and the role of reading specialists.

PAGE, WILLIAM D. (1976b). Semantic acceptability and semantic change. In P.D. Allen & D. Watson (Eds.), *Findings of research in miscue analysis: Classroom implications* (pp. 38–44). Urbana, IL: ERIC and National Council of Teachers of English. (ED 128 762)

> Explains the coding of semantic acceptability and semantic change in miscue analysis.

PAGE, WILLIAM D. (1976c). The three cue systems: #3—semantic. In P.D. Allen & D. Watson (Eds.), *Findings of research in miscue analysis: Classroom implications* (pp. 88–94). Urbana, IL: ERIC and National Council of Teachers of English. (ED 128 762)

> Explains how readers use the semantic cuing system.

PAGE, WILLIAM D. (1976d). Inquiry into an unknown word. *School Review, 83*(3), 461–477.

> Theoretical explanation of how readers cope with unknown words. Includes discussion of Goodman's taxonomy of cuing systems and suggests implications for instruction and research.

PAGE, WILLIAM D. (1976, May). Pseudocues, supercues, and comprehension. *Reading World, 15*(4), 232–238.

> Finds that unacceptable miscues behave as mistakes in relation to cloze, but acceptable miscues are not significantly related to cloze.

PATERRA, MARY ELIZABETH (1976). *A comparison of the Informal Reading Inventory and Reading Miscue Inventory*. (ED 133 706)

> The IRI and RMI are compared as to their purpose, origins, and methods of use.

PIKULSKI, JOHN J. (1976, April). Linguistics applied to reading instruction. *Language Arts, 53*(4), 373–377, 384. (EJ141130)

> Implications for classroom instruction from work in linguistics and psycholinguistics are discussed.

RADER, NANCY LOUISE (1976). *From written words to meaning: A developmental study*. Unpublished doctoral dissertation, Cornell University, Ithaca, NY. (UMI No. AAC 76-18192)

> Examines the direct apprehension theory that suggests written language does not go through the phonemic coding system and the dual coding theory of Paivio that suggests language and nonsymbolic images have separate codes. The direct apprehension theory is supported.

RECHT, DONNA R. (1976, April). The self-correction process in reading. *The Reading Teacher, 29*(7), 632–636. (EJ134376)

> Argues that self-correction indicates that a reader is comprehending.

RIGG, PAT (1976). Reading in ESL. In J. Fanselow & R. Crymes (Eds.), *On TESOL '76* (pp. 203–210). Washington, DC: Teachers of English to Speakers of Other Languages.

> Six Arabic speakers' reading is used to demonstrate the use of miscue analysis and how readers may make miscues and demonstrate high comprehension in their retellings.

ROTHSTEIN, EVELYN (1976, August). *Assessing reading competency: A psycholinguistic perspective.* Paper presented at the 3rd International Scientific Conference of the International Federation of Learning Disabilities, Montreal, PQ. (ED 135 150)

> Discusses an oral reading procedure for children with reading problems that assesses competency through analyzing meaningful versus non-meaningful alterations to the text.

ROUSCH, PETER DESMOND (1976a). Grammatical categories. In P.D. Allen & D. Watson (Eds.), *Findings of research in miscue analysis: Classroom implications* (pp. 49–52). Urbana, IL: ERIC and National Council of Teachers of English. (ED 128 762)

> Explains the coding for grammatical categories in miscue analysis.

ROUSCH, PETER DESMOND (1976b). Semantic word relationships. In P.D. Allen & D. Watson (Eds.), *Findings of research in miscue analysis: Classroom implications* (pp. 52–54). Urbana, IL: ERIC and National Council of Teachers of English. (ED 128 762)

> Explains the coding for semantic word relationships in miscue analysis.

ROUSCH, PETER DESMOND (1976c). Testing. In P.D. Allen & D. Watson (Eds.), *Findings of research in miscue analysis: Classroom implications* (pp. 132–136). Urbana, IL: ERIC and National Council of Teachers of English. (ED 128 762)

> Discusses insights from miscue analysis that are relevant to testing issues.

SHUMAN, R. BAIRD (1976, March). Some reasons for oral reading. *Reading Horizons, 16*(3), 170–176. (EJ139217)

> Suggests that students need to hear literature read orally throughout the grades; less proficient readers should not be embarrassed; and dialect differences should be accepted if meaning is retained.

SIMS, RUDINE (1976a). Structural levels. In P.D. Allen & D. Watson (Eds.), *Findings of research in miscue analysis: Classroom implications* (pp. 46–49). Urbana, IL: ERIC and National Council of Teachers of English. (ED 128 762)

> Explains the coding for structural level (such as submorpheme, bound morpheme, word, phrase, or clause) in miscue analysis.

SIMS, RUDINE (1976b). What we know about dialects and reading. In P.D. Allen & D. Watson (Eds.), *Findings of research in miscue analysis: Classroom implications* (pp. 128–131). Urbana, IL: ERIC and National Council of Teachers of English. (ED 128 762)
> Presents implications for instruction based on knowledge about dialect influences on reading. Examples of children's code switching are included.

SMITH, LAURA A. (1976). Miscue research and readability. In P.D. Allen & D. Watson (Eds.), *Findings of research in miscue analysis: Classroom implications* (pp. 146–151). Urbana, IL: ERIC and National Council of Teachers of English. (ED 128 762)
> Miscue research reveals the limitations of traditional measures of readability.

STEINRUCK, YVONNE SIU (1976). *Reading: Communication and comprehension.* Unpublished; ERIC document only. (ED 124 873)
> Describes the use of retelling as an indicator of comprehension.

TORTELLI, JAMES PETER (1976, April). Simplified psycholinguistic diagnosis. *The Reading Teacher, 29*(7), 637–639. (EJ134377)
> Presents a method for analyzing the miscues of elementary school children.

TOVEY, DUANE R. (1976, March). The psycholinguistic guessing game. *Language Arts, 53*(3), 319–322.
> Discusses the cue systems and strategies students need in reading and follows with suggestions for teaching.

VORHAUS, RENEE POOL (1976). *Analysis and comparison of oral miscues generated by first grade students on four different reading tasks.* Unpublished doctoral dissertation, University of Pennsylvania, Philadelphia. (ED 126 437, UMI No. AAC 76-15602)
> Finds that differences in reading proficiency are not based on ability to identify graphic cues, but on awareness that reading is a meaning-constructing process.

WILLIAMSON, LEON E., ALLEN, SUE, & MCDONALD, BARBARA (1976). *Braille reading is less efficient than visual reading.* Unpublished; ERIC document only. (ED 124 870)
> Cites differences in strategies used by Braille and sighted readers.

WILLIAMSON, LEON E., & YOUNG, FREDA (1976). *The reading performances of monolinguals and bilinguals compared.* Unpublished; ERIC document only. (ED 130 252)

> Results show that monolinguals demonstrate more sensitivity to grammatic and semantic cues than do bilinguals, and that miscues are less apt to result in comprehension loss for monolinguals.

WOOD, MARTHA WINDHAM (1976). *A multivariate analysis of beginning readers' recognition of taught words in four contextual settings.* Unpublished doctoral dissertation, Texas Women's University, Denton. (UMI No. AAC 77-00766)

> Examining Goodman's contextual hypothesis and Samuels' focal attention hypothesis, this study investigates the use of words in isolation, words with pictures, words in sentence context, and words in story context. The results on the trials to criterion variable clearly support Goodman's contextual hypothesis.

1977

ALLINGTON, RICHARD L., & STRANGE, MICHAEL (1977). Effects of grapheme substitutions in connected text upon reading behaviors. *Visible Language*, 11(3), 285–297. (ED 136 248)

> Finds that poor readers' responses to altered words seem less bound to graphic cues than do those of the good readers.

ALLOUCHE, EDITH KROO (1977). *The application of miscue analysis to the oral reading of vocalized and unvocalized Hebrew texts.* Unpublished doctoral dissertation, The Ohio State University, Columbus. (UMI No. AAC 77-31814)

> Concludes that artificial reduction of the graphic display does not seem to promote more efficient or effective use of the various cuing systems.

ARMSTRONG, MAVIE ELIZABETH (1977). *Language centered instruction and its effect upon the process of writing and reading.* Unpublished master's thesis, University of Arizona, Tucson.

> An exploration of a broad interpretation of language centered teaching (incorporating team-teaching, multi-age grouping, and open classroom) that uses miscue analysis in its evaluation of students' development.

AU, KATHRYN HU-PEI (1977, October). Analyzing oral reading errors to improve instruction. *The Reading Teacher*, 31(1), 46–49. (EJ167712)

> Presents an instructional program designed to fit the needs of second grade remedial readers as revealed through an analysis of their oral reading errors.

BALDWIN, R. SCOTT (1977, April). *Psycholinguistic strategies as a factor in estimating the readability of written texts.* Paper presented at the Annual Meeting of the American Educational Research Association, New York, NY. (ED 136 242)

> Examines 56 third graders' reading of passages with varying word order and finds the differences in comprehension and number intonation miscues suggest clause-analysis strategies should be included in syntactic analyses of reading.

BLAIR, H. LYNN (1977). *A psycholinguistic description of the oral reading behavior of mature readers.* Unpublished doctoral dissertation, Arizona State University, Tempe. (UMI No. AAC 77-17863)

> Uses the RMI to study two groups of adults: working class young adults in a community college and retirees in an upscale retirement community.

CAMBOURNE, BRIAN (1977, August). *Some psycholinguistic dimensions of the silent reading process. A pilot study.* Paper presented at the 3rd Annual Meeting of the Australian Reading Conference, Melbourne. (ED 165 087)

> Two studies use cloze to identify five specific reading/language abilities. Readers find clues by looking back or ahead; use their background experience and logical buildup of story line for making predictions; and use letter clues.

CUNNINGHAM, PATRICIA M. (1977, October). Match informal evaluation to your teaching practices. *The Reading Teacher*, 31(1), 51–56. (EJ167713)

> Suggests that informal evaluations should be adjusted to teachers' individual teaching practices so that the evaluations give a truer picture of students' abilities to perform in the classroom.

DANK, MARION E. (1977, June). What effect do reading programs have on the oral reading behavior of children. *Reading Improvement*, 14(2), 66–69. (EJ164028)

> Examines oral reading miscues made by 20 children during their second year of instruction.

DEWITZ, PETER (1977). Criterion-referenced tests and the Reading Miscue Inventory. In M.P. Douglass (Ed.), *All things considered*. (Forty-first Yearbook of the Claremont Reading Conference, pp. 148–158). Claremont, CA: Claremont Graduate School.

> The author compares and notes weaknesses of each procedure's use for diagnostic purposes and suggests it is a weakness for RMI that graphophonic fit is not attended to in the same way syntactic and semantic information is.

DUBOIS, DIANE MARIE (1977). *A psycholinguistic analysis of the oral reading miscues generated by a selected group of Navajo speakers.* Unpublished doctoral dissertation, Wayne State University, Detroit, MI. (UMI No. AAC 77-23967)

> Analyzes miscues of Navajo children at grades 2, 4, and 6 over a two-year period reading basal and culturally relevant materials. Subjects tend to produce fewer low-quality miscues and more semantically acceptable miscues, and are able to retell more of the culturally relevant stories than the basal text stories. Subjects view the purpose of reading as learning English rather than viewing reading as a necessary communicative process.

EWOLDT, CAROLYN (1977). *A psycholinguistic description of selected deaf children reading in sign language.* Unpublished doctoral dissertation, Wayne State University, Detroit, MI. (ED 160 994, UMI No. AAC 77-23972)

> Study of miscues in the signing of four profoundly deaf students of different ages.

FARREN, SEAN N. (1977, October). *A study of reading errors using Goodman's miscue analysis and cloze procedure.* Paper presented at the 2nd Annual Meeting of the Reading Association of Ireland, Dublin. (ED 160 980)

> Studies the reading of 11 boys, ages 12 to 14 with low reading ability, to discover what kinds of errors they make and whether differences might exist between error patterns in silent and oral reading.

FOLMAN, SHOSHANA (1977). *A psycholinguistic analysis of miscues generated by a selected group of Israeli non-native speakers of English during the oral reading of an adapted American story—A descriptive study*. Unpublished doctoral dissertation, New York University, New York, NY. (UMI No. AAC 77-20742)

> The study includes five Israeli high school students in Tel Aviv for whom English is a foreign language. The students read one unadapted English story aloud with retelling. A major finding of this study is that the reading of the subjects is characterized by an excessive preoccupation with an accurate rendition of the word in its acoustic form to the extent of overlooking syntactic and semantic cues.

FROESE, VICTOR (1977, March). How to cause word-by-word reading. *The Reading Teacher*, 30(6), 611–615. (EJ154972)

> Presents several instructional practices that cause children to become word-by-word readers.

GARCIA, RICARDO L. (1977). *Language and reading development of bilinguals in the United States*. Norman, OK: University of Oklahoma. (ED 145 449)

> Recommends that future bilingual research use nonbehavioral science tools and miscue analysis to describe semantic processes and psycholinguistic and sociolinguistic phenomena.

GOODMAN, KENNETH S., & GOODMAN, YETTA M. (1977, August). Learning about psycholinguistic processes by analyzing oral reading. *Harvard Educational Review*, 47(3), 317–333. (EJ167143)

> States that reading is an active language process. The analysis of oral reading miscues can provide windows on reading and other language processes.

GOODMAN, YETTA M., & WATSON, DOROTHY J. (1977, November). A reading program to live with: Focus on comprehension. *Language Arts*, 54(8), 868–879. (EJ171361)

> Addresses teaching questions of "What is reading?" "How do children learn?" "What instruction is compatible with these views of reading and learning?" and "What resources are available?"

HITTLEMAN, DANIEL R. (1977, May). *Adaptive assessment for nonacademic secondary reading*. Paper presented at the 22nd

Annual Convention of the International Reading Association, Miami Beach, FL. (ED 140 240)

> Looks at the quality of reading errors of high school students on different reading materials including narrative, expository, and job related text forms.

HODES, PHYLLIS (1977, May). *Oral reading of bilingual Yiddish/ English children*. Paper presented at the 22nd Annual Convention of the International Reading Association, Miami Beach, FL. (ED 137 731)

> The study shows the RMI to be completely useful with a language having a different alphabetical and directional system.

HUGHES, MARGARET ANN (1977). *Word identification in learning to read*. Unpublished doctoral dissertation, University of Toronto, Toronto, ON.

> Finds that increasing use of language context is related to both better comprehension and learning of new words, especially for lower ability readers.

LAMBERG, WALTER J., & McCALEB, JOSEPH L. (1977, April). Performance by prospective teachers in distinguishable dialect features and miscues unrelated to dialect. *Journal of Reading*, 20(7), 581–584. (EJ158684)

> Examines responses made by prospective teachers when conducting an informal oral reading inventory with a student whose language exhibits some features of black dialect.

LESLIE, LAUREN, & PACL, PENNE (1977, April). *A comparison of oral reading strategies of fourth- and seventh-grade children of fourth-grade instructional level*. Paper presented at the Annual Meeting of the American Educational Research Association, New York, NY. (ED 137 760)

> Disabled readers make more uncorrected miscues that result in meaning loss than do younger average readers. Disabled readers tend to make miscues on high-frequency words.

LINDBERG, MARGARET ANN (1977). *A descriptive analysis of the relationship between selected prelinguistic, linguistic and psy-*

cholinguistic measures of readability. Unpublished doctoral dissertation, Wayne State University, Detroit, MI. (UMI No. AAC 77-23992)

> Compares six readability measures: the Dale-Chall, Fry Readability Graph, Moir's Word-Content Ratio, the Botel-Granowsky Syntactic Complexity Formula, the Cloze Readability Test, and the Miscue Formative Depth Analysis.

MAVROGENES, NANCY A. (1977, May). *The language development of the disabled secondary reader*. Paper presented at the 22nd Annual Convention of the International Reading Association, Miami Beach, FL. (ED 141 763)

> Analysis of the reading of 20 disabled secondary readers shows that they make most of their meaning-affecting miscues on complex structures.

MILLER, BONNIE L. (1977a). *Behind those words: The language cue systems*. Unpublished; ERIC document only. (ED 177 598)

> A review of the literature on miscue analysis supports the assumption that reading is a language process. All three language cue systems—graphophonic, syntactic, and semantic—must interact if reading for meaning is to occur, and a whole language environment is necessary for a student to develop reading proficiency.

MILLER, BONNIE L. (1977b). *Assisted reading as a remedial reading technique at the high school level: A psycholinguistic evaluation*. Unpublished doctoral dissertation, Virginia Polytechnic Institute and State University, Blacksburg. (UMI No. AAC 78-07218)

> Seven problem readers show that appropriate instructional emphasis can increase their use of the syntactic and semantic cuing systems. It is found that standardized testing does not address the readers' developments.

MOTT, BARBARA W. (1977). *A psycholinguistic analysis of native German speakers reading English: Implications for teaching reading*. Unpublished master's thesis, Michigan State University, East Lansing.

> Compares the reading of English and German by seven 16–21-year-old bilingual native German speakers.

NEY, JAMES W. (1977). *Miscue analysis: The writing of three Hispanic American students in a class of twenty fourth graders.* Tempe, AZ: Arizona State University. (ED 161 077)
> Finds that the Hispanic American children in this study do not make writing miscues that are quantitatively different from those of the other students in the predominantly non-Hispanic class.

NORTON, DONNA E., & HUBERT, PATTY (1977). *A comparison of the oral reading strategies and comprehension patterns developed by high, average, and low ability 1st grade students taught by two approaches—phonic emphasis and eclectic basal* (Final Report). College Station, TX: Texas A&M University, College of Education. (ED 145 393)
> Compared to the phonics program, students in the eclectic program produce more semantic and syntactic acceptable miscues, more miscues with no meaning change, and more self-corrections.

OTTO, JEAN A. (1977). *Reading: Cue utilization, achievement, and comprehension in an adolescent population.* Unpublished doctoral dissertation, Indiana University, Bloomington. (UMI No. AAC 77-27010)
> Finds that the primary testing of semantics distinguishes good readers from poor readers.

OTTO, JEAN (1977, March). Reading cue utilization by low achieving college freshman. *Journal of Reading Behavior, 14*(1), 71–84.
> Compares the use of graphic cues with syntactic and semantic processes for low achieving college freshmen.

PAGE, WILLIAM D. (1977). Comprehending and cloze performance. *Reading World, 17*(1), 17–21. (EJ171386)
> Compares comprehending scores from oral reading with scores from an oral cloze test.

PAGE, WILLIAM D. (1977, October). *The altercue continuum: Theoretical considerations.* Paper presented at the Buffalo Conference on Researching Response to Literature and the Teaching of Literature, Buffalo, NY. (ED 155 677)

Describes the altercue continuum, a miscue-based theoretical arrangement of oral reading responses that deviate from the expected responses,
arranged according to their relationship to reading comprehension.

PRENTICE, WALTER C., & PETERSON, JOE (1977, December). *Beyond passage dependency: A closer look at what reading comprehension tests measure.* Paper presented at the 27th Annual
Meeting of the National Reading Conference, New Orleans, LA.
(ED 157 022)
States that K.S. Goodman's naturalistic model of reading is a valid alternative to the manipulative techniques of mainstream comprehension
research.

RIGG, PAT (1977). The miscue–ESL project. In H.D. Brown, D.
Yorio, & R. Crymes (Eds.), *Teaching and learning ESL: Trends in
research and practice* (pp. 106–118). Washington, DC: Teachers
of English to Speakers of Other Languages.
Preliminary presentation of K.S. Goodman's 1978 report on the dialect
of speakers of languages other than English.

RIGG, PAT (1977, April). Getting the message, decoding the message. *The Reading Teacher*, 30(7), 745–749.
Two Chaldean children show two patterns of reading: One makes many
miscues but produces a strong retelling, the other makes few miscues but
produces a poor retelling.

ROUSCH, PETER DESMOND, & CAMBOURNE, BRIAN L. (1977,
May). *Reading in different kinds of Australian children.* Paper
presented at the 22nd Annual Convention of the International
Reading Association, Miami Beach, FL. (ED 140 269)
Constructs a taxonomy for nonoral reading, and compares the performance of Australian children on oral reading with their performance
on the nonoral reading tasks.

RUPLEY, WILLIAM H. (1977, February). ERIC/RCS: Miscue analy-
sis research: Implications for teacher and researcher. *The Reading
Teacher*, 30(5), 580–583. (EJ151282)
Reviews pertinent literature in ERIC.

SCALES, ALICE M. (1977). *An assessment-prescriptive-instructional packet for older learners.* Unpublished; ERIC document only. (ED 153 181)

> Includes Reading Miscue Inventory as part of the assessment-prescriptive-instructional packet, developed for assessment of older readers. Explains how to collect and interpret data on readers' interests, attitudes, and reading abilities.

SCHLIEPER, ANNE (1977, December). Oral reading errors in relation to grade and level of skill. *The Reading Teacher, 31*(3), 283–287. (EJ169507)

> Children learn to use strategies that focus on meaning and language as their reading ability progresses.

SHAFER, ROBERT E. (1977, March). What teachers should know about psycholinguistics in reading and miscue analysis. *English Quarterly, 10*(1), 49–54. (EJ165785)

> Discusses applications of miscue analysis and psycholinguistic work.

SILVA, FATIMA SAMPAIO (1977). *Relationships between selected oral language factors and reading proficiency.* Unpublished doctoral dissertation, University of Arizona, Tucson. (UMI No. AAC 78-02084)

> A study of 25 beginning readers without previous instruction are found to naturally use language constraints while reading. Early linguistic competence is shown to correlate with individual differences in comprehension.

STANSELL, JOHN C. (1977). *An exploratory study of perceptions of the reading process and control of that process in narrative and expository material by selected 8th graders.* Unpublished doctoral dissertation, Indiana University, Bloomington. (UMI No. AAC 77-27013)

> A main finding is that readers' beliefs about the reading process have a stronger influence on miscue patterns and retellings than differences in mode of writing.

STANSELL, JOHN C., HARSTE, JEROME C., & DeSANTI, ROGER J. (1977, December). *The effects of content-area writing patterns upon cue system utilization by second-grade, ninth-grade, and mature adult readers.* Paper presented at the 27th Annual Meeting of the National Reading Conference, New Orleans, LA. (ED 151 791)

> Readers in all three age groups tend to use the same cue systems consistently regardless of the nature of the materials read.

STURDIVANT-ODWARKA, ANNE MARITA (1977). *Relationships between quality of oral reading errors and oral syntactic development of second-grade children.* Unpublished doctoral dissertation, University of Iowa, Iowa City. (UMI No. AAC 77-21174)

> Suggests that as children become more fluent silent readers, their oral reading accuracy decreases in accordance with more efficient silent reading.

TAYLOR, JOELLYN (1977, September). Making sense: The basic skill in reading. *Language Arts, 54*(6), 668–672.

> Suggests ways of encouraging readers to make sense when they read.

WALTZ, PENNIE ALICE (1977). *Reflection-impulsivity and oral reading miscues among fourth-grade boys.* Unpublished master's thesis, Rutgers University, New Brunswick, NJ. (ED 132 510)

> Similarities and differences between reflective and impulsive readers are discussed.

ZINCK, R. ANN (1977). *An investigation of semantic and syntactic language cues utilized during oral and silent reading.* Unpublished doctoral dissertation, University of Georgia, Athens. (UMI No. ACC 77-30523)

> This study examines how performance on a cloze test when qualitatively analyzed using miscue analysis relates to a standardized test of reading comprehension and to oral reading proficiency. It is concluded that oral reading and silent reading processes seem to utilize syntactic and semantic language cues in a similar manner.

ZUTELL, JEROME B., JR. (1977, December). Teacher informed response to reader miscue. *Theory Into Practice, 16*(5), 384–391. (EJ180352)

> Discusses ways teachers use oral reading analysis to understand why students make miscues.

1978

ALLINGTON, RICHARD L. (1978, November). Teacher ability in recording oral reading performance. *Academic Therapy, 14*(2), 187–192. (EJ194157)

> Studies 57 teachers and their abilities to correctly evaluate oral reading.

AMOROSE, HENRY CHARLES (1978). *A psycholinguistic analysis of the oral and silent reading performance of selected standard IV subjects in Trinidad and Tobago, W. Indies* (Tech. Rep. No. 468). Madison, WI: Wisconsin University, Research and Development Center for Individualized Schooling. (ED 162 278)

> Describes the overall reading ability of 200 students and explores the extent that linguistically related reading difficulties are manifested in their oral and silent reading.

BARRERA, ROSALINDA B. (1978). *Analysis and comprehension of the first-language and second-language oral reading behavior of native Spanish-speaking Mexican American children.* Unpublished doctoral dissertation, University of Texas, Austin. (UMI No. AAC 78-17612)

> Uses miscue analysis to study reading of native Spanish speakers in Spanish and in English. The study shows that Spanish reading is very much like English reading.

BEAN, THOMAS WILLIAM (1978, June). Oral reading miscues of Hawaiian Islands dialect speakers in grades four, five, and six. *Reading Improvement, 15*(2), 115–118. (EJ192195)

> Describes differences in strategies employed by average and below average readers in each grade and across succeeding grade levels.

BOUSQUET, ROBERT J. (1978). *A primer of Black English for informal reading inventory error/miscue analysis.* Monograph prepared for the Trenton Public Schools, Trenton, NJ. (ED 181 446)

> Provides information on black English to be used by teachers as they score miscues.

CAREY, ROBERT F. (1978). *A psycholinguistic analysis of the effects of semantic acceptability of oral reading miscues on read-*

ing comprehension. Unpublished doctoral dissertation, University of Connecticut, Storrs. (UMI No. AAC 79-11342)

> Finds that oral reading miscues, when considered on the basis of degree of semantic acceptability and correction behavior, maintain a persistent and significant relationship with comprehension performance.

CHRISTIE, JAMES F. (1978, June). The effect of later appearing syntactic structures on children's oral reading errors. *Reading Improvement, 15*(2), 154–156. (EJ192204)

> Finds more detrimental errors on passages containing later appearing syntactic structures.

ESSELMAN, BIRDLENE (1978). *An investigation of third and fourth grade reading teachers' perceptions as related to those who speak Black dialect in the school district of the city of Highland Park, Michigan.* Unpublished doctoral dissertation, Wayne State University, Detroit, MI. (UMI No. AAC 78-16019)

> Utilizes miscue analysis to document teachers' feedback to children's dialect miscues. The teachers' education level is found to be an influence in judgments of dialect miscues.

EWOLDT, CAROLYN (1978, December). Reading for the hearing impaired: A single process. *American Annals of the Deaf, 123*(9), 945–948.

> The deaf readers in this study demonstrate strategies similar to hearing readers, such as predicting, chunking, using their own language, and developing concepts through reading.

GARDINER, D. ELIZABETH (1978). *The effect of a language-based reading approach upon the reading strategies of first grade children.* Unpublished doctoral dissertation, Pacific States University, Los Angeles, CA. (ED 167 959)

> Uses miscue analysis to support a language-based approach to reading in first grade.

GEISSAL, MARY A., & KNAFLE, JUNE D. (1978, November). *The effects of miscue analysis instruction on judgments of seriousness of oral reading errors.* Paper presented at the 28th Annual Meeting of the National Reading Conference, St. Petersburg Beach, FL. (ED 165 105)

> Studies whether miscue analysis instruction changes undergraduate students' perceptions of the seriousness of certain kinds of errors in children's oral reading.

GLENN, JUNE, & GLENN, HUGH W. (1978). Do children read as they are taught to read? In M.P. Douglas (Ed.), *Reading for life.* (Forty-second Yearbook of the Claremont Reading Conference, pp. 111–117). Claremont, CA: Claremont Reading Conference.

> Miscue research is used as a basis for arguing that what is taught is not what children learn about reading.

GONZALES, PHILLIP C., & ELIJAH, DAVID (1978, December). Stability of error patterns on the Informal Reading Inventory. *Reading Improvement, 15*(4), 279–288. (EJ199350)

> Consistent word recognition patterns are found for 26 third graders who read and reread oral passages at instructional and frustrational levels.

GOODMAN, KENNETH S., & GOODMAN, YETTA M. (1978, August). *Reading of American children whose language is stable rural dialect of English or a language other than English* (Final Report, Project NIE-C-00-3-0087). Washington, DC: National Institute of Education. (ED 173 754)

> Studies of the miscues of 96 students are presented, and K.S. Goodman's model of the reading process is refined.

GOODMAN, KENNETH S., & PAGE, WILLIAM D. (1978). *Reading comprehension programs: Theoretical bases of reading comprehension instruction in the middle grades.* (Revised Final Report). Center for the Expansion of Language and Thinking, Tucson, AZ. (ED 165 092)

> Discussion of the relationship between theories of reading comprehension and instructional practices and program consistency.

GRAHAM, STEVE, & HUDSON, FLOYD (1978). *Oral reading miscues or errors: A bibliography of research.* (Sponsored by the Bureau of Education for the Handicapped, Washington, DC, Grant #G007700460). Lawrence, KS: University of Kansas. (ED 159 604)

Partially annotated bibliography includes 154 reports on the analysis of oral reading miscues.

GRANGER, ROBERT C., & RAMIG, CHRISTOPHER J. (1978, March). *Teacher judgements of the ability of readers with different speech patterns.* Paper presented at the Annual Meeting of the American Educational Research Association, Toronto, ON. (ED 153 197)
> The results are interpreted to indicate that black dialect does influence teacher diagnosis of reading ability.

HART, M. MURLEE (1978, November). *Preventing the proliferation of problem readers.* Paper presented at the 68th Annual Meeting of the National Council of Teachers of English, Kansas City, MO. (ED 172 150)
> Argues that problem readers are created by teachers who stress isolated reading skills and error-free oral reading over reading for understanding.

HOCEVAR, SUSAN PAGE, & HOCEVAR, DENNIS (1978). The effect of meaningful versus non-meaningful reading material on oral reading errors in first through third grade children. *Journal of Reading Behavior, 10*(3), 297–299. (EJ201178)
> Tests whether students reading material related to their backgrounds of experience will produce fewer oral reading errors if material is unfamiliar.

HOOD, JOYCE (1978, December). Is miscue analysis practical for teachers? *The Reading Teacher, 32*(3), 260–266. (EJ939944)
> Describes a modified version of miscue analysis for classroom teachers.

HOWELL, SALLY W., & RILEY, JAMES D. (1978, March). Words for positive growth: Teacher-student interaction in reading instruction. *The Reading Teacher, 31*(5), 664–667. (EJ177567)
> Discusses the importance of positive feedback to children's miscues.

JACKSON, SUSAN M. (1978). *Assessing reading vocabulary of Pima Indian students for curriculum adaptation.* Unpublished doctoral dissertation, Arizona State University, Tempe. (UMI No. AAC 79-11128)
> Differences are found in quantitative vs. qualitative assessment. This paper recommends miscue analysis for assessment of divergent populations.

JONGSMA, EUGENE A. (1978, October). The effect of training in miscue analysis on teachers' perceptions of oral reading behaviors. *Reading World, 18*(1), 85–90. (EJ188590)

> Reports evidence that training in miscue analysis helped 23 teachers become more sensitive to students' strengths and weaknesses in reading.

JURENKA, NANCY ELIZABETH ALLEN (1978). *Psycholinguistic description of the oral reading miscues generated by nine selected Mexican-American students in grades three, four, and five, reading English texts.* Unpublished doctoral dissertation, Indiana University, Bloomington. (UMI No. AAC 79-05970)

> The changes noted as readers get older are: fewer miscues per hundred words, omissions are used differently, and syntactic acceptability increases. Younger readers read ethnic stories more effectively. All readers show better comprehension of ethnic stories and retellings in English and Spanish.

KAMIL, MICHAEL, & PEARSON, P. DAVID (1978, March). Error patterns in oral reading. *Reading Improvement, 15*(1), 33–35. (EJ181398)

> Five examples show how teachers can analyze oral reading errors informally, effectively, and inexpensively.

KOLCZYNSKI, RICHARD GERALD (1978). *A comparative analysis of miscues in content area reading.* Unpublished; ERIC document only. (ED 214 107)

> Findings suggest that the reading process remains stable across passages from various subject areas.

LESLIE, LAUREN, & OSOL, PAT (1978, December). Changes in oral reading strategies as a function of quantities of miscues. *Journal of Reading Behavior, 10*(4), 442–445. (EJ202988)

> Describes miscue patterns in eighth grade children reading material of sixth, eighth, eleventh, and thirteenth grade readability.

MAGUIRE, MARY H. (1978). *Psycholinguistic descriptive analysis of six selected secondary IV students' perceptions of the reading and writing processes and their language performance: Case studies of above average, average, and poor readers.* Unpublished master's thesis, McGill University, Montreal, PQ.

> Uses RMI profiles and interviews to compare students' behavior and awareness of their reading and writing processes. Finds students' metacognitive awarenesses consistent with their practices, with average and above average readers more aware of their own limitations.

MARING, GERALD H. (1978, May). Matching remediation to miscues. *The Reading Teacher, 31*(8), 887–891. (EJ181339)

> Suggests ways to apply psycholinguistic principles in the classroom.

McNAUGHTON, STUART (1978, August). *Learning in one-to-one oral reading interactions: Outcomes of teacher attention to errors.* Paper presented at the 9th Annual Meeting of the International Reading Association New Zealand Conference on Reading, Dunedin, New Zealand. (ED 172 134)

> Analyzes the influence on readers of the attention teachers give to their reading miscues in one-to-one instruction.

MITCHELL, KATHERINE A. (1978a). *Patterns of teacher-student responses to oral reading errors as related to teachers' previous training in different theoretical frameworks.* Unpublished; ERIC document only. (ED 182 716)

> Six teachers judged as expert representatives of either Kenneth Goodman's or Caleb Gattegno's theoretical positions are videotaped while working with remedial readers eight to nine years old.

MITCHELL, KATHERINE A. (1978b). *Patterns of teacher-student responses to oral reading errors as related to teachers' previous training in different theoretical frameworks.* Unpublished doctoral dissertation, New York University, New York, NY. (UMI# AAC 79-11252)

> Study of two groups (Goodman oriented and Gattegno oriented) of teachers' responses to reading errors using the Analytical System for Student-Teacher Interactions in Reading.

NEWMAN, HAROLD (1978, May). Oral reading miscue analysis is good but not complete. *The Reading Teacher, 31*(8), 883–886. (EJ181338)

Discusses differences between oral and silent reading and suggests that each must be evaluated to understand the reading process.

NIERATKA, ERNEST BLAIR (1978). *A psycholinguistic description of the oral and silent reading behavior of persisting and non-persisting non-traditional college freshman reading narrative and expository material.* Unpublished doctoral dissertation, Wayne State University, Detroit, MI. (UMI No. AAC 79-08947)

> Among other findings, reports a significant relationship between reading strategy effectiveness and persistence in college for nontraditional students.

OTTO, JEAN A. (1978, November). *Reading: Cue use, achievement and comprehension in an adolescent population.* Paper presented at the 28th Annual Meeting of the National Reading Conference, St. Petersburg Beach, FL. (ED 165 106)

> Miscues made by 96 eighth and ninth graders suggest that K.S. Goodman's theory of the reading process can be applied to the reading of secondary students.

PFLAUM, SUSANNA W. (1978). *Oral reading in the learning disabled.* Unpublished; ERIC document only. (ED 174 959)

> Reports differences and similarities between disabled children's linguistic cue use and that of normal readers under controlled conditions.

PRATT, LINDA GENDRON (1978). *A psycholinguistic analysis of the oral reading miscues of first grade children made during guided and unguided reading activities.* Unpublished doctoral dissertation, University of Massachusetts, Amherst. (UMI No. AAC 78-18040)

> This study indicates that the instructional Guided Reading Activity procedure has little, if any, effect on either the reading process, its associated reading strategies, or the comprehension of beginning readers of at least average reading ability.

RAISNER, BARBARA KORAL (1978). *Reading strategies employed by non-proficient adult college students as observed through miscue analysis and retrospection.* Unpublished doctoral dissertation, Hofstra University, Hempstead, NY. (UMI No. AAC 78-01410)

> Concludes that nonproficient adult readers exhibit idiosyncratic reading strategies that vary according to the material being read.

RAISNER, BARBARA KORAL (1978, October). Adult reading strategies: Do they differ from the strategies of children? *Reading World*, *18*(1), 37–47. (EJ188585)

> Studies the reading strategies of 14 black adult college students who are not proficient readers and offers suggestions for college remedial reading programs.

RIGG, PAT (1978, March). Dialect and/in/for reading. *Language Arts*, *55*(3), 285–290. (EJ181209)

> Discusses ways students can avoid miscues caused by eye dialects in their reading.

RIVERA-VIERA, DIANA T. (1978). *A descriptive study of reading miscues of Spanish-speaking elementary school children*. Unpublished doctoral dissertation, University of Massachusetts, Amherst. (UMI No. AAC 78-10746)

> An exploratory study of eight Spanish speaking third graders in Puerto Rico finds no important differences in the Spanish reading process and finds that the use of the RMI as a research tool for studies with Spanish-speakers is valid.

ROUSCH, PETER DESMOND, & CAMBOURNE, BRIAN L. (1978). *A psycholinguistic model of the reading process as it relates to proficient, average, and low ability readers*. Wagga Wagga, NSW, Australia: Riverina College of Advanced Education.

> Includes 130 students from grades 2, 4, 6, and 8, and finds differences in how well they control the three kinds of cues. The difference for low ability readers is a failure in semantic processing; the study suggests they are semantically at risk.

SMARR, JUDY LEE (1978). *A psycholinguistic study of the miscues and selected dialect features exhibited in the oral readings and retellings of two groups of down east Maine dialect speakers*. Unpublished doctoral dissertation, Wayne State University, Detroit, MI. (UMI No. AAC 78-16085)

> Supports the theory that there is a single reading process. Dialect features have no effect on the comprehension or reconstruction of meaning during the reading process.

SMITH, LAURA A. (1978). *Psycholinguistic comparison of use of syntactic cues by monolingual and bilingual subjects during oral reading in English basal readers*. Unpublished doctoral dissertation, Wayne State University, Detroit, MI. (UMI No. AAC 79-08964)

> Finds that while bilingual subjects' ability to use English syntax in oral language increases from second to fourth to sixth grades, the sixth grade group does not become more proficient in using this ability in reading.

SMITH, LAURA A., & WEAVER, CONSTANCE (1978). A psycholinguistic look at the informal reading inventory Part I: Looking at the quality of readers' miscues: A rationale and an easy method. *Reading Horizons, 19*(1), 12–22. (EJ201226)

> Discusses the importance of quality rather than quantity when analyzing oral reading miscues and presents ways to analyze miscues for insights into appropriate instruction.

SMITH, MABEL GLOVER (1978a). *A comparison between oral reading miscues of readers with normal intelligence and educable mentally retarded readers* (Tech. Rep. No. 469). Madison, WI: Research and Development Center for Individualized Schooling. (ED 162 280)

> Reports that normal and mentally retarded readers are similar in their use of graphophonic cues, but differ in their use of syntactic and semantic cues and in self-correction.

SMITH, MABEL GLOVER (1978b). *A comparison between oral reading miscues of readers with normal intelligence and educable mentally retarded readers*. Unpublished doctoral dissertation, University of Wisconsin, Madison. (UMI No. AAC 78-15075)

> Twenty-six students from first, second, and third grades are compared with 26 mentally retarded students ages 9 to 16. Although differences do exist between the groups, it is apparent that mentally retarded readers are utilizing the reading strategies tapped by the Goodman RMI. The majority of these reading strategies, however, are not used as efficiently.

STANSELL, JOHN C. (1978, December). Instructional needs in secondary reading: An illustrative case study. *Reading World, 18*(2), 156–165. (EJ203024)

Presents a case study of a high school reader whose miscue patterns reveal an instructionally-induced over-reliance on graphophonic cues at the expense of meaning. Suggests instructional strategies to help the reader.

STANSELL, JOHN C., HARSTE, JEROME C., & DESANTI, ROGER J. (1978). The effect of differing materials on the reading process. In P.D. Pearson & J. Hansen (Eds.), *Reading: Disciplined inquiry in process and practice.* (Twenty-seventh Yearbook of the National Reading Conference, pp. 27–35). Clemson, SC: National Reading Conference.

Second and ninth graders and elderly readers read narrative and expository text. Suggests that the reading process is relatively stable across content areas and text types. Concern for accurate decoding is related to poor comprehension, even among ninth graders and elderly.

THOMAS, KEITH J. (1978). Psycholinguistic implications regarding the development of reading rate. In G. Enright (Ed.), *Learning assistance: Charting our course.* (Proceedings of the 11th Annual Conference of the Western College Reading Association, pp. 83–87). San Francisco, CA: Western College Reading Association.

Comparing Frank Smith and Ken Goodman's theories of reading finds Goodman's work more appropriate for teachers due to its attention to the mediating nature of each of the cueing systems.

THOMSON, M. (1978). A psycholinguistic analysis of reading errors made by dyslexics and normal readers. *Journal of Research in Reading, 1*(1), 7–20.

Children labeled dyslexic in this study make more errors at the graphophonic level than at the syntactic and semantic level, whereas the control group makes more errors at the bound morpheme, phrase, and sentence level.

WATSON, DOROTHY J. (1978, December). Reader selected miscues: Getting more from sustained silent reading. *English Education, 10*(2), 75–85. (EJ195974)

Describes a technique that involves junior high students in identifying and dealing with their own miscues.

WEAVER, CONSTANCE (1978, March). *Grammar and what to do with it.* Paper presented at the 10th Annual Meeting of the National Conference on Language Arts in the Elementary School, Indianapolis, IN. (ED 155 730)

> Argues that recognition and appreciation of children's intuitive understanding of sentence structure and their ability to apply this understanding as they read can be gained through the use of miscue analysis.

WHITMER, JOAN ELIZABETH A. (1978). *A psycholinguistic description of oral reading miscues of third grade linguistically different Spanish surnamed and Anglo children.* Unpublished doctoral dissertation, University of Colorado, Boulder. (UMI No. AAC 79-03099)

> Study concludes that middle class children make higher quality miscues than lower class children across ethnic backgrounds.

WOLF, ANNE ELIZABETH (1978). *Generalizability of Reading Miscue Inventory scores generated by average readers in grade three on basal-reader fictional selections of comparable length and readability level.* Unpublished doctoral dissertation, University of Wisconsin, Madison. (UMI No. AAC 78-11755)

> A statistical study of the RMI has third grade readers reading three basal reader stories of the same readability score. Findings based on inconsistency of readers' miscues across the stories lead to questioning the use of miscue analysis findings for research or diagnosis.

YOUNG, KELVIN K.K. (1978, March). Language cues and effective reading. *Educational Perspectives, 17*(1), 18–23. (EJ186279)

> Discusses the ways language cues are used in reading, describes methods for evaluating readers' processing of cues, and suggests ways to promote more effective reading strategies.

1979

AKURAL, KATHRYN RIDER (1979). *Kenneth S. Goodman's theory of reading: A psycholinguistic and epistemological analysis.* Unpublished doctoral dissertation, Indiana University, Bloomington. (UMI No. AAC 80-00674)

The study asks what Goodman's theory of reading has to say about is- sues ranging from the nature of knowledge to the nature of language. The major concern is the identification of the epistemological problems raised by Goodman's view of reading and the examination of his philo- sophical positions and methodology.

AULLS, MARK W. (1979, November). *QASOR: A framework for interpreting silent and oral reading.* Paper presented at the 29th Annual Meeting of the National Reading Conference, San Anto- nio, TX. (ED 189 594; See also ED 184 103)
> Presents guidelines for using Qualitative Analysis of Silent and Oral Reading instrument, an adaptation of the Reading Miscue Inventory.

AUTERI, VIOLETTE T. (1979). *Oral reading miscues made by chil- dren in high, medium and low reading groups in grade one through six.* Unpublished doctoral dissertation, Temple Universi- ty, Philadelphia, PA. (UMI No. AAC 79-24041)
> Studies types of miscues across elementary grades and ability groups. In the medium group, graphic miscues decrease as grade level increases, and semantic miscues increase as grade level increases.

BALDAUF, RICHARD B., JR., & PROPST, IVAN K. (1979, October). *Measuring ESL reading achievement with matching cloze.* Paper presented at the Micronesian Educators' Conference, Saipan, Pacific Islands. (ED 186 468)
> Goodman's theory of the strategies used by good readers is described as it relates to the construction of matching cloze tests.

BEAN, THOMAS WILLIAM (1979, May). The miscue mini-form: Re- fining the informal reading inventory. *Reading World, 18*(4), 400–405. (EJ203052)
> Presents a miniform of miscue analysis to be used in identifying reading levels and error patterns.

BIEMILLER, ANDREW (1979, December). Changes in use of graph- ic and contextual information as a function of passage difficulty and reading achievement level. *Journal of Reading Behavior, 11*(4), 307–318. (EJ234081)

Reports that first grade children instructed with a "meaning emphasis" shift toward greater reliance on graphic information when confronted with materials where words are harder to identify.

BRADY, MARY ELLA (1979). *Effect of teacher responses to pupil miscues on pupil strategies of decoding and comprehending.* Unpublished doctoral dissertation, Indiana University, Bloomington. (UMI No. AAC 79-16885)

> Research on how teacher response to miscues impacts reading strategies. Finds readers receiving instruction in "sounding out" make significantly more sound/nonsense miscues than readers in other groups.

CAREY, ROBERT F. (1979). Reading the content areas: Some implications from psycholinguistics. In R. Vacca & J. Meagher (Eds.), *Reading through content* (pp. 43–50). Storrs, CT: University of Connecticut.

> Poses possible links between psycholinguistic research in reading and reading instruction in the content areas. The intended audience is teachers.

CAREY, ROBERT F. (1979, March). Cloze encounters of a different kind. *Reading Horizons, 19*(3), 228–231. (EJ210774)

> Describes the use of a cloze test after an oral reading of the same passage.

CHIPPENDALE, ENE KAJA HARM (1979). *A psycholinguistic model of reading comprehension based on language competence, reading proficiency, and discourse analysis.* Unpublished doctoral dissertation, University of Missouri, Columbia. (UMI No. AAC 80-02344)

> Finds that mismatches, where textual expectations exceed the linguistic background of the child or where effective reading strategies have not been developed, result in comprehension loss.

CUTHBERTSON, BEVERLY J. (1979). *A comparative study relating to oral reading miscues and first language influence for Mexican-American junior high school students.* Unpublished doctoral dissertation, Northern Arizona University, Flagstaff. (UMI No. AAC 80-04773)

> RMI is used in this study of first language influence in relation to sex, intelligence, socioeconomic status, and literacy.

D'ANGELO, KAREN, & WILSON, ROBERT M. (1979, February). How helpful is insertion and omission miscue analysis? *The Reading Teacher*, 32(5), 519–520.

> Suggests that time spent analyzing insertions and omissions is better spent on comprehension-distorting substitutions.

DANK, MARION E., & McEACHERN, WILLIAM (1979, March). A psycholinguistic description comparing the native language oral reading behavior of French immersion students with English language students. *Canadian Modern Language Review*, 35(3), 366–371. (EJ203198)

> Compares oral reading strategies of students in a primary French immersion program with those of students in a traditional English language program.

DESANTI, ROGER JOSEPH (1979, July). Cue system utilizations among older readers. *Educational Gerontology*, 4(3), 271–277. (EJ210499)

> Miscue analysis reveals that mature, older readers are consistent in the cue systems they utilize.

DILENA, MICHAEL JAMES (1979). *Conceptual knowledge and the construction of meaning from written texts*. Unpublished doctoral dissertation, Harvard University, Cambridge, MA. (UMI No. AAC 80-14038)

> Study uses miscue analysis to test the hypothesis that young, relatively inexperienced readers retain information from text only when they can relate it to existing knowledge.

DONALD, D.R. (1979, July). The remedial evaluation of oral reading errors: A methodological synopsis. *Reading*, 13(2), 16–24. (EJ212284)

> Proposes a system for analyzing oral reading errors of remedial readers.

DUBOIS, DIANE MARIE (1979, March). Getting meaning from print: Four Navajo students. *The Reading Teacher*, 32(6), 691–695. (EJ202894)

> Analyzes the reading of four Navajo children and notes that they believe the purpose of reading is to produce acceptable English grammar.

EATON, ARLINDA JANE (1979). *Psycholinguistic analysis of the oral reading miscues of selected field-dependent and field-independent native Spanish-speaking Mexican American first-grade children.* Unpublished doctoral dissertation, University of Texas, Austin. (UMI No. AAC 79-28279)

> First graders draw on the same linguistic cue systems in their attempts to reconstruct meaning from print while reading in both English and Spanish.

ELLIOTT, CYNTHIA MARGOT (1979). *Reading strategy development in beginning reading.* Unpublished doctoral dissertation, University of Massachusetts, Amherst. (UMI No. AAC 80-04919)

> Study of 30 beginning readers finds diversity in their approaches to print though readers can be grouped according to the similarity in their use of the cuing systems. Over time readers begin to rely heavily on graphophonic cuing to the point of producing graphophonically accurate non-words, indicating considerable graphophonic instruction seems to have an effect.

EWOLDT, CAROLYN, & GARNER, D. (1979, December). Psycholinguistic theory and practice: Facilitating the reading of the hearing impaired. *Washington Reading Quarterly, 5*(1), 12–14.

> The authors describe the reading of a basal story by deaf students, offering instructional suggestions for using the story to aid reading and writing development, language development, and intercurricular development.

FEELEY, JOAN T. (1979, March). Adding the Reading Miscue Inventory to the reading case study. *Reading Improvement, 16*(1), 75–81. (EJ206222)

> Describes the use of the RMI as an addition to the case studies of two primary grade students and one seventh grader who have been referred to a college reading clinic.

GOODMAN, KENNETH S. (1979, September). The know-more and the know-nothing movements in reading: A personal response. *Language Arts, 56*(6), 657–663.

> A 1979 restatement of the Goodman Model of Reading.

GOODMAN, KENNETH S., & GOODMAN, YETTA M. (1979). Learning to read is natural. In L.B. Resnik & P.A. Weaver (Eds.), *The-*

ory and practice of early reading, Vol. 1, (pp. 137–154). Hillsdale, NJ: Erlbaum. (See: ED 155 621)

> Discusses a holistic view of early reading development.

GRAHAM, STEVE, & MILLER, LAMOINE (1979). Miscue analysis: Application with handicapped students. *Diagnostique, 4*(1), 35–41. (EJ223624)

> Presents a technique for miscue analysis that has been used with handicapped students.

HARSTE, JEROME C., & CAREY, ROBERT F. (EDS.). (1979). *New perspectives on comprehension: Monographs in language and reading studies, No. 3.* Bloomington, IN: Indiana University. (ED 325 821)

> Includes 11 essays describing issues, problems, and trends in contemporary reading research and theory, with an emphasis on comprehension research. Chapters include those by K.S. Goodman, W.D. Page, P.D. Pearson, R. Spiro, and R. Tierney.

HOFFMAN, JAMES V. (1979, May). On providing feedback to reading miscues. *Reading World, 18*(4), 342–350. (EJ203043)

> Discusses the importance of teacher feedback to oral reading miscues.

KIBBY, MICHAEL W. (1979, January). Passage readability affects the oral reading strategies of disabled readers. *The Reading Teacher, 32*(4), 390–396. (EJ197685)

> Suggests that teachers should use less difficult materials in miscue analysis in order to get a true picture of a child's syntactic and semantic strategies.

KNAFLE, JUNE D., & GEISSAL, MARY ANN (1979, November). *Variations in attitudes toward children's oral reading errors.* Paper presented at the 29th Annual Meeting of the National Reading Conference, San Antonio, TX. (ED 182 741)

> Describes and compares the attitudes toward dialect demonstrated by several kinds of teachers.

LAMBERG, WALTER J. (1979, April). Assessment of oral reading which exhibits dialect and language differences. *Journal of Reading, 22*(7), 609–616. (EJ202912)

Describes procedures for assessing the oral reading of readers who exhibit dialect or second language influences in their speech.

Laws, William Ernest (1979). *A comparative psycholinguistic study of miscues generated by selected matched pairs of non-Distar and Distar readers who are special education pupils from junior opportunity classes.* Unpublished doctoral dissertation, Wayne State University, Detroit, MI. (UMI No. AAC 80-10153)

Fourteen Distar EMR readers are matched with 14 non-Distar (taught by traditional methods) EMR readers. Miscues are similar with respect to measures of graphic proximity, sound proximity, grammatical function, correction, grammatical acceptability, semantic acceptability, and grammatical strength. Distar readers differ significantly on comprehension measures and retelling scores from non-Distar readers, who do significantly better on these measures.

Love, Fannye Epps (1979). *An investigation of reading strategy lessons employing miscue analysis in psycholinguistic approaches to second grade reading instruction.* Unpublished doctoral dissertation, Kansas State University, Manhattan. (UMI No. AAC 79-26565)

Finds some gain in retelling scores for an experimental group of second graders given reading strategy lessons over a six week period.

MacLean, Margaret (1979, November). *QASOR: A framework for qualitatively analyzing silent and oral reading.* Paper presented at the 29th Annual Meeting of the National Reading Conference, San Antonio, TX. (ED 184 103; See also ED 189 594)

Suggests QASOR, an alternative to the RMI, can be used to investigate individual variations in oral and silent reading behaviors.

Marsden, Fleur Sybil (1979). *A psycholinguistic analysis of the reading strategies of early readers.* Unpublished doctoral dissertation, Peabody College for Teachers of Vanderbilt University, Nashville, TN. (UMI No. AAC 80-6109)

Fourteen kindergarten children make efficient use of graphophonic, syntactic, and semantic reading strategies. Relationship strategies, which are not as competently used, appear to be highly correlated to meaningful reading. The more efficient readers focus directly on meaning while the less efficient readers limit themselves more closely to the surface structure of print.

MUTTER, DAVIDA WARRINGTON (1979). *A psycholinguistic investigation of the influence of prior knowledge on the oral reading miscues and comprehension of selected high school seniors.* Unpublished doctoral dissertation, University of Massachusetts, Amherst. (UMI No. AAC 79-20876)

> Ten high school seniors read six informational passages taken from a textbook, standardized test, car manual, consumer magazine, and one self-selected passage. The influence of the reader's depth of prior knowledge and interest on processing strategies and comprehension is examined and described. The data suggest that comprehending and prompted retelling performances are dependent upon readers' background knowledge in the content of a passage.

NICHOLSON, TOM, PEARSON, P. DAVID, & DYKSTRA, ROBERT (1979, December). Effects of embedded anomalies and oral reading errors on children's understanding of stories. *Journal of Reading Behavior, 11*(4), 339–354. (EJ234084)

> Calls for a model of reading that accounts for prior knowledge, complexity of the comprehension task, familiarity with the text, and the level of understanding required by readers.

PAGE, WILLIAM D. (1979). *Theoretically derived variants of the comprehending score: Relationships between oral reading, cloze performance, and classroom reading ability.* (Study prepared at University of Connecticut). Unpublished; ERIC document only. (ED 181 406)

> Explores relationships between post oral reading cloze test scores and seven theoretically constructed variants of the comprehending score.

PAGE, WILLIAM D. (1979, December). Oral reading error correction behavior and cloze performance. *Reading World, 19*(2), 168–176. (EJ214132)

> Correction behavior in the reading of 48 elementary school children is related to comprehension and is measured by cloze procedure.

RHODES, LYNN K. (1979a). Comprehension & predictability: An analysis of beginning reading materials. In R.F. Carey & J.C.

Harste (Eds.), *New perspectives on comprehension: Monographs in Language and Reading Studies, No. 3* (pp. 100–131). Bloomington, IN: Indiana University. (ED 325 821)

> Reports the variation in comprehending (miscue analysis) and comprehension.

RHODES, LYNN K. (1979b). *The interaction of beginning readers' strategies and texts reflecting alternate models of predictability.* Unpublished doctoral dissertation, Indiana University, Bloomington. (UMI No. AAC 80-00619)

> Relationships between reader performance and semantic text structures suggest selections that focus the reader on semantics build comprehension through more effective use of available cues.

SHAFER, ROBERT EUGENE (ED.). (1979). *Applied linguistics and reading.* Newark, DE: International Reading Association. (ED 170 711)

> Presents linguistic theory as it applies to teaching reading. Includes a discussion of miscue analysis with an emphasis on comprehension.

SHAW, MARGARET HELEN (1979). *A psycholinguistic analysis of the oral reading miscues and the cognitive control of distractibility of remedial readers.* Unpublished doctoral dissertation, University of Oklahoma, Norman. (UMI No. AAC 80-04395)

> A study of 28 elementary students' reading miscues demonstrates that high distractibility remedial readers move from lesser use of graphic cues to higher use of those cues to generate meaning from print. Low distractibility remedial readers move from greater use of those cues to lesser use of those cues to generate meaning.

SHEARER, ARLEEN P. (1979). *A psycholinguistic comparison using cloze and oral miscue analysis of good and poor readers.* Unpublished; ERIC document only. (ED 255 870)

> Fourth grade good and poor readers show miscue analysis is more closely related to teacher rating and the California Test of Basic Skills than phoneme cloze procedures. Syntactic and nonsense error rate discriminate the fourth grade groups.

SHERMAN, BARRY W. (1979, November). Reading for meaning: Don't let word study blind your students. *Learning, 8*(3), 41–44. (EJ216872)

> Discusses common misconceptions about children's reading and presents practical suggestions for the classroom.

SIEGEL, FLORENCE (1979, October). Adapted miscue analysis. *Reading World, 19*(1), 36–43. (EJ209317; See also ED 154 349, 1977)

> Presents a form of miscue analysis for use by classroom teachers.

SILVA, AURELIA DAVILA DE (1979). *Oral reading behavior of Spanish-speaking children taught by a meaning-based program*. Unpublished doctoral dissertation, University of Texas, Austin. (UMI No. AAC 80-09928)

> Miscue analysis is used to describe the reading of Spanish-speaking children.

SIMS, RUDINE (1979). Miscue analysis—emphasis on comprehension. In R.E. Shafer (Ed.). *Applied Linguistics and Reading* (pp. 101–111). Newark, DE: International Reading Association.

> A discussion of how miscue analysis provides information about comprehending/comprehension in reading.

SIU-RUNYAN, Y. (1979). Using the retelling technique to investigate and enhance comprehension. *Illinois Reading Council Journal, 7*, 24–27.

> Author explains the retelling technique and discusses how to use it to develop and investigate comprehending strategies.

SPITZER, ROSINA (1979). *Psycholinguistic processes in reading*. Unpublished doctoral dissertation, The Fielding Institute, Santa Barbara, CA. (UMI No. AAC 80-19357)

> Twenty-four subjects in grades 5–8 who are labeled problem readers receive psycholinguistic-based instruction. After not making much progress in reading for as much as four to seven years, these students show a statistically significant breakthrough in reading comprehension through the increased quality of their miscues in only eight hours of overtime instruction.

TANNER, MICHAEL LOWELL (1979). *The effect of high and low interest on the reading miscues, strategies and behaviors of secondary students while reading American history materials.* Unpublished doctoral dissertation, University of Northern Colorado, Greeley. (UMI No. AAC 80-04477)

> While high school sophomores and juniors do not differ in cue system use, they make fewer miscues, use more effective reading strategies, and give better retellings when reading material of high interest versus material of low interest.

TOVEY, DUANE R. (1979, June). Teachers' perceptions of children's reading miscues. *Reading Horizons, 19*(4), 302–307. (EJ212193)

> Evaluates teachers' responses to students' miscues and finds that teachers object most strongly to dialect-related miscues.

WATSON, DOROTHY J. (1979). Breaking the barriers: What miscue analysis offers the classroom teacher. In A.M. Scales & J.D. Peebles (Eds.), *Reading and writing: Concepts for teaching and learning.* (Proceedings of the 30th and 31st Language Communications Conferences, pp. 11–30). Pittsburgh, PA: University of Pittsburgh. (ED 229 765)

> Lists and examines six traditional beliefs about reading and what miscue analysis reveals about these beliefs. Classroom implications are discussed and strategy lessons are suggested.

WEAVER, CONSTANCE, & SMITH, LAURA (1979, December). A psycholinguistic look at the Informal Reading Inventory Part II: Inappropriate inferences from an Informal Reading Inventory. *Reading Horizons, 19*(2), 103–111. (EJ202927)

> Points out the importance of distinguishing between the quality of miscues and the quantity of miscues.

WILLEKENS, MARY GUERRA (1979). *A descriptive analysis of reading miscues of Spanish-surnamed readers in grades three and five.* Unpublished doctoral dissertation, Arizona State University, Tempe. (UMI No. AAC 79-17946)

> This study of 32 students finds third graders rely more on the use of graphophonic strategies than do fifth graders.

WILLIAMS, LINDA K. (1979). *The risks of initial reading instruction in an immersion English as a second language situation.* Unpublished master's thesis, San Diego State University, San Diego, CA. (ED 185 844)

> Traces the progress and problems of five Spanish-speaking fourth graders who have learned to read only in English.

WIXSON, KAREN L. (1979, June). Miscue analysis: A critical review. *Journal of Reading Behavior, 11*(2), 163–175. (EJ214092)

> Discusses trends in miscue analysis and states that miscue patterns are the result of complex interactions among many variables.

PART 5

1980–1984

1980

ANDERSON, JONATHAN (1980, August). *New miscue analysis: A tool for comprehending reading.* Paper presented at the 8th Meeting of the World Congress on Reading, Manila, Philippines. (ED 198 516)

> Presents a form of miscue analysis that combines cloze with the traditional RMI.

BEEBE, MONA JANE (1980). The effect of different types of substitution miscues on reading. *Reading Research Quarterly, 15*(3), 324–336. (EJ221382)

> Finds that not all substitutions detract from comprehension to the same degree in the reading of 46 fourth grade boys.

BIANCHI, ANNE M. (1980). *Qualitative and descriptive analysis of the oral reading of narrative and expository material by 8th grade students in the 1st and 3rd year of a bilingual program.* Unpublished doctoral dissertation, University of Northern Colorado, Greeley. (UMI No. AAC 81-08216)

> Several differences in patterns of miscues and retellings are found between first and third year students in the same bilingual program.

BOTTHOF, RICHARD NELS (1980). *Reading strategies and comprehension of average second-grade readers reading a basal text with or without illustrations.* Unpublished doctoral dissertation, University of Oklahoma, Norman. (UMI No. AAC 80-7506)

> Concludes that miscues reflect responses to the text to a greater extent than they reflect responses to alternative cues, such as illustrations.

BROWN, SUSAN COHEN (1980). *The efficacy of the Reading Miscue Inventory in evaluating the reading performance of college freshmen.* Unpublished doctoral dissertation, New Mexico State University, Las Cruces. (UMI No. AAC 80-19218)

> Looks at beginning college students reading content materials. Compares groups with high and low ACT scores. Finds the RMI is useful for evaluating college reading.

BUTTON, LINDA JEAN (1980). *Standardized reading test scores & informal reading inventory results with miscue analysis for above and below average 3rd graders: A comparison.* Unpublished doctoral dissertation, University of Northern Colorado, Greeley. (UMI No. AAC 80-28320)

> Uses a modified form of miscue analysis and finds reading strategies for below average students use graphophonic, syntactic, and semantic cues in nearly equal proportions.

CASHEN, CAROL JOAN (1980). *A study of the effect of the test environment on the reading comprehension, comprehending, and processing of text by junior high school readers.* Unpublished doctoral dissertation, Indiana University, Bloomington. (UMI No. AAC 81-03408)

> Uses the RMI to study comprehending defined as in-process construction of meaning. Demonstrates that pupils vary in response to the test situation. Some pupils perform more poorly in test situations than in nontest or classroom conditions.

CHRISTIANSEN, JANET C., ANNESLEY, FREDERICK R., & SCOTT, EDWARD (1980, August). *Relationship between cognitive style and the acquisition of meaning in content reading.* Paper presented at the 8th Meeting of the World Congress on Reading, Manila, Philippines. (ED 200 915)

> Reports findings of a study concerned with the effectiveness and efficiency with which ninth grade field-dependent and field-independent readers process prose at three levels of difficulty.

CHRISTIE, JAMES F., & ALONSO, PATRICIA A. (1980, March). Effects of passage difficulty on primary-grade children's oral reading error patterns. *Educational Research Quarterly, 5*(1), 40–49. (EJ231264)

Studies effects of passage difficulty on the oral reading error patterns of first and third grade students.

CLARKE, MARK A. (1980, June). The short circuit hypothesis of ESL Reading—Or when language competence interferes with reading performance. *Modern Language Journal*, 64(2), 203–209. (EJ251161)

> The results of these studies suggest that, although some form of the universals hypothesis may be justified, the role of language proficiency may be greater than has previously been assumed. Apparently, limited control over the language short circuits the good reader's system, causing him or her to revert to poor reader strategies when confronted with a difficult or confusing task in the second language.

CORTEZ, JESUS (1980). *Miscue corrections by bilingual and monolingual teachers when teaching bilingual children to read: A comparative study of Wales, Spain and two regions of the United States.* Unpublished doctoral dissertation, University of Washington, Seattle. (UMI No. AAC 80-26219)

> Studies teacher responses to miscues on typescripts of Welsh-English, Catalan-Castellano, and Spanish-English readers. Subjects are teachers asked to indicate which miscues they would correct in a child's reading. Bilingual teachers appear to do better than monolingual teachers in choosing which miscues need correction.

CRAM, RUBY VICTORIA (1980). *A psycholinguistic investigation of the cloze responses of secondary school students.* Unpublished doctoral dissertation, University of British Columbia, Vancouver, BC.

> Investigates the role of exact and nonexact replacements of cloze responses in the assessment of reading comprehension. Two modes of discourse, narrative fiction and expository prose, are investigated. Responses are tested for an exact match to the author's word (Bormuth, 1975). To evaluate nonexact replacements, the investigator adapts the Cambourne Reading Assessment Procedure (1978), based on the Goodman Taxonomy of Reading Miscues.

D'ANGELO, KAREN (1980, March). *Clinical research: Miscue analysis and phonics inventories.* Paper presented at the 3rd Annual Meeting of the Eastern Regional Conference of the International Reading Association, Niagara Falls, NY. (ED 190 982)

Compares adapted miscue analysis and phonics skill inventory in grades 1–12. Suggests a focus on substitutions and finds that poor readers rely more on graphics and use graphic based distortions to make corrections.

DEFORD, DIANE E., MEEKER, LORELEI, & NIERATKA, ERNEST B. (1980, March). An effective screening profile in reading for high risk students: A matter of convenience or service? *Viewpoints in Teaching and Learning, 56(2),* 65–73.

> The authors argue that reliance upon standardized test scores as a sole means of predicting success or failure in university programs is not effective or efficient.

DEVINE, JOANNE MARY (1980). *Developmental patterns in native and non-native reading acquisition.* Unpublished doctoral dissertation, Michigan State University, East Lansing. (UMI No. AAC 81-01095)

> Fourteen Mexican adults studying in a summer program are ranked according to reading proficiency level. The study supports the existence of developmental trends in the reading of adults attempting to master reading in a foreign language. The research also establishes a relationship between changes in reading behavior, as a function of increased reading proficiency, for children learning to read in their native language and nonnative adults learning to read in a foreign language.

DONALD, D.R. (1980, September). Analysis of children's oral reading errors: A current perspective. *Journal of Research in Reading, 3(2),* 106–114. (EJ234050)

> Discusses the current interest in oral reading error analysis, including the resultant theoretical shifts.

ELLIS, ROD (1980, July). Learning to read through a second language. *Reading, 14(2),* 10–16. (EJ231972)

> Reports a study of the oral reading of 12 Asian children. Discusses strategies used by children learning to read a second language.

EWALD, HELEN ROTHSCHILD (1980). *Error-analysis for correctness, effectiveness, and composing procedure.* (ED 218 626)

> Miscue analysis is suggested as a process-oriented method of evaluating both the composing process and its products.

FELDMAN, DAVID, & WISEMAN, DONNA L. (1980, November). *A description of moderately mentally retarded adolescents' responses to written language.* Paper presented at the 7th Annual Conference of the Association for the Severely Handicapped, Los Angeles, CA. (ED 199 939)

> Includes miscue analysis on the oral reading of 12 moderately mentally retarded adolescents.

FLEISHER, BARBARA MARY (1980). *Meaning identification and word calling: Changes in strategies of good and poor readers as text gradually increases in difficulty.* Unpublished doctoral dissertation, University of San Francisco, San Francisco, CA. (UMI No. AAC 81-03660)

> This study investigates the hypothesis that better readers tend to perceive reading as primarily a meaning identification task compared to poorer readers who tend to perceive reading as a word calling task. Data from 16 fourth grade subjects supports the theory that as materials increase in difficulty, efficient readers tend to differ from poorer readers because they hold meaning identification as the higher priority, whereas poorer readers tend to prioritize graphic similarity.

GOLLASCH, FREDERICK V. (1980). *Readers' perception in detecting and processing embedded errors in meaningful context.* Unpublished doctoral dissertation, University of Arizona, Tucson. (UMI No. AAC 81-07445)

> Two hundred forty junior and college level students read text with letter and word level embedded errors. Readers demonstrate that comprehension inhibits attention to graphic detail and is central to their reading. More efficient readers show greater flexibility in their use of the reading process.

GOODMAN, KENNETH S., & GOLLASCH, FREDERICK V. (1980). Word omissions: Deliberate and non-deliberate. *Reading Research Quarterly, 16*(1), 6–31. (EJ234110)

> Explores why omissions take place and their effects on the reading process. Classifies word level omissions as being either deliberate or non-deliberate.

GOODMAN, KENNETH S., & GOODMAN, YETTA M. (1980). *Linguistics, psycholinguistics, and the teaching of reading: An an-*

notated bibliography. (3rd ed.). Newark, DE: International Reading Association. (ED 190 994)

> Topics include: beginning reading; comprehension, semantics, and meaning; curriculum; language differences; discourse analysis; application of linguistics and psycholinguistics to reading; instruction; miscue analysis; oral and written language; syntax, grammar, and intonation; testing; reading theory; and words.

GRIFFIN, MARGARET, & JONGSMA, KATHLEEN (1980, May). *Adaptations of retelling: Two variations on a theme.* Paper presented at the 25th Annual Meeting of the International Reading Association, St. Louis, MO. (ED 190 984)

> Presents a five-step adaptation of the Reading Miscue Inventory.

HAYES, CHRISTOPHER G. (1980, March). *An overview of psycholinguistic reading theory.* Paper presented at the 31st Annual Meeting of the Conference on College Composition and Communication, Washington, DC. (ED 188 114)

> Discusses the importance of comprehension to a theoretical view of reading, and how miscue analysis and cloze procedure can be useful in understanding the reading process.

HITTLEMAN, DANIEL R. (1980). Adaptive assessment for nonacademic secondary reading. In D.J. Sawyer (Ed.), *Disabled readers: Insight, assessment, instruction*, (pp. 74–81). Newark, DE: International Reading Association.

> Case study of a high school dropout reading narrative, expository, and job related passages. Shows that the number and types of miscues vary with the text topic, format, and organization (See also ED 140 240, 1977).

HOFFMAN, JAMES V. (1980, December). Weighting miscues in informal inventories: A precautionary note. *Reading Horizons, 20*(2), 135–139. (EJ215878)

> States that weighting miscues on an informal inventory can result in an inappropriate independent reading level designation.

HOFFMAN, JAMES V., & BAKER, CHRISTOPHER (1980). *Observing communication during oral reading instruction: A critique of past research and a report on the development of a taxonomy of behaviors useful in field based research*. Paper presented at the 30th Annual Meeting of the International Communication Association, Acapulco, Mexico. (ED 189 541)

> Reports on the development of an observation instrument useful in characterizing the communication between teacher and student during oral reading instruction.

HOFFMAN, JAMES V., GARDNER, C.H., & CLEMENTS, RICHARD O. (1980). *FORMAS— Feedback to oral reading analysis system* (Training Manual No. 5058). Washington, DC: National Institute of Education. (ED 192 291)

> Presents six lessons designed to teach FORMAS in 10 hours.

KALMBACH, JAMES ROBERT (1980). *The evaluation of narrative retellings by sixth grade students*. Unpublished doctoral dissertation, Michigan State University, East Lansing. (UMI No. AAC 81-06393)

> Looks at retellings of sixth grade pupils who have been studied with the RMI and uses Labov's definition of narratives in examining the retellings.

KING, DOROTHY F. (1980). *A psycholinguistic analysis and propositional comparison of the reading of selected middle school children of self-authored and professionally-authored text*. Unpublished doctoral dissertation, University of Missouri, Columbia. (UMI No. AAC 81-08814)

> The study describes some of the behaviors that contribute to different performances on text that is self-authored and professionally authored and supports a psycholinguistic tenet that what the reader brings to the reading act is more important than the print encountered there.

KITA, MARY JANE (1980). *Children's concepts of reading and writing*. Unpublished doctoral dissertation, University of Virginia, Charlottesville. (UMI No. AAC 81-01063)

> An analysis of interviews and writing samples demonstrates that kindergarten children know more than they could articulate and suggests teachers should better understand students' tacit knowledge.

LESLIE, LAUREN (1980, June). The use of graphic and contextual information by average and below-average readers. *Journal of Reading Behavior, 12*(2), 139–149. (EJ246969)

Examines the use of graphic and contextual information by average and below-average readers when reading with equal rates of miscues.

MACAUL, SHERRY LYNN (1980). *The influence of linguistic context on word recognition accuracy and miscues.* Unpublished doctoral dissertation, Kent State University, Kent, OH. (UMI No. AAC 81-12886)

> Finds that context more than isolated graphic presentation seems to effect an increase in the single most acceptable combinatorial type miscue while serving to reduce the two most unacceptable combinatiorial miscues. The study also supports viewing the reader as an active participant, who exercises various degrees of strategic control over the material read.

MACMULLIN, M. RODERICK (1980). *Substitution errors in the oral reading of words from a list, and of the same words in context.* Research prepared at Temple University, Philadelphia, PA. (ED 191 002)

> In this study of 80 second graders, the recognition in context of a word unknown in isolation depends upon its grammatical function, difficulty, frequency of use, repetition in context, and the adequacy of context cues.

NEY, JAMES W. (1980, August). *Cognitive styles and miscue analysis of reading and writing.* Paper presented at the 3rd Annual International Conference on the Teaching of English, Sydney, Australia. (ED 194 886)

> Fourth graders' miscues in signaled sentence combining exercises are compared with their reading miscues in a study relating cognitive style (impulsive/reflective) to miscue analysis of reading and writing.

NG, SEOK M. (1980, August). *The strategies children use in learning to read.* Paper presented at the 8th Meeting of the World Congress on Reading, Manila, Philippines. (ED 205 901)

> This one-year descriptive study of beginning readers suggests that teaching programs emphasizing one particular strategy may not take full advantage of other equally valid strategies children can develop.

PARK, DONNA ANN (1980). *A study of the Goodman sociopsycholinguistic approach to beginning reading instruction in a first grade classroom.* Unpublished doctoral dissertation, University of Massachusetts, Amherst. (UMI No. AAC 81-01377)

An evaluation of a first grade reading program based on Goodman's sociopsycholinguistic approach.

POLLOCK, JOHN F., & BROWN, GARTH H. (1980, August). *Observing the effects of reading instruction.* Paper presented at the 8th Meeting of the World Congress on Reading, Manila, Philippines. (ED 198 500)
> Investigates ways of establishing links between different methods of reading instruction, children's conceptualizations of the reading process, and children's actual reading behavior.

POTTER, FRANK (1980, September). Miscue analysis: A cautionary note. *Journal of Research in Reading*, 3(2), 116–128. (EJ234051)
> Presents a modified form of miscue analysis that claims to avoid the confounding effects of a reader's ability to use graphic cues.

PROSAK, LESLIE ANN (1980). *A study and investigation of the perception of the reading process of preservice and inservice teachers.* Unpublished doctoral dissertation, University of Toledo, Toledo, OH. (UMI No. AAC 80-28553)
> Four hundred fifty preservice and inservice teachers are given the Siu Test of Teacher Perception of the Reading Process (STORP) to determine differences in their understandings of the reading process.

RAMIG, CHRISTOPHER J., & HALL, MARY ANNE (1980, March). Reading strategies of first grade children taught by a language experience approach and a basal approach. *Reading World*, 19(3), 280–289. (EJ217603)
> Studies first graders taught with either a language experience approach or a basal approach and concludes that there are no significant differences in the cues used by the two groups.

SADOSKI, MARK C. (1980). A unitive psycholinguistic comprehension measure: The comprehension process score. In J. Meagher & W.D. Page (Eds.), *Language centered reading instruction* (pp. 86–89). Storrs, CT: University of Connecticut: Reading Language Arts Center.

Describes the comprehension process score (a ratio of miscues that are positive predictors of comprehension to those that are negative). The study derives from principles of W.D. Page's altercue continuum.

SCHLIEPER, ANNE (1980, March). Reversal and sequence errors in a meaningful text. *Reading Improvement*, 17, 74–79.
Finds that reversals occur infrequently and do not seem to signal reading problems for first, second, and third graders reading a meaningful text.

SCOTT, EDWARD, ANNESLEY, FREDERICK R., MAHER, KAREN, & CHRISTIANSEN, JANET (1980, August). *Cognitive style and reading miscue in eighth graders*. Paper presented at the 8th Meeting of the World Congress on Reading, Manila, Philippines. (ED 200 914)
Presents a study of the oral reading miscues of field-dependent and field-independent above-average eighth graders on content area materials.

SMITH, CHRISTINE C. (1980). The relationship between oral reading miscues and comprehension: A study of developmental reading at the college level. In G. Enright (Ed.), *The 1980's: New sources of energy for learning*. (Proceedings of the 13th Annual Conference of the Western College Reading Association, San Francisco, CA, Vol. 13, pp. 65–69). Whittier, CA: Western College Reading Association. (ED 247 536)
Profiles of 27 college students who are seeking help in reading show (1) a word level focus; (2) their experience of timed testing supports a word level focus; and (3) there is a need for broader exposure to reading material.

SPIEGEL, DIXIE LEE, & ROGERS, CAROL (1980). Teacher responses to miscues during oral reading by second-grade students. *Journal of Educational Research*, 74(1), 8–12. (EJ237783)
Suggests that some teachers view exact word identification to be the goal of oral reading and they often miss opportunities to guide students toward a focus on meaning.

THOMAS, SHARON KAY (1980). *The effect of reader-authored materials on the performance of beginning readers*. Unpublished doctoral dissertation, Michigan State University, East Lansing. (UMI No. AAC 81-06451; Summary in ED 203 283)

Shows that readers perform more proficiently on their dictated stories than on a basal reader story, despite the more difficult vocabulary and syntactic complexity of dictated story.

TORRES, FRANK JOHN (1980). *College freshman detection of encoded semantic, syntactic, grammatical, and morphological errors and this detection's relationship to reading comprehension.* Unpublished doctoral dissertation, New Mexico State University, Las Cruces. (UMI No. AAC 80-22967)

This study of 120 freshman finds proficient readers are more prone to detect encoded errors; detection of syntactic errors is the most accurate variable in the prediction of reading comprehension. The finding that the detection of semantic encoded errors accounts for virtually the same amount of variability in comprehension indicates that the recognition of one of these types of encoded errors may be used to check for comprehension.

TUMARKIN, SANDRA RITA (1980). *A psycholinguistic analysis of the cloze responses of selected readers of varying abilities during silent and oral reading.* Unpublished doctoral dissertation, The American University, Washington, DC. (UMI No. AAC 81-10554)

Uses an adapted form of Goodman's miscue taxonomy to classify and analyze nonexact replacements in cloze passages.

TURNER, GLADYS H. (1980). *Oral reading errors of fifth grade students.* Unpublished doctoral dissertation, Temple University, Philadelphia, PA. (UMI No. AAC 80-14568)

This investigation looks at the differences in the oral reading among the mean percentages of graphic, syntactic, and semantic errors and graphic, syntactic, and semantic self corrections made by fifth graders who score higher on word knowledge subtests versus those scoring higher on comprehension subtests of the MAT.

WANGBERG, ELAINE G., & THOMPSON, BRUCE (1980, November). *Cognitive development and miscue patterns of differentially skilled readers.* Paper presented at the Annual Meeting of the Mid-South Educational Research Association, New Orleans, LA. (ED 193 603)

This study investigates which cue strategies readers of different abilities utilize, and whether these strategies are mediated by levels of cognitive development.

WATSON, DOROTHY J., & STANSELL, JOHN C. (1980, March). *Miscues we have known and loved*. *Reading Psychology, 1*(2), 127–132. (EJ217658)
> Uses miscue examples to illustrate the nature of the reading process and how it is influenced by various kinds of situations.

WEED, FLOY BAUGHMAN (1980). *An analysis of student self diagnosis of reading problems using miscue techniques*. Unpublished doctoral dissertation, University of Houston, Houston, TX. (UMI No. AAC 80-27028)
> One of two fifth grade classes is given instruction derived from RMI that acquaints students with the three cue systems, provides practice in students' recognizing their own problem areas, and provides practice in classifying students' own miscues using the three cue systems. Results indicate the experimental group uses the cue systems in a more efficient manner.

WORSNOP, CHRIS M. (1980). *A procedure for using the technique of the Reading Miscue Inventory as a remedial teaching tool with adolescents*. Unpublished master's thesis, Queen's University, Kingston, ON. (ED 324 644)
> Early study that explores retrospective miscue analysis. Transcripts and case studies are included.

1981

ALTWERGER, BESS I., & GOODMAN, KENNETH S. (1981). *Studying text difficulty through miscue analysis*. (Occasional Paper No. 3) Tucson, AZ: University of Arizona, Program in Language and Literacy. (ED 209 657)
> Reports a study of three texts using the miscue data base to identify points of text difficulty.

ANGEL, CAROLYN LINDBERG (1981). *A psycholinguistic description of internal consistency and predictability in the oral reading process*. Unpublished doctoral dissertation, University of Southern California, Los Angeles.

> A correlational study to see if oral reading is consistent and predictable across contexts. Findings support the psycholinguistic view of reading that cuing systems in language operate similarly throughout the reading process within and across texts. Supports the view of a single generalizable reading process.

BURK, BARBARA JUNE (1981). *A psycholinguistic description of the oral reading miscues of students labeled 'developmental reader'*. Unpublished doctoral dissertation, University of Missouri, Columbia. (UMI No. AAC 82-05371)

> Describes the oral reading behavior of 20 age 12- to 14-year-olds who are identified as developmental readers in a reading lab. Implications for corrective instruction are considered.

CHRISTIE, JAMES F. (1981, July). The effects of grade level and reading ability on children's miscue patterns. *Journal of Educational Research*, *74*(6), 419–423. (EJ250511)

> Miscues that are acceptable in context increase by grade level and ability for second, fourth, and sixth graders of high and low reading ability.

COLES, RICHARD E. (1981). *The reading strategies of selected junior high students in the content areas*. Unpublished doctoral dissertation, University of Arizona, Tucson.(UMI No. AAC 82-18454)

> Investigates the reading strategies selected junior high school students employ when reading social studies, science, and literature in school and when reading a self-selected passage in a nonschool setting.

D'ANGELO, KAREN (1981, December). Correction behavior of good and poor readers. *Reading World*, *31*(2), 123–129. (EJ255009)

> Finds good readers correct more miscues than poor readers, who rely more on graphic information to make corrections. Finds small differences in the use of syntactic and semantic cues to make corrections, except as the difficulty of material increases.

DAGOSTINO, LORRAINE (1981). *An exploratory study of how ninth grade boys read short stories and science selections*. Unpublished doctoral dissertation, Syracuse University, Syracuse, NY. (UMI No. AAC 81-23894)

96

Study of ninth grade boys reports on the silent reading processes they use while reading short stories and scientific material. Generally, the data suggest that although readers draw from a common core of strategies, readers also have individual preferences.

DENOBLE, ALEXANDER JAMES (1981). *A comparison of the qualitative and retelling performances of learning disabled middle school students while reading expository passages under three conditions.* Unpublished doctoral dissertation, University of Northern Colorado, Greeley. (UMI No. AAC 82-02697)

Uses RMI to compare oral and silent preparation and oral reading. Preparation improves the quality of miscues but no differences are found in effects of oral and silent preparation.

DRIVER, D.C., & ELKINS, J. (1981, April). Oral reading strategies among high school boys of Australian and Italian descent. *Australian Journal of Education, 25*(1), 73–80.

Australian and immigrant Italian high school students show similar miscue patterns when reading in English except for the low comprehension Italian group that also shows greater accuracy.

EHRLICH, SUSAN F. (1981, June). Children's word recognition in prose context. *Visible Language, 15*(3), 219–244. (EJ253738)

Reviews research in which children's processing of individual words is examined in prose context. When taken together, the data suggest that the reader's dependence on contextual constraint for individual word identification decreases with age.

ENGELS, SHIRLEY EUNICE (1981). *A descriptive analysis of the miscues associated with the construction of meaning by three bilingual Spanish-English-speaking students reading in their second language, English.* Unpublished doctoral dissertation, University of Illinois, Urbana-Champaign. (UMI No. AAC 81-27587)

Four case studies look at the first language logic used by Spanish-English bilingual students while reading in their second language, English. They are 12- to 14-year-olds in sixth and seventh grades. Each student reads one 13-sentence passage into a tape recorder three times. A much modified miscue analysis looks for reduction of uncertainty.

ENGLERT, CAROL S., & SEMMEL, MELVYN I. (1981, December). The relationship of oral reading substitution miscues to comprehension. *Reading Teacher*, 35(3), 273–280. (EJ254993)

> Reports that specific types of miscues made by poor readers do not predict comprehension level. Suggests that comprehension might involve processes not revealed by miscue analysis alone.

EWOLDT, CAROLYN (1981a). A descriptive analysis of reading behavior exhibited by one hearing-impaired child. *Directions*, 2, 55–56.

> The strengths and weaknesses of one nonproficient deaf reader are described, and instructional implications are given.

EWOLDT, CAROLYN (1981b). Factors which enable deaf readers to get meaning from print. In S. Hudelson (Ed.), *Learning to read in different languages* (pp. 45–53). Washington, DC: Center for Applied Linguistics.

> The argument is presented that deaf readers are not cognitively different from hearing readers and that the same factors that enable a hearing child to become a reader can be made available to the deaf child.

EWOLDT, CAROLYN (1981c). New techniques for research and evaluation in the reading of the deaf. In G. Propp (Ed.), *1979 CAID Convention Proceedings* (pp. 240–246). Washington, DC: 1981 Convention of American Instructors of Deaf.

> This paper discusses the use of miscue analysis and discourse analysis as tools for studying the reading process of the deaf.

EWOLDT, CAROLYN (1981d). A psycholinguistic description of selected deaf children reading in sign language. *Reading Research Quarterly*, 16(1), 58–89.

> Data gathered from deaf readers' miscues, cloze responses, and retellings while reading are used to develop a model of the reading of the deaf and to evaluate the relationship between that model and the model developed by Goodman in his miscue research.

EWOLDT, CAROLYN, FRICK, CHARLENE, LEWIS, LESLIE, & WALKER, ELIZABETH (1981). *Program objectives for reading and writing: The Kendall Demonstration Elementary School language arts curriculum guide*. Washington, DC: Gallaudet College, Pre-College Programs. (ED 225 325)

> Discusses and lists objectives and evaluation forms for deaf and hearing-impaired students in reading and writing at Kendall Demonstration Elementary School.

GOODMAN, KENNETH S., & GOLLASCH, FREDERICK V. (1981). *Word omissions in reading: Deliberate and non-deliberate*. (Occasional Paper No. 2), Tucson, AZ: University of Arizona, Program in Language and Literacy. (ED 210 631)

> A study of omission substitutions that lead to an elaboration of Goodman's Model of Reading.

GOODMAN, KENNETH S., & GOODMAN, YETTA M. (1981). *A whole- language, comprehension-centered reading program*. (Occasional Paper No. 1). Tucson, AZ: University of Arizona, Program in Language and Literacy. (ED 210 630)

> Written for teachers and school administrators, this paper on whole language as a holistic approach outlines key principles for whole language learning, examines the shortcomings of other than whole language practices, and presents essentials of an in-school program that recognizes learners' knowledge.

GOODMAN, KENNETH S., & GOODMAN, YETTA M. (1981, June). To err is human. *New York University Education Quarterly*, *12*(4), 14–19. (EJ249531)

> Suggests that miscues show the effects of psycholinguistic processes that have led to unexpected responses. Miscues reveal cognitive schema that guide comprehension and verbalization. Expanded form in R.B. Ruddell, M.R. Ruddell, & H. Singer, (Eds.), (1994). *Theoretical models and processes in reading* (pp. 104–123). Newark, DE: International Reading Association.

HATT, CLIFFORD VAN (1981). *Effects of verbal mediation on serial recall task with subtypes of disabled readers*. Unpublished doctoral dissertation, University of Northern Colorado, Greeley. (UMI No. AAC 81-19798)

> It is concluded that low readers identified by miscue patterns in this study perform as well as normal readers on the probe-type serial recall

task and neither low reading nor normal readers benefit from verbal training prior to the task.

HENRICHS, MARGARET (1981, April). *Strategies for language expansion: A college reading program.* Paper presented at the 26th Annual Meeting of the International Reading Association, New Orleans, LA. (ED 207 034)

> Describes a whole language based reading improvement program at Westminster College, Fulton, Missouri.

HOBSON, CHARLES DAVID (1981). *Language and Black children: The effects of dialects in selected passages on Black third graders' reading strategies as revealed by oral reading miscues.* Unpublished doctoral dissertation, Georgia State University, Atlanta. (UMI No. AAC 81-20115)

> Primary children's reading shows bidialectal speakers/readers produce miscues that differ in the semantic proximity category when reading a black dialect literary passage and an English literary passage. Miscues in the dialect text are closer in meaning to text items than are miscues in the English passage.

HODES, PHYLLIS (1981). Reading: A universal process. In S. Hudelson (Ed.), *Learning to read in different languages* (pp. 27–31). Washington, DC: Center for Applied Linguistics. (ED 198 744)

> Discusses the use of RMI with Hasidic children reading English, Yiddish, and Hebrew, and finds a number of miscues directly related to retelling scores.

HOFFMAN, JAMES V., & BAKER, CHRISTOPHER (1981, January). *A study of students' perceptions of the teacher's role during guided oral reading.* Paper presented at the 9th Annual Meeting of the Southwest Regional Conference of the International Reading Association, San Antonio, TX. (ED 200 900)

> Report on a study where students adopt the role of teacher during oral reading. Discusses the kinds and frequency of miscues student "teachers" respond to and the attitudes of readers.

100

HOFFMAN, JAMES V., & BAKER, CHRISTOPHER (1981, May). Characterizing teacher feedback to student miscues during oral reading instruction. *Reading Teacher*, 34(8), 907–913. (EJ245507)

> Presents Feedback to Oral Reading Miscue Analysis System as a procedure for teachers to use in evaluating their own feedback to students' oral reading miscues.

HOFFMAN, JAMES V., & CLEMENTS, RICHARD (1981). *A descriptive study of the characteristics of miscue focused verbal interactions between teacher and student during guided oral reading.* Report to National Institute of Education. (ED 200 946)

> Good and poor readers are found to be significantly different in their miscue patterns and subsequent reaction strategies; teachers are significantly different in their verbal response patterns to the second group.

HOFFMAN, JAMES V., & KUGLE, CHERRY L. (1981, April). *A study of the theoretical orientation to reading and its relationship to teacher verbal feedback during reading instruction.* Paper presented at the Annual Meeting of the American Educational Research Association, Los Angeles, CA. (ED 203 304)

> Reports that for most teachers in the study there is no strong relationship between stated theoretical orientation and their behavior during reading instruction.

HUDELSON, SARAH (ED.). (1981). *Learning to read in different languages: Linguistics and literacy papers in applied linguistics, Series 1.* Washington, DC: Center for Applied Linguistics. (ED 198 744)

> Includes papers on the acquisition of reading skills, several of which are based on insights from miscue analysis. Includes discussions regarding adult, bilingual, deaf, German, Polish, and Spanish reading proficiency.

HUTSON, BARBARA A., & NILES, JEROME A. (1981, June). How similar are patterns of miscue in oral reading and cloze tasks? *Reading Improvement*, 18(2), 144–149. (EJ249839)

> Examines differences in the patterns of responses of primary school children in oral reading and an auditory cloze task. Finds that the proportions of wrong responses and morphemically acceptable responses are greater for the cloze tasks.

JONES, RUTH ELLEN (1981). *Patterns of three selected groups of learning disabled and normal children on the Reading Miscue Inventory*. Unpublished doctoral dissertation, Ball State University, Muncie, IN. (UMI No. AAC 82-01894)

> Uses RMI to study differences between learning disabled and normal readers.

KEITH, CLAIRE, CARNINE, DOUGLAS, CARNINE, LINDA, & MAGGS, ALEX (1981, March). Miscues and oral language proficiency. *Reading Improvement, 18*(1), 68–72.

> Compares high and low readers and oral presentation rate of sentences with readers' identification of semantic and syntactic violations.

KNELL, SUSAN MARCIA (1981). *Reading and language performance in deaf children: A comparison between oral and manual communication approaches*. Unpublished doctoral dissertation, Case Western University, Cleveland, OH. (UMI No. AAC 82-00352 .

> Twenty-one children, six from oral classrooms for the deaf, eight from total communication classrooms for the deaf, and seven hearing children are given a number of reading and language sampling tasks. When the reading process is considered, children in the total communication classes tend to resemble their hearing peers more than children in oral classes do.

LOVE, FANNYE EPPS (1981, December). Reading strategy lessons employing miscue analysis in psycholinguistic approaches to second grade reading instruction. *Reading Improvement, 18*(4), 298–301. (EJ257757)

> Finds no differences in the reading proficiency of second grade students taught with an experimental reading strategy technique and those taught with traditional techniques.

MCARTHUR, JANICE RAE (1981). *An analysis of reading miscue patterns and comprehension performance made by fourth and sixth grade students in regular and remedial classrooms*. Unpublished doctoral dissertation, Northern Arizona University, Flagstaff. (UMI No. AAC 81-25649)

> The miscues of 55 fourth and sixth grade students show fourth grade students have a higher mean for percent of miscues than sixth grade

students. Sixth grade students have a higher mean score for the percent of semantic errors and two types of meaning errors.

MCCULLOUGH, MICHELE PAGE (1981). *Teachers' knowledge of and attitudes toward Black English and correction of dialect-related reading miscues.* Unpublished doctoral dissertation, University of Michigan, Ann Arbor. (UMI No. AAC 82-04712)

> Looks at the patterns of 63 elementary school teachers in their response to and correction of dialect miscues.

MCNAUGHTON, STUART (1981, December). The influence of immediate teacher correction on self-corrections and proficient oral reading. *Journal of Reading Behavior, 13*(4), 365–371. (EJ259276)

> Finds that teacher correction reduces later independent self-correction and accuracy in word identification behavior in readers.

NICKOLAUS, CHARLENE WILLSON (1981). *A psycholinguistic description of the use of whole language lessons with older adult readers.* Unpublished doctoral dissertation, University of Missouri, Columbia. (UMI No. AAC 82-05409)

> Six adults ages 69 to 90 experience psycholinguistic-based reading lessons for six weeks. It is determined that the reader with the least existing proficiency before the lessons and the reader with the greatest existing proficiency before the lessons make the least gains. The four remaining readers make the greatest gains on retelling and comprehending scores after the lessons.

SADOSKI, MARK C. (1981). *The relationships between student retellings and selected comprehension measures.* Unpublished doctoral dissertation, University of Connecticut, Storrs. (UMI No. AAC 81-25458)

> Establishes construct validity for comprehension process score and miscue retelling format through correlation, regression, and factor analysis. Provides interrater reliability for retelling. Summary in ED214127.

SADOSKI, MARK C., PAGE, WILLIAM D., & CAREY, ROBERT F. (1981). Empirical testing of new miscue scoring technique. *New England Reading Association Journal, 16,* 41–47.

> Provides criterion-related validity for the comprehension process score through correlation with cloze scores and standardized test scores.

SOUTHGATE, V., ARNOLD, H., & JOHNSON, S. (1981). *Extending beginning reading.* Portsmouth, NH: Heinemann. (ED 263 543)
> Discusses the development and nature of a University of Manchester, England, research project aimed at helping beginning readers. Part six of the book discusses miscue analysis, children's strategies, and views of reading.

STANSELL, JOHN C. (1981, February). The language of print. *English Education, 13*(1), 23–31. (EJ243718)
> Uses miscue examples and writing samples to illustrate the effects of instruction on written language use.

STOCKDALE, BETSY S., & CRUMP, W. DONALD (1981, September). Alternative reading strategies: A case study. *Learning Disabilities Quarterly, 4*(4), 401–405.
> Follows a 14-year-old learning disabled child for four years through a change from skills instruction to RMI informed meaning-centered instruction. Positive changes in reading and attitude are recorded.

TWYFORD, C.W., DIEHL, WILLIAM, & FEATHERS, KAREN (EDS.). (1981). *Reading English as a second language: Moving from theory. Monographs in teaching and learning No. 4*, Bloomington, IN: ERIC Clearinghouse on Reading and Communication Skills, Indiana University. (ED 325 822; See also ED 198 590 and ED 323 564)
> Looks at ESL from a psycholinguistic perspective. A chapter is included on applying miscue analysis to the diagnosis of ESL readers.

WOLFE, VICKI TRASOFF (1981). *Miscues and reading strategies of native Spanish speaking and nonproficient native English speaking college students reading English.* Unpublished doctoral dissertation, Hofstra University, Hempstead, NY. (UMI No. AAC 82-12764)
> Uses miscue analysis to identify strategies of two different groups of college students reading in English.

ZAMORA, NORMA IBANEZ (1981). *An analysis of oral reading miscues of Mexican-American bilingual children in grades first, third, and fifth and implications for improvement of reading in-*

struction. Unpublished doctoral dissertation, Texas A & I University, Kingsville.

> A study of the miscues of Mexican-American children reading English.

1982

ALTWERGER, BESS I. (1982). *A psycholinguistic analysis of sixth, eighth, and tenth grade readers' processing of naturally occurring text metaphors.* Unpublished doctoral dissertation, University of Arizona, Tucson. (UMI No. AAC 82-17493)

> Utilizes the Goodman taxonomy with metaphor feature matrix, finding processing of text as a whole and retelling scores positively relate to the processing of metaphors, though processing of metaphors is generally less successful than text processing.

ALTWERGER, BESS I., & BIRD, LOIS (1982, January). Disabled: The learner or the curriculum? *Topics in Learning and Learning Disabilities, 1*(4), 69–78.

> Discussion of two college nonreaders who significantly advance when they discover reading should be a meaning-centered activity.

ANASTASIOW, NICHOLAS J., HANES, MADLYN LEVINE, & HANES, MICHAEL L. (1982). Developing proficient readers. In N.J. Anastasiow, M. Hanes, & M.L. Hanes (Eds.), *Language and reading strategies for poverty children* (pp. 183–203). Baltimore, MD: University Park Press.

> Does not consider dialect to interfere with reading comprehension and suggests focus on meaning and RMI strategy use.

ANDERSON, JONATHAN (1982, July). *The measurement of the perception of cohesion: A second language example.* Paper presented at the 9th Meeting of the World Congress on Reading, Dublin, Ireland. (ED 222 885)

> Students' perception of textual cohesion is measured by asking them to read texts containing deletions. Miscue analysis does not indicate serious weaknesses in the students' reading.

BAGHBAN, MARCIA (1982, January). *Practicality and literacy.* Paper presented at the 26th Annual Convention of the International Reading Association, New Orleans, LA. (ED 206 411)

> Argues for natural literacy development and a process orientation in instruction.

BARBER, WILFRED CLIFTON (1982). *The oral reading behaviors of early readers.* Unpublished doctoral dissertation, University of Texas, Austin. (UMI No. AAC 82-17823)

> Uses miscue analysis to investigate the oral reading behaviors of 20 kindergarten children who learn to read before entering school.

BEARDSLEY, GILLIAN (1982, September). Context cues in early reading. *Journal of Research in Reading, 5*(2), 101–112. (EJ269753)

> Details a study showing that for young children, proactive semantic cues are the most helpful in reading. Also reveals that the children make miscues displaying semantic associations across cue types.

BETTELHEIM, BRUNO, & ZELAN, KAREN (1982). *On learning to read.* New York: Alfred A. Knopf.

> Explores misreadings in terms of previous experience in a reader's life, misdirected instruction, poor text quality, and argues that reading should be a meaningful experience for readers.

BOARD, PETER EMILE (1982). *Toward a theory of instructional influences: Aspects of the instructional environment and their influence on children's acquisition of reading.* Unpublished doctoral dissertation, University of Toronto, Toronto, ON. (UMI No. AAC 05-51889)

> Looks at children learning to read in classrooms with very different instructional theories. Finds that it is the less proficient readers whose miscues show the most specific instructional influences.

BOWER, JUDITH A. (1982, April). Intrasentence contextual facilitation in children's oral reading. *Reading Psychology, 3*(2), 91–103.

> Examination of the qualitative and quantitative assessment of oral reading errors respective to reading words in sentence context and in isolation.

BURKE, SUZANNE M., PFLAUM, SUSANNA W., & KNAFLE, JUNE D. (1982, January). The influence of Black English on diagnosis of reading in learning disabled and normal readers. *Journal of Learning Disabilities, 15*(1), 19–22. (EJ258030)

> On all three tests, learning disabled children score lower than control children. Also, the effect of removing dialect miscues as errors causes an overall increase in reading scores on all three tests.

BUSCH, ROBERT F., & JENKINS, PATRICIA W. (1982, September). Integrating the language arts for primary-age disabled readers. *Reading Horizons, 23*(1), 41–46. (EJ271054)

> Describes a program of reading instruction for young disabled readers that is based on a theory of the reading process developed by Kenneth Goodman that integrates speaking, reading, listening, and writing activities.

CAVUTO, GEORGE JOHN (1982). *Teacher feedback to students' miscues as a reflection of teacher theoretical orientation.* Unpublished doctoral dissertation, Hofstra University, Hempstead, NY. (UMI No. AAC 82-23616)

> Investigates the relationship between the feedback teachers give to students who miscue during oral reading instruction and the teacher's theoretical orientations to reading.

CEPRANO, MARIA A. (1982, December). *The influence of two methods of teaching reading on beginners' perceptions of the reading process.* Paper presented at the 4th Eastern Regional Conference of the International Reading Association, Boston, MA. (ED 230 895)

> Discusses how measurement techniques associated with instructional strategies bias research. The study finds word level instruction does not differ from context instruction at word level. Based on syntactic and semantic levels, context instruction proves more effective.

COX, JOYCE TIPTON (1982). *An exploration of the relationship between teachers' responses to oral reading miscues, their theoretical orientation, and their purposes.* Unpublished master's thesis, Sonoma State University, Rohnert Park, CA.

> A study of how theoretical orientation relates to teachers' responses to miscues.

CRAWFORD, LESLIE W. (1982, April). *Providing effective reading instruction for refugee students*. Paper presented at the 27th Annual Convention of the International Reading Association, Chicago, IL.

> Review of the literature for L2 (second language) readers suggests effective reading strategies should emphasize five principles: cultural orientation, background experience, inclusion of syntactic and semantic clues, miscue analysis based evaluation, and links between reading and writing.

CUNNINGHAM, JAMES W., & CAPLAN, ROBERT M. (1982, May). Investigating the concurrent validity of miscue analysis as a measure of silent reading processes. *Reading World, 21*(4), 299–310. (EJ261454)

> Finds concurrent validity for syntactic and semantic categories in miscue analysis through measuring the silent reading processes of elementary school children.

CURTIS, A. CHERYL (1982). *A study of the effects of process-oriented reading instruction and self-concept enhancement on reading achievement among community college students*. Unpublished doctoral dissertation, University of Massachusetts, Amherst. (UMI No. AAC 82-29539)

> Miscue analysis shows that participation in process-oriented instruction does not significantly improve the students' ability to process syntactic information, but does significantly improve semantic processing.

D'ANGELO, KAREN (1982, January). Correction behavior: Implications for reading instruction. *Reading Teacher, 35*(4), 395–398. (EJ256288)

> Presents a review of the literature on correction behavior and suggests techniques for encouraging students to correct miscues.

DIXON, NANCE DEES (1982). *Reading disability, language impairment and reading strategies: Implications for differential diagnosis*. Unpublished doctoral dissertation, University of Colorado, Boulder. (UMI No. AAC 82-21065)

> Investigates how reading disabled youngsters with oral language impairments use the semantic, syntactic, and graphophonic language systems during oral reading.

DYBDAHL, CLAUDIA S. (1982). *A theoretical analysis of revision strategies employed by proficient and less proficient readers for underlying model construction in narrative text.* Unpublished doctoral dissertation, University of Arizona, Tucson. (UMI No. AAC 82-27349)

> Explores the contribution psycholinguistics can make in understanding comprehension.

EBERWEIN, LOWELL (1982, March). Do dialect speakers' miscues influence comprehension? *Reading World, 21*(3), 255–263. (EJ257835)

> Suggests that when asked to read material at their instructional level, students' abilities to comprehend are not adversely affected by their dialects.

EWOLDT, CAROLYN (1982). Teaching new vocabulary? Skip it! In J. Price (Ed.), *Teaching handicapped students in the English classroom* (pp. 26–27). Urbana, IL: National Council of Teachers of English.

> The author suggests alternatives to preteaching vocabulary to deaf students.

EWOLDT, CAROLYN (1982, September). Diagnostic approaches and procedures and the reading process. Reading and the hearing impaired individual. *Volta Review, 84*(5), 83–94.

> The article critiques a variety of widely used reading tests based on an interactive reading model and the author's research and experience with deaf readers; offers criteria for the development of diagnostic instruments for deaf readers; and describes administration of the RMI.

GOLDSMITH, JOSEPHINE SPIVACK, NICOLICH, MARK J., & HAUPT, EDWARD J. (1982). A system for the analysis of word and context-based factors in reading. In J.A. Niles & L.A. Harris (Eds.), *New inquiries in reading research and instruction* (Thirty-first Yearbook of the National Reading Conference, pp. 185–190). Rochester, NY: National Reading Conference.

> Discusses and modifies the RMI with a concern for extracting more information about the reader's use of the graphophonic cueing system and for use of more standard statistical analysis techniques.

GOLLASCH, FREDERICK V. (ED.). (1982). *Language and literacy: The selected writings of Kenneth S. Goodman: Volume I: Process, theory, research, and Volume II: Reading, language, and the classroom teacher.* Boston, MA: Routledge & Kegan Paul. (ED 261 358, Vol. 1)

> A collection of the major psycholinguistic papers, including those on miscue analysis, by K.S. Goodman. Included is an evaluation of the Goodman model.

GOODMAN, KENNETH S., & BIRD, LOIS B. (1982). *The wording of texts: Intra-text word frequency* (Occasional Paper No. 6). Tucson, AZ: University of Arizona, Program in Language and Literacy. (ED 277 977)

> A study of texts used in miscue analysis to study relative word frequency within texts. (See *Research in the Teaching of English*, 18(2), 119–145).

GOODMAN, YETTA M. (1982). Retellings of literature and the comprehension process. *Theory Into Practice, 21*(4), 300–307. (EJ275419)

> Students' retellings are analyzed to document how readers predict information, form concepts, and relate material to their own background experience. Classroom implications are discussed.

GOODMAN, YETTA M. (1982, May). Making connections. *Language Arts, 49*(5), 433–436. (EJ264222)

> Presents examples of young children using written language. Shows teachers and parents what they can learn from children's developing sense of written language. Suggests activities by which parents and teachers can spur child language development.

GOODMAN, YETTA M. (1982, August). Kidwatching: Evaluating written language development. *Australian Journal of Reading, 5*(3), 120–128. (EJ269808)

> Points out that all good teachers can use kidwatching in the classroom to monitor children's knowledge and growth in literacy.

GOODMAN, YETTA M., HAUSSLER, MYNA, & STRICKLAND, DOROTHY (Compilers). (1982). *Oral and written language de-*

velopment research: Impact on the schools. Proceedings from the 1979 and 1980 IMPACT Conferences. (ED 214 184, 1981)

> Includes "Three aspects of children's language development: Learning language, learning through language, learning about language" by M.A.K. Halliday, and "Language development: Issues, insights, and implementation" by K.S. Goodman.

GUZZETTI, BARBARA JEAN (1982). *A psycholinguistic analysis of the reading strategies of high, average, and low ability readers across selected content areas.* Unpublished doctoral dissertation, University of Colorado, Denver. (UMI No. AAC 82-21081.

> Finds that high, average, and low ability readers are consistent in using syntactic and semantic cues to reconstruct meaning; the application of these strategies does not vary with reading content.

HAUSSLER, MYNA MATLIN (1982). *Transitions into literacy: A psycholinguistic analysis of beginning reading in kindergarten and first grade children.* Unpublished doctoral dissertation, University of Arizona, Tucson. (UMI No. AAC 82-17497)

> Miscue techniques are used to analyze the reading of eight children as part of this study of early readers.

HEYDORN, BERNARD L., & CHEEK, EARL H. (1982, June). Reversals in reading and writing: Perceptual, developmental, diagnostic and remedial aspects. *Reading Improvement, 19*(2), 123–128.

> Suggests that reversals are a developmental phenomenon that may persist in some children who may or may not have reading difficulties.

HOFFMAN, JAMES V. (1982). *Feedback to oral reading miscues. Parts I, II & III* (Final Report, Project No. 9-1289). Washington, DC: National Institute of Education. (ED 227 455 and ED 227 456, Part III)

> A three-part report on a series of studies that examines the nature and effects of verbal feedback to student reading miscues.

HONEYCUTT, CHARLES ALLEN (1982). *A study of the second-language reading process using cloze procedure, miscue analysis, and story retelling with 3rd year high school French students.* Unpublished doctoral dissertation, The Ohio State University, Columbus. (UMI No. AAC 83-00268)

> The researcher concludes that cloze, miscue analysis, and retelling are valid measures of the reading ability of the subjects in French and that they are successful in differentiating between two levels of reading ability.

HOOD, JOYCE (1982). The relationship of selected text variables to miscue scores of second graders. *Journal of Reading Behavior, 14*(2), 141–158.

> Separates miscue scores and accuracy levels respective to text influence. Results indicate percent of corrections and comprehension are related to text characteristics; meaning loss is associated with accuracy level differences.

LAMM, JILL SIMPSON (1982). *Sentence combining: A case study of its effect on reading ability*. Unpublished doctoral dissertation, Indiana University of Pennsylvania, Indiana, PA. (UMI No. AAC 82-26163)

> Uses miscue analysis (among other measures) to investigate the effect of sentence combining exercises on reading ability. Finds relatively little positive effect.

LIPSON, MARJORIE YOUMANS (1982, December). *The relationship between oral reading miscues and category of replacement errors of cloze passages*. Paper presented at the 32nd Annual Meeting of the National Reading Conference, Clearwater Beach, FL. (ED 230 915)

> Presents findings of a study examining the relationship between types of miscues made by readers during oral reading and the errors made by the same readers on a cloze task.

LOEFFLER, RUTH EDDLEMAN (1982). *The relationship between understanding grammatical conjunction and reading comprehension in Native American children*. Unpublished doctoral dissertation, University of Oklahoma, Norman. (UMI No. AAC 82-25508)

> Among other findings, a variation of miscue analysis indicates a maturational tendency to move from syntactic dominance at the fourth grade level to semantic focus at the sixth grade level.

LONGNION, BONNIE OWNBY (1982). *The effects of selected variables on miscue patterns of adult readers.* Unpublished doctoral dissertation, Texas A&M University, College Station. (UMI No. AAC 82-19121)

> Investigates the reading strategies of adult readers (adult basic education students, high-risk college freshmen, college senior education majors) and examines possible sources of variance for producing miscues.

MALICKY, GRACE V., & NORMAN, CHARLES A. (1982, May). Reading strategies of adult illiterates. *Journal of Reading*, 25(8), 731–735. (EJ261378)

> Suggests that strategies employed by adults are different than those used by children and that adult education programs should take this factor into account.

MARTIN, ELAINE RUSSO (1982, December). Theoretical orientation to reading and teacher verbal feedback: A selected review of recent literature. *Journal of Classroom Interaction*, 18(1), 8–10. (EJ 277 417)

> A review of the literature on verbal feedback, including feedback to miscues.

MONTANER, ARMANDO HUMBERTO BALTRA (1982). *Reading for academic purposes: An eclectic exploration into reading theories and practical classroom applications.* Unpublished doctoral dissertation, Linguistica aplicada ao ensino de linguas, Sao Paulo.

> Investigates the psycholinguistic nature of reading comprehension for the purpose of assessing reading programs for Brazilian professionals seeking to read English, and an analysis of models finds the Goodman model is the most appropriate for development of instructional practices.

MOSS, R. KAY, & STANSELL, JOHN C. (1982, April). *Comprehension in context: Social and situational influences on story retellings.* Paper presented at the 27th Annual Convention of the International Reading Association, Chicago, IL. (ED 216 338)

> Examines the influences of differing contexts on the story retellings of three different readers.

NEWMAN, HAROLD (1982, November). *Utilizing psycholinguistic insights in teaching via the basal reader.* Paper presented at the 16th Annual Meeting of the New York State Reading Association, Kiamesha Lake, NY. (ED 227 471)

> Suggests methods for combining psycholinguistic theory with ideas presented in current basal reader manuals to help teachers teach reading more effectively.

PAGE, WILLIAM D. (1982). A response to Donald Leu's (1982) seriously misleading review of oral reading. *Reading Research Quarterly, 18*(1), 123–124.

> Points out two relevant studies overlooked by Donald Leu in his critique of miscue analysis (Leu, D. [1982]. *Reading Research Quarterly 17*[3], 420–437).

PINSON, SHARON LESLEY (1982). *Reading strategies of four early readers.* Unpublished bachelor of education dissertation, Deakin University, Allansford, Victoria, Australia. (ED 222 853)

> Four young children are studied in depth by means of family questionnaires, reading age tests, diagnostic subskill tests, and miscue analysis.

SADOSKI, MARK C. (1982, April). *The relationship between student retellings and selected comprehension measures.* Paper presented at the 27th Annual Convention of the International Reading Association, Chicago, IL. (ED 214 127)

> The results of this study suggest construct validity for oral recall, miscue, post oral-reading cloze, and passage dependent multiple choice reading comprehension indicators.

SCHAMROTH, MARILYN VINE (1982). *The relationship of personality assessment and oral reading miscue assessment for sixth grade girls and boys.* Unpublished doctoral dissertation, Hofstra University, Hempstead, NY. (UMI No. AAC 82-25120)

> Aspects of 36 sixth graders' reading is compared to personality factors assigned via the Eysenck personality questionnaire. This study supports the contention that there may be unique patterns of interaction based on the relationship between reading and sex and personality.

SHEARER, ARLEEN PASETTI (1982). *A psycholinguistic comparison of second grade readers and 4th grade good and poor readers on their oral reading miscues and standard and phoneme cloze responses.* Unpublished doctoral dissertation, University of South Florida, Tampa. (UMI No. AAC 82-16888)

> Analysis of oral reading miscues shows that syntactic and nonsense variables might be used as predictors of reading failure.

SHELTON, ROSEMARY RIGGEN (1982). *A description of the change in reading proficiency, model of reading and reading behavior of college students after instruction in a psycholinguistically-based reading program.* Unpublished doctoral dissertation, University of Missouri, Columbia. (UMI No. AAC 83-10358)

> Six college self-described poor readers are given one semester of psycholinguistically-based reading instruction. It is determined that the reader with the greatest proficiency and the two readers with the least proficiency make the least gains. The three remaining readers make the greatest gains on retelling and comprehending scores.

SHERMAN, NANCY JO (1982). *Reading in English: Insights from intermediate ESOL adults.* Unpublished doctoral dissertation, Memphis State University, Memphis, TN. (UMI No. AAC 82-27419)

> Investigates the extent to which Goodman's model of the reading process can describe reading in English by adult ESOL students.

SWAN, DESMOND (ED.). (1982). *Perspectives on reading: A symposium on the theory and teaching of reading.* Dublin, Ireland: Glendale. (ED 258 148)

> Irish conference papers include an "Experimental Investigation of the Psycholinguistic Model of the Reading Process" and "A Study of Reading Errors Using Goodman's Miscue Analysis and Cloze Procedure."

TERRY, PAMELA R. (1982, April). *Assessing teacher skill in the detection and description of reading miscues before and after training using the hypothesis/test reading modules.* Paper presented at the 60th Annual International Convention of the Council for Exceptional Children, Houston, TX. (ED 219 894)

Effects of training in miscue analysis via hypothesis/test reading modules show increased use of syntactic and meaning descriptors for children's reading miscues. The study suggests more teachers should be trained in miscue analysis.

WANGBERG, ELAINE G., & THOMPSON, BRUCE (1982, June). Miscue and cognitive development patterns of differentially skilled readers. *Reading Improvement, 19*(2), 98–103. (EJ266953)

Cognitive development tasks show that proficient readers are especially sensitive to semantic cues. Suggests that these tasks may be used to evaluate reading readiness.

1983

ALLEN, JoBETH (1983). *Theoretical models of reading: Implications for the beginning reader.* Unpublished; ERIC document only. (ED 240 518)

Argues that teachers need to make students aware of the different models available to them.

BARKET, B. (1983). *The effect of graphic and phonemic similarity on syntactic acceptability.* Unpublished doctoral dissertation, University of North Florida, Jacksonville.

Graphic and phonemic similarity are only slightly related to syntactic acceptability. Graphic similarity appears to be more independent of syntactic acceptability than does phonemic similarity.

BARRERA, ROSALINDA B. (1983). Bilingual reading in the primary grades: Some questions about questionable views and practices. In T.H. Escobedo (Ed.), *Early childhood bilingual education: A Hispanic perspective* (pp. 164–184). New York: Teachers College Press.

Discusses issues about bilingual language arts programs from a psycholinguistic viewpoint.

CAREY, ROBERT F. (1983, September). Theory and research in reading: Insights from socio-psycholinguistics. *Reader: Essays in Reader-Oriented Theory, Criticism, and Pedagogy, 10,* 1–14.

Reviews, for an audience of literacy theorists, major developments in reading during the last ten years. Includes comments on the Goodman Model of Reading.

CARTER, M.J. (1983). Developing a computer program to cater for children's special needs in reading. In D. Dennis (Ed.), *Reading: Meeting children's special needs* (pp. 134–143). Exeter, NH: Heinemann.

Provides the author's own miscue analysis as a computer program and uses a prescriptive point of view for teachers.

CHEEK, DALLAS HENDERSON (1983, July). A physiognolinguistic approach to reading assessment: An alternative form of miscue analysis. *Reading Psychology, 4*(3–4), 365–368.

A lighthearted look at miscue analysis analogizing miscue codes to nonverbal cues, retellings to mime.

D'ANGELO, KAREN, & MAHLIOS, MARC (1983, April). Insertion and omission miscues of good and poor readers. *The Reading Teacher, 36*(8), 778–782. (EJ276255)

Suggests that because insertion and omission miscues of both good and poor readers seldom cause syntactic or semantic distortions, time spent coding these miscues is unwarranted.

DAVEY, BETH, & THEOFIELD, MARY (1983, June). An investigation of miscue analysis training for teachers. *Reading Improvement, 20*(2), 105–110. (EJ283775)

Concludes that miscue analysis training has valuable effects on teachers' perceptions of reading and on their ability to judge patterns of readers' strengths and weaknesses.

EATON, ARLINDA JANE (1983). The oral reading miscues of field-dependent and field-independent Mexican American children. In T.H. Escobedo (Ed.), *Early childhood bilingual education: A Hispanic perspective* (pp. 222–238). New York: Teachers College Press. (ED 235 680)

Eighteen first graders read English and Spanish stories. Although both field-dependent and field-independent groups use the same cuing systems and strategies in both languages, their emphases vary. Field-independent produces more nonword substitutions than field-dependent, considered a result of more substitutions overall.

ENGLERT, CAROL S., & SEMMEL, MELVYN I. (1983, November). Spontaneous teacher decision making in interactive instructional contexts. *Journal of Educational Research*, 77(2), 112–121. (EJ290761)
> Teachers prompt respective to meaning disruption of miscues and tend not to interrupt when problems are graphophonic related. Yet, they also interrupt poor readers with prompts more often and emphasize skills and phonics strategies.

EWOLDT, CAROLYN (1983, May). Text simplification: A solution with many problems. *Perspectives for Teachers of Hearing Impaired*, 1(5), 23–25.
> The practice of simplifying the syntax for deaf readers is opposed and instructional alternatives are offered.

FELDMAN, DAVID, & FELDMAN, BRIAN (1983, April). *The responses to written language by elementary level learning disabled students.* Paper presented at the 61st Annual International Convention of the Council for Exceptional Children, Detroit, MI. (ED 242 148)
> Uses 11 language tasks to explore the reading and writing behavior of 13 upper elementary learning disabled students and finds psycholinguistic principles applicable.

FROESE, VICTOR (1983, November). *A comparison of first-graders' ability in three modes of expression: dictation, independent writing, and story retelling.* Paper presented at the 33rd Annual Meeting of the National Reading Conference, Austin, TX. (ED 243 131)
> Compares independent writing, dictation, and retelling. Finds little difference between the three when T-units, dependent clauses, mazes, dependent clauses per T-unit, and total words produced are compared.

GARCIA, PHYLLIS M. (1983). *An investigation of miscue analysis with bilingual children.* Unpublished doctoral dissertation, University of Northern Colorado, Greeley. (UMI No. AAC 83-28493)

Compares reading miscues of fifth grade Chicano students in bilingual classrooms with reading miscues of fifth grade Chicano students in regular classrooms.

GONZALEZ, TERESA ARTOLA (1983). *Analisis de los errores de la lectura oral.* Unpublished doctoral dissertation, Universidad Complutense, Madrid, Spain.

Finds the Goodman model promising for reading analysis and examines the model in terms of methodological issues. Also discusses possibilities for sources of reader's errors.

GOODMAN, KENNETH S. (1983a). A linguistic study of cues and miscues in reading (with critique and response). In L.M. Gentile, M.L. Kamil, & J.S. Blanchard (Eds.), *Reading research revisited* (pp. 187–203). Columbus, OH: Charles E. Merrill.

Reprint of original "A linguistic study of cues and miscues in reading" (1965) with critique by Jay S. Blanchard and response by Kenneth S. Goodman.

GOODMAN, KENNETH S. (1983b). *Text features as they relate to miscues: Determiners* (Occasional Paper No. 8). Tucson, AZ: University of Arizona, Program in Language and Literacy. (ED 297 260)

Uses the miscue data base to study miscues on determiners by second, fourth, and sixth graders.

GOODMAN, KENNETH S., & GESPASS, SUZANNE (1983). *Text features as they relate to miscues: Pronouns* (Occasional Paper No. 7). Tucson, AZ: University of Arizona, Program in Language and Literacy. (ED 297 259)

Uses the miscue data base to study miscues on pronouns by second, fourth, and sixth grade readers.

GOODMAN, KENNETH S., & GOODMAN, YETTA M. (1983, May). Reading and writing relationships: Pragmatic functions. *Language Arts, 60*(5), 590–599. (EJ280832)

Describes the interrelationship of reading and writing and proposes a full-school program for reading and writing development that builds on the full range of personal use of written language.

HOGE, GLENDA SHARON (1983). *A study of reading comprehension monitoring using reader selected miscues with selected tenth, eleventh, and twelfth grade students.* Unpublished doctoral dissertation, University of Missouri, Columbia. (UMI No. AAC 83-10398)

> The results of this study demonstrate the utility of the reader-selected miscue procedure as the basis for classroom instruction.

HOGE, SHARON (1983, October). A comprehension-centered reading program using reader selected miscues. *Journal of Reading, 27*(1), 52–55. (EJ289473)

> Describes an approach for discovering difficulties students have in their reading and suggests how strategy lessons can be designed to help students.

JOHNSON, JOHN R. (1983, August). Understanding misunderstanding: A key to effective communication. *Training and Development Journal, 37*(8), 62–68.

> Business journal article that applies Goodman's insights to business transactions.

KLIGMAN, PHILIP SIMON (1983). *An analysis of the oral reading miscues of learning disabled fourth, fifth and sixth grade children taught reading by three different instructional approaches.* Unpublished doctoral dissertation, Claremont Graduate School, Claremont, CA. (UMI No. AAC 83-09661)

> The study supports the suggestion that naturalistic approaches to reading might be employed as effectively as other commonly used reading programs for learning disability students.

McDANIEL, RUTH ROGERS (1983). *A description of the psycholinguistic dimensions of oral and silent reading processes by third grade readers of high and average ability and sixth grade readers of high and low ability.* Unpublished master's thesis, Texas Women's University, Denton. (ED 228 605)

> Oral reading substitutions and silent reading cloze substitutions are used to compare five dimensions of the reading process.

MCKENNA, MICHAEL C. (1983, March). Informal reading inventories: A review of the issues. *Reading Teacher, 36*(7), 670–679. (EJ276104)

> Discusses question choice, scoring criteria, and allowable miscues.

MILLER, LYNNE D., & WOODLEY, JOHN W. (1983). Retrospective miscue analysis: Procedures for research and instruction. *Research on reading in secondary schools: A semi-annual report*, (Vol. 10–11, pp. 53–67). Tucson, AZ: University of Arizona.

> Authors present procedures for RMA as a tool for individual and group instruction with adolescents for the purpose of supporting readers in the evaluation of their own reading and facilitating reading development.

POWERS, WILLIAM (1983). Relationships between reader-response and the research of Kenneth and Yetta Goodman. *Reader: Essays in Reader-Oriented Theory, Criticism, and Pedagogy*, (10), 28–36.

> Explores characteristics and findings of Goodmans' work that are important to reader-response theory.

RODRIGUEZ-BROWN, FLORA V., & YIRCHOTT, LYNNE S. (1983). *A comparative analysis of oral reading miscues made by monolingual versus bilingual students*. Washington, DC: Office of Bilingual and Minority Languages Affairs (Bilingual Education Paper Series, Vol. 7, No. 5). (ED 258 460; See also ED 192 273, 1980)

> Suggests more work needs to be done comparing miscues in first and second languages.

SADOSKI, MARK C. (1983, Fall). An exploratory study of relationships between reported imagery and the comprehension and recall of a story. *Reading Research Quarterly, 19*(1), 110–123. (EJ289565)

> Demonstrates relationships between the comprehension process score, miscue format retellings, and reported mental imagery. Provides validity and reliability for comprehension process scores and retellings.

SHAJARI, JALEH (1983). *A psycholinguistic analysis of miscues generated by bilingual subjects during the oral reading of mate-*

rials in Persian and English. Unpublished doctoral dissertation, University of Southern California, Los Angeles.

> The purpose of this study is to determine the extent to which miscue analysis in the oral reading of the native language can be used to predict reading problems in the second language.

SHANNON, ALBERT J. (1983, September). Diagnosis, remediation and management of reading miscues among children of limited English proficiency. *Reading Improvement, 20*(3), 224–229. (EJ288077)

> Argues that children with limited oral proficiency in English are often mistakenly judged as poor readers on formal and informal measures. Suggests strategies for dealing with true miscues in oral reading.

SHEARON, LINDA ANNE (1983). *A comparison of miscues made during oral and silent reading.* Unpublished doctoral dissertation, Auburn University, Auburn, AL. (UMI No. AAC 83-17563)

> Finds significant differences in the categories of dialect involvement, semantic acceptability, grammatical transformation, grammatical category, or peripheral involvement in analyzing 1,950 miscues.

SILVA, AURELIA DAVILA DE (1983). The Spanish reading process and Spanish speaking Mexican American children. In T.H. Escobedo (Ed.), *Early childhood bilingual education: A Hispanic perspective* (pp. 185–200). New York: Teachers College Press.

> Discusses six extensive research studies dealing with Spanish reading. The study dispels common misconceptions and offers insights for teachers.

STANSELL, JOHN C., & MOSS, R. KAY (1983). *Dealer's choice: The language processing game.* College Station, TX: Texas A&M University, College of Education. (ED 234 362)

> Describes the influence of context upon reading and retelling and proposes that teachers, as critical features of instructional contexts, largely determine the nature and quality of students' written language use.

STICE, CAROLE F. (1983, April). Reading, dialect, and the low-achieving black college student. *Negro Educational Review, 34*(2), 84–87. (EJ284953)

Examination of the oral reading performance of dialect speakers shows dialect does not interfere with reading.

TAYLOR, BARBARA M., & NOSBUSH, LINDA (1983, December). Oral reading for meaning: A technique for improving word identification skills. *The Reading Teacher*, 37(3), 234–237. (EJ289453)

Suggests that poor readers need to correct their miscues in order to read for meaning. Presents a four-step technique for encouraging corrections.

TAYLOR, JANET B. (1983, October). Influence of speech variety on teachers' evaluation of reading comprehension. *Journal of Educational Psychology*, 75(5), 662–667.

Finds that attitudes of teachers toward dialect significantly influence their ratings of readers only when the attitudes are negative.

TIEN, SU O. LIN (1983). *Chinese adult reader: A psycholinguistic and transactional study of the reading process in Chinese, with comparison to English*. Unpublished doctoral dissertation, Michigan State University, East Lansing. (UMI No. AAC 83-15514.

This study compares the reading miscues of 10 proficient adult Chinese readers reading Chinese with adult American readers' reading of English. Some variation in graphic vs. sound similarities is found.

WADE, BARRIE, & DEWHIRST, WENDY (1983, February). *Readers' Digest*: The implementation of research in reading comprehension. *Educational Review*, 35(1), 89–95. (EJ273932)

A review of research in reading comprehension is presented. The role of language in comprehension is analyzed and implications are drawn for actual practice by primary teachers in the reading curriculum.

WEATHERILL, DAVID W. (1983, March). Lucas: A reader and his reading. *Reading Education*, 8(2), 53–59.

Examines the reading of one self-described poor reader using the RMI and retrospective miscue analysis. The reader is found to base his self-description on quantity not quality of miscues.

WEAVER, CONSTANCE (1983, February). *Dialects and reading.* Paper presented at the East York/Scarboro Reading Conference, Toronto, ON. (ED 233 302)

> States that teachers can create an effective reading program for black students not by giving instruction in standard English but by changing their own attitude toward black dialect.

WILSON, MARILYN (1983, March). *Developmental patterns of reading proficiency in adult ESL students: Implications for ESL classrooms.* Revised version of a paper presented at the Annual Meeting of the Teachers of English to Speakers of Other Languages, Toronto, ON. (ED 248 709)

> By examining seven ESL adults, the author concludes that second language acquisition is like acquisition language processes in first language acquisition: reading modes are important; total English proficiency is not necessary for literacy; and learners who rely too much on certain strategies need to refocus.

WOODLEY, JOHN (1983). *Perception of tachistoscopically presented lines of print.* Unpublished doctoral dissertation, University of Arizona, Tucson. (UMI No. AAC 83-24467)

> A study of the perception of lines of print as viewed through the Goodman Model of Reading that demonstrates the importance of readers' expectations and use of all three cuing systems.

1984

ANDERSON, GORDON S. (1984, April). *Handbook for a self-programmed reading diagnostic/remediation approach.* Paper presented at the 3rd Annual Meeting of the National Council of Teachers of English Spring Conference, Columbus, OH. (ED 247 522)

> This handbook is used as a supplement to a course and for staff development. Theory and practice, use of miscue inventory, and diagnostic and instructional procedures are discussed.

ANTES, CAROLE A. (1984). *Teacher self-assessment and analysis of feedback to student miscues during oral reading.* Unpublished doctoral dissertation, Indiana State University, Terre Haute. (UMI No. AAC 85-09130)

> Looks at self-assessment patterns as teachers analyze the feedback given elementary students about students' miscues. Increased flexibility in the form of feedback is noted.

BEEBE, MONA JANE (1984, May). *The Integration of psycholinguistic and discourse processing theories of reading comprehension*. Paper presented at the 29th Annual Convention of the International Reading Association, Atlanta, GA. (ED 245 191)

> Ninety-four fourth graders reading *Space Pet* demonstrate reading strategies. Regression analysis demonstrates readers generating new knowledge vs. information recall.

BENITEZ, DIANA (1984). *A study of the reading process of selected groups of seventh grade bilingual Spanish/English-speakers reading in Spanish and English*. Unpublished doctoral dissertation, Georgetown University, Washington, DC. (UMI No. AAC 85-27450)

> Spanish/English bilingual speakers who had instruction both in Spanish and English or only English for at least three years are examined. Reading process is similar in both groups, with those instructed in Spanish using more efficient strategies in both languages than those instructed in English only.

BROWN, DOROTHY LLOYD (1984). *A psycholinguistic analysis of the oral reading behavior of selected urban students: A five-year longitudinal descriptive study*. Unpublished doctoral dissertation, Georgia State University, Atlanta. (UMI No. AAC 84-25841)

> Study shows 14 proficient readers' growth in dealing with increasingly complex text over time and their movement toward conventional forms of language use.

CARNINE, LINDA, CARNINE, DOUGLAS, & GERSTEN, RUSSELL (1984, Spring). Analysis of oral reading errors made by economically disadvantaged students taught with synthetic-phonics applications. *Reading Research Quarterly, 19*(3), 343–356. (EJ296722)

> In beginning reading, substitution miscues tend to be graphically constrained if instruction has focused on phonics. If instruction emphasizes meaning, substitutes are more contextually constrained. Few nonsense miscues are made on familiar words.

CORLISS, JULIA CANDACE (1984). *Readers and story: The expressed and revealed concepts of story of three children responding to fantasy fiction.* Unpublished master's thesis, Sonoma State University, Rohnert Park, CA.

> A study of children's response to fantasy fiction.

CUNNINGHAM, JAMES W. (1984, December). A simplified miscue analysis for classroom and clinic. *Reading Horizons, 24*(2), 83–89. (EJ293060)

> Presents an alternate miscue analysis system that claims to keep the strengths of the original system but eliminates its weaknesses.

DAVIDSON, EDWARD B. (1984). *Examining the influence of educational cognitive style on reading comprehension.* Unpublished doctoral dissertation, University of Michigan, Ann Arbor. (UMI No. AAC 85-02789)

> Compares 15 third graders' comprehension of their own and others' dictated stories; cognitive style match is shown as a significant factor in reading comprehension.

EARLE-CARLIN, SUSAN E. (1984). *Bilingual reading strategies of native-speaking college ESL students.* Unpublished doctoral dissertation, Hofstra University, Hempstead, NY. (UMI No. AAC 84-18832)

> Compares the types of language miscues made in native language Spanish and in second language Spanish and investigates the relationships of reading skills and strategies between L1 (first language) and L2 (second language).

GOURLEY, JUDITH W. (1984). Discourse structure: Expectations of beginning readers and readability of text. *Journal of Reading Behavior, 16*(3), 169–188.

> Identifies the least readable portions of three primer and trade texts through miscue analysis data from nine beginning readers. Results suggest beginning readers are more successful when texts meet their expectations about the discourse structure.

GUZZETTI, BARBARA JEAN (1984, September). The reading process in content fields: A psycholinguistic investigation. *American Educational Research Journal, 21*(3), 659–668. (EJ303681)

Finds 36 fifth graders' strategies appear similar across ability and content. The article argues that background experience and interest relate to comprehension.

HOFFMAN, JAMES V., & CLEMENTS, RICHARD (1984, March). Reading miscues and teacher verbal feedback. *Elementary School Journal*, 84(4), 423–439. (EJ297103)
> Explores teacher responses to oral reading miscues made by second graders. Finds that poorer readers receive less constructive feedback than do better readers.

HOFFMAN, JAMES V., O'NEAL, SHARON Y., KASTLER, LESA A., CLEMENTS, RICHARD O., SEGAL, KERRY W., & NASH, MARCIA F. (1984, Spring). Guided oral reading and miscue focused verbal feedback in second-grade classrooms. *Reading Research Quarterly*, 19(3), 367–384. (EJ296724)
> Explores relationships between readers' miscues and their teachers' verbal responses.

KIRK, BARBARA VANDYKE (1984). *Effects of prior aural exposure on the oral reading performance and comprehension of Mexican American migrant children.* Unpublished doctoral dissertation, Michigan State University, East Lansing. (UMI No. AAC 85-07507)
> Prior aural exposure results in significantly higher comprehension and fewer miscues though no change in types of miscues. Miscues on ethnically related material maintain meaning and corrections on unrelated material are more successful.

LASS, BONNIE (1984, March). Do teachers individualize their responses to miscues?: A study of feedback during oral reading. *Reading World*, 23(3), 242–254. (EJ294667)
> Primary grade teachers show evidence of individualizing their responses to reading miscues. They disregard semantically acceptable miscues, provide instruction when letter cues are misused, and provide words when children hesitate on a word.

LONG, PATRICIA C. (1984). *The effectiveness of the Reading Miscue Inventory and the Reading Appraisal Guide in graduate read-*

ing programs. Unpublished doctoral dissertation, University of Arizona, Tucson. (UMI No. AAC 84-21975)

> Experimentally compares RMI with Reading Appraisal Guide and finds full RMI is used more appropriately by teachers in appraising children's reading.

MARKS, NANCY LOUISE (1984). *The relationship of the cognitive style pair of risk taking and cautiousness to the quality of oral reading miscues*. Unpublished doctoral dissertation, Case Western Reserve University, Cleveland, OH. (UMI No. AAC 84-26279)

> Explores the importance of risk taking to the psycholinguistic model of reading. Correlations of ring toss (one measure of risk taking) to corrections and sound similarity are not as expected.

McCLELLAN, JEAN GODSMAN (1984). *Signs of attention to meaning: An ethnographic study of comprehension in the beginning reading process*. Unpublished doctoral dissertation, University of Massachusetts, Amherst. (UMI No. AAC 85-00099)

> Miscue patterns and signs of attention on meaning are studied. Finds that comprehension is of concern to beginning readers and important to the beginning reading process.

O'BRIEN, DAVID GERARD (1984). *The relation between surface processing variables and comprehension product measures in oral and silent reading*. Unpublished doctoral dissertation, University of Georgia, Athens. (UMI No. AAC 84-21139)

> The findings for 37 seventh grade average readers indicate that the ability to orally produce grammatically acceptable language is inversely related to gist-level recall for familiar texts and positively related to inferential comprehension for unfamiliar texts.

ROBINSON, NANCY MARGARET (1984). *The effects of increasing academic learning time on the reading comprehension of learning disabled students*. Unpublished doctoral dissertation, Indiana University, Bloomington. (UMI No. AAC 85-16630)

> Self-correction behavior is facilitated when teachers' instructional focus is on the strategy of self-correction rather than on direct teacher correction.

SACHS, ARLENE (1984, May). The effects of previewing activities on oral reading miscues. *Remedial and Special Education (RASE)*, 5(3), 45–49. (EJ304115)

> Miscue scores are compared to assess teaching techniques.

SADOSKI, MARK C., & PAGE, WILLIAM D. (1984, October). Miscue combination scores and reading comprehension: Analysis and comparison. *Reading World*, 24(1), 43–53. (EJ306599)

> Provides directions for, validity for, and comparison of several miscue combination process scores and the altercue index.

SASKI, JIM, & CARTER, JADE (1984, March). Effective reading instruction for mildly handicapped adolescents. *Teaching Exceptional Children*, 16(3), 162–166. (EJ299700)

> An emphasis on meaning with handicapped adolescents suggests using adapted miscue analysis, informal reading inventory, guided reading, previewing, and study strategies.

SHUMAN, R. BAIRD (1984). How classroom teachers can use the research in miscue analysis. *Illinois Schools Journal*, 64(1–4), 18–26. (EJ336952)

> Reviews findings on miscue analysis. Discusses the classification of miscues, oral reading vs. silent reading, and the importance of context.

STUART-HAMILTON, IAN (1984, September). *The role of phonemic awareness in the reading style of beginning readers*. Paper presented at the Meeting of the British Psychological Society, Lancaster, UK. (ED 258 142)

> Using miscue analysis, this British study finds that greater graphemic awareness in 20 beginning readers (vs. 20 lacking graphemic awareness) is related to fewer nonsense errors when reading schoolbooks.

SWAGER, CHRISTINE LOUISE (1984). *The relationship of level of schema to selected reading variables*. Unpublished doctoral dissertation, University of South Carolina, Conway. (UMI No. AAC 84-19082)

> The possession of a schema for material is related to increased speed and lack of hesitation. No effect related to graphophonic and syntactic lev-

els suggests their constancy for readers. Semantic level effect suggests schema is passage specific.

UMANSKY, BARRON MARSHA (1984). *Teacher feedback and practices during guided oral reading for high and low first-grade reading groups: A descriptive study.* Unpublished doctoral dissertation, Texas Woman's University, Denton. (UMI No. AAC 85-02641)

> Positive and negative feedback, engaged time, and teacher interruptions are analyzed respective to high and low groups showing significantly more teacher interruption behavior toward the low group.

WATSON, DOROTHY J. (1984, May). *Two approaches to reading: Whole language and skills.* Paper presented at the 29th Annual Convention of the International Reading Association, Atlanta, GA. (ED 247 546)

> Compares one skills teacher and one whole language teacher using Theoretical Orientation to Reading Profile interview and videotapes to determine if and how the teachers adhere to their theoretical model of reading. The whole language teacher focuses on larger units of language, allows miscues, and involves children in planning and thinking about what they read.

WEBELER, MARY ELIZABETH (1984). *Oral reading of high and low reading achievement fourth grade students taught by an integrated language arts approach and skills approach to reading.* Unpublished doctoral dissertation, The Ohio State University, Columbus. (UMI No. AAC 84-26498)

> In this study, groups experiencing different reading instruction methods differ in their perceptions of the reading process but not in the strategies they use. Community context is suggested for failure of more substantial findings.

PART 6

1985–1989

1985

ADKINS, TREANA, & NILES, JEROME (1985, December). *The influence of sustaining feedback on the oral reading performance of low ability readers*. Paper presented at the 35th Annual Meeting of the National Reading Conference, San Diego, CA. (ED 267 377)

> Treatments do not differentially affect the graphic similarity of readers' responses. Results indicate no significant differences in the percent of miscues corrected by each of three groups. However, all three groups increase in the use of correction.

ANDERSON, GORDON S. (1985, May). *Applying discourse analysis, miscue and cohesive analysis to reader and text: Classroom implications related to comprehension*. Paper presented at the 30th Annual Convention of the International Reading Association, New Orleans, LA. (ED 269 726)

> This study looks at the use of story grammar, propositional analysis, miscue analysis, and cohesive analysis to gain information about one reader's interaction with a text.

BISAGNA-VILLAFANE, JOANNE (1985). *"!Me *sabi esas palabras!" ("I *knowed those words!"): A linguistic analysis of the reading performance of three- and four-year-old Spanish speakers learning to read in a bilingual preschool early reading program*. Unpublished doctoral dissertation, Georgetown University, Washington, DC. (UMI No. AAC 86-13926)

> The statistics given of very young readers' miscues demonstrate a high graphic similarity while maintaining strength in grammatical anticipation, correction, and comprehension. Comments show that readers monitor reading, analyze sound-letter relations, and are proud of their accomplishments.

BROMLEY, KAREN D'ANGELO, & MAHLIOS, MARC (1985, September). Good and poor readers' cue utilization and views of the reading process. *Educational and Psychological Research*, 5(4), 257–274.

> Few differences are found in reading between good and poor readers; however, their views differ because good readers think more about meaning; poor readers orient toward decoding skills.

CENTURION, CESAR ENRIQUE (1985). *The use of the informal reading inventory and miscue analysis to evaluate oral reading, reading comprehension and language interference/transfer in English as a second language students.* Unpublished doctoral dissertation, Texas A&I University, Kingsville. (UMI No. AAC 85-27088)

> Informal Reading Inventories are unreliable when used with ESL students. A qualitative differentiation of miscues is required, such as a form of modified miscue analysis that takes into account language interference/transfer factors.

CLEMENS, LYNDA PRITCHARD (1985). *The simultaneous/successive model of intelligence: Relationship to reading and spelling acquisition and the cognitive developmental shift.* Unpublished doctoral dissertation, Temple University, Philadelphia, PA. (UMI No. AAC 85-09380)

> Miscue analysis is used in the assessment of a model of intelligence. The study finds that the simultaneous/successive model is limited to use with children over 7 years of age. Linguistic development is found to be a causal factor in cognitive and reading ability.

COKELY, DENNIS R. (1985). *Towards a sociolinguistic model of the interpreting process: Focus on ASL and English.* Unpublished doctoral dissertation, Georgetown University, Washington, DC. (UMI No. AAC 86-02362)

> Miscue taxonomy is adapted for development of a model of interlingual interpretation that accounts for cultural and individual as well as linguistic factors in six certified sign language interpreters.

EDITORS. (1985, March). Research report: Patterns of comprehension in third grade. *Australian Journal of Reading*, 8(2), 44–48.

Discusses the use of miscue analysis to examine third graders' use of cohesives.

ELLINGER, ROMONA J. (1985). *An analysis of reading strategies used by a high and low proficiency group of students learning English as a second language.* Unpublished doctoral dissertation, Oklahoma State University, Stillwater. (UMI No. AAC 85-28094)

> The higher group utilizes a syntactic and semantic system, predicts more, and uses redundancy and punctuation clues, and the lower group relies more on graphophonic information.

FEATHERS, KAREN M. (1985). *The semantic features of text: Their interaction and influence on comprehending.* Unpublished doctoral dissertation, Indiana University, Bloomington. (UMI No. AAC 85-07850)

> Investigates interaction among semantic features of text and reader behavior described by the Reading Miscue Inventory. Results suggest a definite relationship between these features and reader behavior.

GOODMAN, KENNETH S. (1985). Growing into literacy. *Prospects: Quarterly Review of Education, 15*(1), 57–65. (EJ320362)

> Children who grow up in literate societies, surrounded by the printed word, begin to read and write long before they start school. The extent and scope of early literacy development is examined, theoretical explanations of this development are offered, and implications for schools are presented.

GOODMAN, KENNETH S. (1985, February). Commentary: On being literate in an age of information. *Journal of Reading, 28*(5), 388–392. (EJ311423)

> Points out that the expansion of written language to serve the full range of functions for all people in an information age is a manifestation of our ability as individuals and societies to create new language forms as they are needed in the context of their use.

GOODMAN, YETTA M. (1985, September). Developing writing in a literate society. *Educational Horizons, 64*(1), 17–21. (EJ324884)

> The author shares her insights about the principles and knowledge of the writing system that children discover, develop, and learn to control. She categorizes these principles as functional principles, linguistic principles, and relational principles.

HAHN, LOIS BLACKBURN (1985). *Correlations between reading music and reading language with implications for music instruction.* Unpublished doctoral dissertation, University of Arizona, Tucson. (UMI No. AAC 85-25597)

> Uses the Goodman model in appraising music instruction.

HOFFMAN, JAMES V. (1985, March). *Instruction: The implications of research on teacher responses toward reading miscues.* Paper presented at the Annual Meeting of the American Educational Research Association, Chicago, IL. (ED 263 071)

> This paper presents a review of literature; suggestions are made for more research.

HOFFMAN, JAMES V., & BAKER, CHRISTOPHER J. (1985). Feedback to oral reading miscues analysis system. In W.T. Fagan, C.R. Cooper, & J.M. Jensen (Eds.), *Measures for research and evaluation in the English language* (Vol. 2, pp. 85–86). (ED 255 933)

> An overview of the FORMAS with an example of the coding sheet.

HOWARD, CHERYL (1985). *An analysis of the relationship between textual features and five 4th graders' processing and comprehension of three full length narratives.* Unpublished master's thesis, Sonoma State University, Rohnert Park, CA.

> Examines textual features of whole text with fourth grade readers.

HUGHES, DELORA JOYCE M. (1985). *An investigation of the relationship between teacher perception of reader need and teacher feedback to oral reading miscues during oral reading group instruction.* Unpublished doctoral dissertation, University of Texas, Austin. (UMI No. AAC 85-29862)

> No verbal, sustaining, or terminal feedback of teachers to student miscues is examined. Teachers' perceptions of students influence feedback, and less feedback results in continued reading and increased self correction behaviors in students.

HURTADO, ROSEMARY (1985). *The bilingual reading process of adult Spanish speakers reading English as a second language.* Unpublished doctoral dissertation, University of San Francisco, San Francisco, CA. (UMI No. AAC 85-18654)

> An interaction effect is noted between proficiencies in the two languages of bilingual readers. There are no clear strategy differences except that better readers, regardless of oral proficiency, use semantic and syntactic cues better at a sentence level when they have problems at the passage level.

KELLY, NANCY JEAN (1985). *The effects of a 'key strategy' on the map reading abilities of early and late adolescents.* Unpublished doctoral dissertation, University of Miami, Miami, FL. (UMI No. AAC 85-19231)

> Looking at the value of a legend or key on maps related to quiz questions demonstrates a relationship between comprehension and question type. Some map reading miscues are found to indicate equal difficulty across age groups. Potential causes are identified.

KOBLITZ, COURTLAND WILLIAM, JR. (1985). *A post-hoc analysis of oral reading miscues generated by second, fourth and sixth grade students taught to read with two different writing systems: ITA and traditional orthography.* Unpublished doctoral dissertation, Southern Illinois University, Edwardsville. (UMI No. AAC 85-16495)

> Miscue analysis is used to compare the visual and nonvisual focus of readers with writing systems; the analysis shows high corrections but in different directions in different grades.

LAGBARA, MAYA SNOWTON (1985). *The influence of teachers' conceptions of reading on the instructional model used to teach good and poor readers: A descriptive study.* Unpublished doctoral dissertation, Texas Woman's University, Denton. (UMI No. AAC 86-08493)

> The manner in which teachers conceive the reading process is found to be significant in feedback to readers. No relation to model used suggests teachers' conceptions are in conflict with school policy.

LASKO, THEODORE WILLIAM (1985). *The effects of reading and writing the answers to random cloze passages on the generation of oral reading substitution, omission, and insertion miscues by second-grade average readers.* Unpublished doctoral dissertation,

Pennsylvania State University, University Park. (UMI No. AAC 85-26042)

> The use of cloze as a teaching device does not significantly increase the reading comprehension of second grade average readers.

LAZARUS, PEGGY (1985, March). *The relationship of oral language features to reading achievement.* Paper presented at the Annual Meeting of the American Educational Research Association, Chicago, IL. (ED 262 394)

> The oral language of 14 kindergarteners (metalinguistic, correction behavior, use of interactive function of language) shows a trend to be increasingly related to their fourth and fifth grade reading achievement.

MANSFIELD, SUSAN (1985). *Foreshadowing in the composing process: Miscues as predictors of revision.* Unpublished doctoral dissertation, Rutgers University, New Brunswick, NJ. (UMI No. AAC 85-24229)

> Concludes that miscues in oral reading of a first draft do predict revision. Miscue related revisions are also surface level revisions, not oriented to meaning change.

MIKDADI, MOHAMMAD FAKHRI AHMAD (1985). *An investigation of oral reading miscues generated by bilingual college students reading expository materials in Arabic and English.* Unpublished doctoral dissertation, Indiana University, Bloomington. (UMI No. AAC 85-27024)

> Compares the oral reading miscues generated by a college student reading expository materials in Arabic and English; this study confirms studies that suggest there is one reading process across languages.

MIRAMONTES, OFELIA (1985). *Bilingual oral reading miscues of hispanic learning disabled and non-learning disabled fourth, fifth and sixth grade students: Implications for transition into English reading.* Unpublished doctoral dissertation, Claremont Graduate School, Claremont, CA. (UMI No. AAC 85-03784)

> Primary Spanish readers attend more to graphophonic strategies; primary English readers do not when reading English, but when reading Spanish switch to graphophonic strategies. Good readers differ from learning disabled readers in reading for meaning.

MUDD, NORMA R. (1985). *Strategies used in the early stages of learning to read: A comparison of children and adults*. Unpublished doctoral dissertation, University of Manchester, Manchester, UK.

> The subjects read two passages orally. Graphic and semantic aspects of their miscues are examined to determine their strategies. Adults show more reliance on semantic cues.

NILES, JEROME A. (1985). Research on teacher-pupil interactions during oral reading instruction. In B.A. Hudson (Ed.), *Advances in reading language research: A research annual* (Vol. 3, pp. 207–226). Greenwich, CT: JAI Press.

> Examines pupil-teacher interactions that occur as a result of miscues made by the pupil.

PEHRSSON, ROBERT S., & DENNER, PETER R. (1985, October). *Assessing silent reading during the process: An investigation of the open procedure*. Paper presented at the 3rd Annual Meeting of the Northern Rocky Mountain Educational Research Association, Jackson, WY. (ED 265 529)

> Discusses an evaluation technique that has students fill in the second half of every other sentence. Correlations are found with miscue scores.

POLLOCK, JOHN F. (1985). *A psycholinguistic analysis of oral reading miscues involving pronoun-referent structures among selected 2nd, 4th, and 6th grade children*. Unpublished doctoral dissertation, University of Arizona, Tucson. (UMI No. AAC 85-29405)

> Results indirectly show readers do construct texts with a different basis from those of the published texts, but these comprehended texts are tentative and often revised as reading proceeds.

PUMFREY, PETER DAVID (1985). *Reading: Tests and assessment techniques* (2nd ed.). Kent, UK: Hodder and Stoughton; United Kingdom Reading Association. (ED 298 448)

> A British publication dealing with reading assessment that includes a chapter on miscue analysis.

RENAULT, LOUISE HELEN (1985). *First language in developing second-language literacy: Genesis and generation for Spanish/*

English readers. Unpublished doctoral dissertation, Indiana University, Bloomington. (UMI No. AAC 86-05810)

> This study examines the miscues and retelling from English texts and intermixed English/Spanish texts. Analysis demonstrates how prior knowledge in first language literacy plays a positive role in second language literacy learning. A second language reading model is developed.

RIGG, PAT, & KAZEMEK, FRANCIS E. (1985, May). For adults only: Reading materials for adult literacy students. *Journal of Reading*, *28*(8), 726–731.

> In a discussion of the difficulties instructors have locating appropriate reading materials for adults, six criteria are given for selection: (1) meaningfulness; (2) completeness; (3) literary merit; (4) availability; (5) affordability; and (6) promotion of integration of a student's language abilities.

ROSE, LEONIE MARIE ATKINS (1985). *A psycholinguistic analysis of oral and silent reading miscues, comprehension, and their relationships*. Unpublished doctoral dissertation, Indiana State University, Terre Haute. (UMI No. AAC 85-19951)

> The comparison shows the product of comprehension is the same for oral and silent reading while the process patterns are similar but not identical.

SADOSKI, MARK C. (1985). Comprehension process score. In W.T. Fagan, C.R. Cooper, & J.M. Jensen (Eds.), *Measures for research and evaluation in the English language arts* (Vol. 2, pp. 103–105). Urbana, IL: National Council of Teachers of English. (ED 255 933)

> Describes the comprehension process score and gives evidence of reliability and validity through correlation with measures including standardized test scores. Reports a significant negative correlation between comprehension process scores and miscues per 100 words.

SMITH, JUDITH, & ELKINS, JOHN (1985). The use of cohesion by underachieving readers. *Reading Psychology*, *6*(1–2), 13–25. (EJ319712)

> Finds underachieving readers make less use of phonemic, graphic, and grammatical features of text when responding to cohesive items vs. whole text.

STONE, RUTH J. (1985). *Effects of English/Spanish language pattern differences on ESL learners' comprehension of English text.* Unpublished doctoral dissertation, George Peabody College for Teachers, Vanderbilt University, Nashville, TN. (UMI No. AAC 85-27856)

    No significant language pattern is reported.

STONE, RUTH J., & KINZER, CHARLES K. (1985, December). *Effects of English/Spanish language pattern differences on ESL learners' comprehension of English text.* Paper presented at the 35th Annual Meeting of the National Reading Conference, San Diego, CA. (ED 266 434)

    Miscue and literal comprehension questions are used to compare the language pattern effects on the reading of fifth grade ESL students. Miscue and literal comprehension questions are used.

TAFT, MARY LYNN, & LESLIE, LAUREN (1985). The effects of prior knowledge and oral reading accuracy on miscues and comprehension. *Journal of Reading Behavior, 17*(2), 163–179. (EJ395024)

    Prior knowledge is found to decrease meaning-loss miscues and graphic similarity of miscues.

TCHACONAS, TERRY NICHOLAS (1985). *Oral reading strategies in Greek and English of second grade bilingual children and their relationships to field-dependence and field-independence.* Unpublished doctoral dissertation, Teachers College at Columbia University, New York, NY. (UMI No. AAC 85-25527, ED 295 497)

    Although all strategies are present in either language, the field-independent children use syntax, semantics, and predict more. Languages are distinguished by stronger reliance on syntax when reading Greek and stronger reliance on semantics when reading English.

TERDAL, MARJORIE S. (1985). *Learning to read and write in English: Case studies of two southeast Asian students in a northwest urban high school.* Unpublished doctoral dissertation, University of Oregon, Eugene. (UMI No. AAC 85-29545)

    Points out connections between reading and writing theory and implications for the ESL classroom.

WATSON, KEN (1985, May). Miscuing: Everybody does it. *English Education, 17*(2), 67–68. (EJ315142)

> Relates the miscues beginning teachers make as they read aloud to their peers.

WEIDLER, SARAH DARLINGTON (1985). The remediation of disabled readers' metacognitive strategies via cognitive self-instruction. Unpublished doctoral dissertation, Pennsylvania State University, University Park. (UMI No. AAC 85-25671)

> When cognitive self-instruction is introduced, a shift occurs toward an increase in the quality of miscues.

WOODLEY, JOHN W. (1985). *Computer applications and research utilization of retrospective miscue analysis.* Unpublished; ERIC document only. (ED 285 121)

> Explores the benefits of using computer programs for readers to look at their miscues and analyze why miscues are made. (Apple and IBM program available from Richard C. Owen Publishing, Katonah, NY).

WOODLEY, JOHN W. (1985, March). *Retrospective miscue analysis as a tool in teacher preparation in reading.* Paper presented at the 4th Annual Meeting of the National Council of Teachers of English, Spring Conference, Houston, TX. (ED 259 324)

> Explains and gives questions for Retrospective Miscue Analysis.

1986

ADAMS, ARLENE (1986). The self-correction behaviors of normal and learning disabled readers, grades 5, 6, and 11. (ED 311 630)

> Fifth, eighth and eleventh grade normal and learning disabled readers self-correct similarly across instructional and frustration range texts.

ASLANIAN-NEMAGERDI, YEGHIA (1986). *An investigation of the reading strategies of five proficient and five less proficient advanced ESL students.* Unpublished doctoral dissertation, Teachers College at Columbia University, New York, NY. (UMI No. AAC 86-20334)

Finds advanced readers more often look at larger portions of text, work at a semantic level, use background knowledge, inference, and read on or reread. Their miscues tend to preserve meaning.

BARRERA, ROSALINDA B., VALDES, GUADALUPE, & CARDENAS, MANUEL (1986). Analyzing the recall of students across different language-reading categories: A study of third-graders' Spanish-L1, English-L2, and English-L1 comprehension. In J.A. Niles & R.V. Lalik (Eds.), *Solving problems in literacy: Learners, teachers, and researchers.* (Thirty-fifth Yearbook of the National Reading Conference, pp. 375–381). Rochester, NY: National Reading Conference.

> This study examines 30 third graders' recall along the dimensions of quantity, type, and structure of information. Retellings are propositionalized, tabulated, and analyzed for miscues.

CHATEL, REGINA GRYCZEWSKI (1986). *A psycholinguistic analysis of the effects of varying the purpose of oral reading on reading comprehension.* Unpublished doctoral dissertation, University of Connecticut, Storrs. (UMI No. AAC 86-19102)

> Study of 56 ninth graders' comprehension using the post-oral reading cloze and a miscue based Altercue 15 Index comprehension measure respective to the explicit stating of the purpose of reading. (The purpose here is to rebuild the author's message.)

COKELY, DENNIS R. (1986, December). The effects of lag time on interpreter errors. *Sign Language Studies*, *53*, 341–376. (EJ345652)

> Studies sign language interpretive skills. Provides evidence of a definite relationship between lag time and miscue occurrence. Fast interpretation produces more miscues.

CURRIE, PAULA S. (1986). *Reading and writing miscues and revisions of selected learning disabled students.* Unpublished doctoral dissertation, University of New Orleans, New Orleans, LA. (UMI No. AAC 86-17838)

> Whereas correction occurs most frequently on miscues that affect comprehension, the more likely miscorrected surface-only and grammar-only miscues suggest these to be weaknesses in the students' revision process.

141

CUSUMANO, JOE DENNIS (1986). *Comparing traditional teacher responses to the Bettelheim-Zelan response when 7th grade remedial reading students commit seemingly meaningless oral substitution errors.* Unpublished doctoral dissertation, Saint Louis University, St. Louis, MO. (UMI No. AAC 86-28766)

> The experimental group shows fewer substitution miscues, higher cued and unsolicited corrections, and increased comprehension scores.

DASCH, ANNE LOUISE (1986). *The use of mapping as an instructional technique with difference model readers.* Unpublished doctoral dissertation, University of the Pacific, Stockton, CA. (UMI No. AAC 86-24544)

> Qualitative RMI comparisons show substantial positive change in comprehension in middle to high school students who practice mapping to provide meaning to oral word-calling reading. An accompanying statistical analysis does not reach significance.

FREEMAN, DAVID E. (1986). *Use of pragmatic cohesion cues to resolve degrees of pronoun reference ambiguity in reading.* Unpublished doctoral dissertation, University of Arizona, Tucson. (UMI No. AAC 86-13816)

> Looks at readers' use of pronoun reference to examine two aspects of proficient readers: tentativeness and scope of focus. Concludes reading whole texts for meaning provides conditions to develop use of these practices.

FREEMAN, DAVID E. (1986, December). *Assignment of pronoun reference: Evidence that young readers control cohesion.* Paper presented at the 36th Annual Meeting of the National Reading Conference, Austin, TX. (ED 280 012)

> Shows the use of certain strategies and features of text in determining pronoun reference by 32 sixth graders and 24 second graders.

GOODMAN, KENNETH S. (1986, March). Basal readers: A call for action. *Language Arts, 63*(4), 358–363. (EJ331248)

> Explores several concepts relevant to instructional materials that emerged from seminars sponsored by the National Council of Teachers of English and the International Reading Association. Describes how basal readers—so prevalent in instruction—fall short of these concepts, and what can be done to improve instruction.

142

GREEN, FRANK (1986, February). Listening to children read: The empathetic process. *The Reading Teacher, 39*(6), 536–543.

> Discusses teachers as partners in reading and how they can learn from children's reading. Ways to respond to miscues are addressed.

HANNON, PETER, JACKSON, ANGELA, & WEINBERGER, JO (1986, March). Parents' and teachers' strategies in hearing young children read. *Research Papers in Education, 1*(1), 6–25.

> Parents' and teachers' interactions with 52 children reading are taped and analyzed. Both provide words and give reading directions. Parents' concern for children's understanding of text tends to be restricted to times of miscues.

HENRICHS, MARGARET (1986). *Characteristics of highly proficient freshman college readers.* Unpublished doctoral dissertation, University of Missouri, Columbia. (UMI No. AAC 87-16682)

> An examination of four college readers demonstrates process reading. The study suggests passing these students' metacognitive/ metalinguistic insights to less proficient readers.

HODGES, MARCELLA JANE V. (1986). *Children's reading miscues in three types of instructional manuals.* Unpublished doctoral dissertation, East Texas State University, Commerce. (UMI No. AAC 86-14725)

> Compares dictated, basal, and structured language texts; students' proficiency is strongest with language experience (dictated text).

HORVATH, FRANK G., & MACHURA, SHIRLEY (1986, November). *Development of the Alberta Diagnostic Reading Program.* Paper presented at the Annual Meeting of the Alberta Provincial Conference of the International Reading Association, Lethbridge. (ED 277 981)

> Description of the Alberta Diagnostic Reading Program, a psycholinguistic based program addressing strategies for evaluation, instruction, and interpretation.

KOLCZYNSKI, RICHARD GERALD (1986, June). Meaning change miscues across four modes of writing. *Perceptual and Motor Skills, 62*(3), 753–754.

> Miscue analysis of 20 college students reading four genres finds no significant difference. Reading process is considered stable.

KUHNS, CAROLYN O., MOORE, DAVID W., & MOORE, SHARON A. (1986, March). The stability of modified miscue analysis profiles. *Reading Research and Instruction, 25*(3), 149–159.

> Suggests that reading researchers and diagnosticians be cautious when inferring readers' strategies based on a subset of miscues.

LLABRE, MARIA M. (1986, March). A methodological note on an erroneous approach to score equating: A reaction to Sadoski and Lee. *Reading Research and Instruction, 25*(3), 168–170.

> Argues that linear transformations suggested by Sadoski and Lee for comparing comprehension scores give misleading results. Recommends publishers' scaled scores. (Sadoski and Lee respond, pp. 171–172).

LONG, PATRICIA C. (1986). *The effectiveness of reading miscue instruments* (Occasional Paper No. 13). Tucson, AZ: University of Arizona, Program in Language and Literacy. (ED 277 980)

> Experimentally compares Reading Miscue Inventory with Reading Appraisal Guide and finds full RMI is used more appropriately by teachers in appraising children's reading.

MARTINEZ, REBECCA ANN (1986). *The relationship between silent reading comprehension and oral reading miscues.* Unpublished doctoral dissertation, University of Texas, Austin. (UMI No. AAC 87-00239)

> Further suggests the use of cloze with miscue analysis for the more accurate assessment of silent reading comprehension as measured by the Test of Reading Comprehension.

MEYER, LINDA A. (1986, November). Strategies for correcting students' wrong responses. *Elementary School Journal, 87*(2), 227–241. (EJ346019)

> Reviews research on elementary school teachers' feedback to students' miscues in basal and content area reading. Describes the sustained feedback paradigm that develops from the direct instruction programs.

PARKER, MARGARET, & BARROSO, JUAN, VIII (1986, September). Strategies for teaching and testing reading. *Hispania, 69*(3), 720–722. (EJ344010)

Describes a method of intensive guided reading instruction in a second language that reduces frustration, ensures success, and implements the processes of reading instruction set forth by Kenneth Goodman and elaborated by others.

RIGG, PAT (1986). Reading in ESL: Learning from kids. In P. Rigg & D.S. Enright (Eds.), *Children and ESL: Integrating perspectives* (pp. 55–91). Washington, DC: Teachers of English to Speakers of Other Languages.

An examination of one Laotian and three Cambodian readers using miscue analysis includes an analysis of the texts used.

RIVERA-VIERA, DIANA T. (1986). Remediating reading problems in a Hispanic learning disabled child from a psycholinguistic perspective: A case study. *Journal of Reading, Writing, and Learning Disabilities International*, 2(1), 85–97. (EJ341249)

The study examines the usefulness of the Reading Miscue Inventory to develop a remedial reading program with a Hispanic learning disabled 7-year-old male. The RMI aids the examination of the child's reading strategies leading to the selection of appropriate remedial reading activities .

ROSENBERG, MIMI (1986). *Assessment of speech variation in oral reading by teachers: Special, regular, bilingual and teachers of English as a second language.* Unpublished doctoral dissertation, Teachers College at Columbia University, New York, NY. (UMI No. AAC 86-11697)

ESL, bilingual, special education, and classroom teachers' assessments of an English speaking and a Spanish speaking child's reading are compared. Training for all groups in assessing Hispanic children is recommended.

SADOSKI, MARK C., & LEE, SHARON (1986, March). Reading comprehension and miscue combination scores: Further analysis and comparison. *Reading Research and Instruction*, 25(3), 160–167.

Examines five comprehension scoring systems. Results add to validity and check for miscue analysis and miscue combination scores. (A reply and response in same issue).

SALEM, LYNN L. (1986). *First graders' ability to read their creative writing (Invented spelling vs. conventional text)* (Final Report).

Urbana, IL: National Council of Teachers of English, Research Foundation, BBB08361. (ED 274 958)

> Fourteen first graders read invented spelling and conventional versions of their own stories. Miscue analysis indicates neither version is read significantly better. Results suggest the existence of stages, one being invented spelling.

SHAKE, MARY C. (1986, September). Teacher interruptions during oral reading instruction: Self-monitoring as an impetus for change in corrective feedback. *Remedial and Special Education (RASE)*, 7(5), 18–24. (EJ343924)

> Teacher interruptions can interfere with reader progress. It is suggested that teachers' self-monitoring helps teachers better support independent reading in students.

SOWELL, VIRGINIA, & SLEDGE, ANDREA (1986, December). Miscue analysis of braille readers. *Journal of Visual Impairment and Blindness*, 80(10), 989–992. (EJ347250)

> Explores similarities of braille and sighted readers, finding strong relationships in the areas of substitutions, omissions, and insertions.

STEPHENS, DEBORAH ANNE (1986). *Linguistic aspects of codeswitching among Spanish/English bilingual children*. Unpublished doctoral dissertation, University of Arizona, Tucson. (UMI No. AAC 86-13450)

> Results indicate a developmental trend in codeswitching. A modified interdependence model can account for dual grammars. Written language environment affects codeswitching.

STOLWORTHY, DORIAN LENADINE (1986). *The Navajo reader and writer: Academic, social, and emotional factors*. Unpublished doctoral dissertation, New Mexico State University, Las Cruces. (UMI No. AAC 86-26085)

> Looks at 18 Navajo fourth graders' literacy strategies looked at for reading and writing relationships and examines the influences of cultural, emotional, social, school, and instructional orientations.

THOMPSON, MERTEL E. (1986, March). *Literacy in a Creole context: Teaching freshman English in Jamaica*. Paper presented at the 37th Annual Meeting of the Conference on College Composition and Communication, New Orleans, LA. (ED 276 054)

> Examines problems Jamaican Creole speaking college students have with English. Suggests a writing workshop approach to help the students in code switching.

WARD, ANNITA MARIA (1986). *Cognitive and metacognitive skills of nonliterate adults as compared to kindergarten and second-grade children.* Unpublished doctoral dissertation, West Virginia University, Morgantown. (UMI No. ACC 86-27736)

> In this study, nonliterate adults differ cognitively but not metacognitively from second graders studied. The adults appear to have difficulty with complex discriminations and synthesizing information into new forms.

YURKOWSKI, PETER, & EWOLDT, CAROLYN (1986, July). A case for the semantic processing of the deaf reader. *American Annals of the Deaf, 13*(3), 243–247.

> This case study of a proficient deaf reader supports the notion that print can be processed by the deaf without being mediated through syntax and that semantics can guide deaf readers' processing of syntax.

1987

ANDERSON, RICHARD C., WILKINSON, IAN, MASON, JANA M., SHIREY, LARRY, & WILSON, PAUL T. (1987). *Do errors on classroom reading tasks slow growth in reading?* (Tech. Rep. No. 404). Cambridge, MA: Bolt, Beranek and Newman. (ED 284 182)

> Comprehension of non-turntakers is helped by oral reading errors when accurate reading is emphasized. Comprehension is not changed when emphasis is placed on story understanding.

ASPDEN, KATHRYN JANE (1987). *An examination of the effect of selected context factors on the reading comprehension of high-average and low-average fifth-grade readers.* Unpublished doctoral dissertation, Georgia State University, Atlanta. (UMI No. AAC 87-27189)

Compares comprehension, as assessed by miscue analysis, with children's awareness of author purposes (narrative/exposition/ instruction). Awareness is considered to affect comprehension. All students recall expository text less than narrative.

BEVERIDGE, MICHAEL, & GRIFFITHS, VALERIE (1987, February). The effect of the pictures on the reading processes of less able readers: A miscue analysis approach. *Journal of Research in Reading, 10*(1), 29–42. (EJ350636)

Suggests that, in the majority of the aspects of the reading process examined, there is a statistically significant interaction between illustration and difficulty levels. The study finds that reading performance in the illustrated conditions is superior to that in the unillustrated conditions at the lower level of difficulty.

BROPHY, NANCY ELLEN (1987). *A longitudinal investigation of the reading performance of learning disabled and non–learning disabled students.* Unpublished doctoral dissertation, University of Missouri, Columbia. (UMI No. AAC 88-18913)

Learning disabled development is found to level off in fifth to sixth grade. Overall, reading scores on the Iowa Test of Basic Skills correlate with the RMI's results in miscue analysis.

BUNNEY, KAREN SUE (1987). *A comparison of third grade readers and readers with learning-disabilities on a measure of oral reading miscues, rate, and comprehension.* Unpublished doctoral dissertation, University of Texas, Austin. (UMI No. AAC 87-28527)

Respective to number of miscues, 31 on-level third graders and 31 learning disabled third grade level readers differ on reading rate, graphophonic, meaning function similarity, self-correction, and use of multiple sources miscues. Respective to comprehension, both groups are similar.

CHANG, YE LING (1987). *Four children's use of prediction strategies and predictable materials in reading instruction in a Chinese/English bilingual classroom.* Unpublished doctoral dissertation, University of Missouri, Columbia. (UMI No. AAC 87-26913)

The use of prediction strategy with predictable reading material in Chinese is successful for four Chinese children. Some modification is indicated for prediction in Chinese.

DEYES, TONY (1987, March). Towards a minimum discourse grammar for ESP reading courses. *Reading in a Foreign Language*, 3(2), 417–428. (EJ370501)

> Miscue analysis is one procedure in ongoing research used to find a minimum discourse grammar for Brazilian English for Special Purposes students. (English for Special Purposes, Portuguese, and English scientific materials are compared.)

DIXON, JANET S. (1987). *A study of average third grade readers' oral reading performance in material of varying Fry determined readabilities*. Unpublished doctoral dissertation, Michigan State University, East Lansing. (UMI No. AAC 87-22829)

> By count, number of miscues does not describe text difficulty. Broader analysis reveals miscues are predictable and miscue research has already identified these factors.

DOKES, MARION A. (1987). *The effect of a reading comprehension instructional strategy on the reading comprehension of average first grade readers*. Unpublished doctoral dissertation, Texas Woman's University, Denton. (UMI No. AAC 88-16794)

> RMI discriminates between basal and reading comprehension instruction strategy on comprehension; adapted version notes no meaning-based strategy difference.

EWOLDT, CAROLYN (1987, March). Reading tests and the deaf reader. *Perspectives for Teachers of the Hearing Impaired*, 5(4), 21–24.

> Looks at standardized tests from a meaning-based perspective.

GOODMAN, KENNETH S. (1987, September). Beyond basal readers: Taking charge of your own teaching. *Learning*, 16(2), 62–65. (EJ361863)

> The whole language approach to reading instruction integrates, rather than fragments, the reading process. The article suggests ways teachers can take responsibility for their students' literacy by modifying or even putting aside basal readers.

GOODMAN, KENNETH S., SMITH, E. BROOKS, MEREDITH, ROBERT, & GOODMAN, YETTA M. (1987). *Language and thinking in the elementary school: A whole-language curriculum* (3rd ed.). Katonah, NY: Richard C. Owen. (ED 278 987)

> A comprehensive look at education. Includes discussions of the psycholinguistic view of reading and writing, and strategies for comprehending. Teaching and learning perspectives are addressed.

GOODMAN, YETTA M., WATSON, DOROTHY J., & BURKE, CAROLYN L. (1987). *Reading miscue inventory: Alternative procedures*. Katonah, NY: Richard C. Owen. (ED 280 009)

> This latest edition of the RMI is the 'how to' book for understanding and doing miscue analysis of readers. It includes discussion of the Goodman model, an explanation of miscue analysis, several alternative procedures, and coding information.

HORNING, ALICE S. (1987, March). The trouble with writing is the trouble with reading. *Journal of Basic Writing*, 6(1), 36–47. (EJ381732)

> Two case studies are used in illustrating a relationship between syntactic and semantic writing miscues and reading miscues.

JOHNSON, RHONDA S. (1987). *Syntactic utilization in a group of adult basic readers*. Unpublished doctoral dissertation, University of Pittsburgh, Pittsburgh, PA. (UMI No. AAC 88-07319)

> Cross relating several measures demonstrates no interrelationship between syntactic measures, reading achievement, and syntactically correct substitution miscues.

LIM, HWA JA LEE (1987). *Literacy development of limited English proficient (LEP) children in a whole language classroom using predictable language materials*. Unpublished doctoral dissertation, University of Missouri, Columbia. (UMI No. AAC 87-28827)

> A naturalistic study of five LEP children in a literacy rich classroom environment with holistic instruction finds kids use meaning in their hypothesis testing about the new language, and have increased motivation to read.

LINDBERG, SHARRYL ANN (1987). *The relationship between product and in-process assessments of reading of third-grade students*. Unpublished doctoral dissertation, University of Southern California, Los Angeles. (UMI No. AAC 05-61034)

Finds that performance on a product (Stanford diagnostic reading test) assessment would not predict or reflect performance on an in-process (RMI) assessment.

MAREK, ANN (1987). *Retrospective miscue analysis as an instructional strategy with adult readers.* Unpublished doctoral dissertation, University of Arizona, Tucson. (UMI No. AAC 88-03262)
> Retrospective miscue analysis is instrumental in moving readers toward effective use of reading strategies and improving perceptions about themselves as readers.

MIRAMONTES, OFELIA (1987). Oral reading miscues of Hispanic good and learning disabled students: Implications for second language reading. In S.R. Godman & H.T. Trueba (Eds.), *Becoming literate in English as a second language: Cognition and literacy* (pp. 127–154). Norwood, NJ: Ablex.
> Similarities and differences are explored between good and learning disabled Hispanic readers' text and meaning acceptable miscues.

MIRAMONTES, OFELIA (1987, December). Oral reading miscues of Hispanic students: Implications for assessment of learning disabilities. *Journal of Learning Disabilities*, 20(10), 627–632. (EJ363488)
> Twenty Hispanic good readers and 20 learning disabled readers reading English and Spanish show differences in the reading of English in grammatical relationships, grammatical function, and comprehension.

MUDD, NORMA R. (1987, June). Strategies used in the early stages of learning to read: A comparison of children and adults. *Educational Research*, 29(2), 83–94. (EJ356452)
> Shows 72 adults' beginning reading strategies are similar to those of 96 children. Children's reading ages range from 7 yrs, to 7 yrs-11 months.

MURPHY, SHARON M. (1987). *The application of causal modeling to the Goodman model of reading.* Unpublished doctoral dissertation, University of Arizona, Tucson. (UMI No. AAC 88-03265)
> Causal modeling using the LISTREL program shows distinctions between process and product theories of reading; process variables are more interrelated.

SAHU, SHANTILATA, & PATTNAIK, SUSMITA (1987, January). Reading proficiency and strategies of disadvantaged children. *Psycho-Lingua*, 17(1), 39–54.

> Miscue analysis indicates advantaged second and fifth grade children's use of semantic level cues increases with time while disadvantaged children's does not.

SCHNEEBECK, JUDITH H. (1987). *Using written expression to improve reading comprehension.* Unpublished doctoral dissertation, Drake University, Des Moines, IA. (UMI No. AAC 88-25161)

> Considers comprehension as meaning composing and therefore suggests writing should be included in reading instruction. Miscue findings: When reading their own writing vs. familiar writing, the two students make fewer miscues and shift from graphophonic to syntactic and semantic cueing.

SCIBIOR, OLGA S. (1987). *Reconsidering spelling development: A socio-psycholinguistic perspective.* Unpublished doctoral dissertation, Indiana University, Bloomington. (UMI No. AAC 87-22916)

> An ethnographic study in a grade 3–4 classroom finds a socio-psycholinguistic view to be more explanatory than a purely cognitive-developmental view.

SHUMAN, R. BAIRD (1987). *The first R: Fundamentals of initial reading instruction. Developments in classroom instruction.* Washington, DC: National Education Association. (ED 293 115)

> Presents many facets of beginning reading instruction, pro and con. Includes a chapter on miscue analysis.

SIMONS, HERBERT D., & AMMON, PAUL R. (1987). *The language of beginning reading texts* (Final Report). Urbana, IL: National Council of Teachers of English, Research Foundation. (ED 284 165)

> Looks at changes in miscue patterns in 64 first graders when basal stories are rewritten in naturally occurring language. Fewer graphic and punctuation miscues are made.

VIPOND, DOUGLAS, HUNT, RUSSELL A., & WHEELER, LYNWOOD C. (1987, March). Social reading and literary engagement. *Reading Research and Instruction*, 26(3), 151–161.

The miscue analysis of 99 college readers shows social reading means greater attempts to convey meaning, but readers report less engagement with the text as a literary work.

WHELDALL, KEVIN, MERRETT, FRANK, & COLMAR, SUSAN (1987, February). "Pause, prompt and praise" for parents and peers: Effective tutoring of low progress readers. *Support for Learning*, 2(1), 5–12.

Describes a reading instructional technique called "pause, prompt, and praise" in which miscue analysis is suggested for use by teachers.

1988

ARELLANO-OSUNA, ADELINA E. (1988). *Oral reading miscues of fourth-grade Venezuelan children from five dialect regions*. Unpublished doctoral dissertation, University of Arizona, Tucson. (UMI No. AAC 88-14206)

Compares five dialect regions and finds that a definition of reading as meaning construction is supported, and dialect is considered an unrelated factor to readers' proficiency.

BARKSDALE, MARY ALICE (1988). *Anxiety and attention in beginning readers*. Unpublished doctoral dissertation, Virginia Polytechnic Institute and State University, Blacksburg. (UMI No. AAC 88-17398)

Uses miscue analysis as one measure of text difficulty. Results indicate an interaction effect between anxiety levels and text difficulty.

BRISTOW, PAGE SIMPSON, & LESLIE, LAUREN (1988, Spring). Indicators of reading difficulty: Discrimination between instructional- and frustration-range performance of functionally illiterate adults. *Reading Research Quarterly*, 23(2), 200–218. (EJ370072)

Checking for indicators of text difficulty for functionally illiterate adults, finds that accuracy, comprehension, and rate and miscue quality are significant.

CAMPBELL, ROBIN (1988). Learning about reading during pupil-teacher reading interaction. *Cambridge Journal of Education, 18*(3), 377–386.

> Explores teachers' interactions with readers to see what is communicated to children by teachers about reading, conversational rights, oral reading as a shared activity, and classroom interaction.

DANIELS, HARRY (1988, March). Misunderstandings, miscues and maths. *British Journal of Special Education, 15*(1), 11–13. (EJ370485)

> A miscue analysis of math is used in a case study of a 10-year-old boy (considered learning disabled).

DENNER, PETER R., MCGINLEY, WILLIAM J., & BROWN, ELIZABETH (1988). *Effects of providing story impressions as a prereading/writing activity on the story comprehension and oral reading miscues of second-grade readers* (Final Report). Pocatello, ID: Idaho State University, The Faculty Research Committee. (ED 301 855)

> A study of the effect of writing speculatively about an unread story in which no effect on miscues and a strong effect on comprehension by 60 second graders is demonstrated.

FLEISHER, BARBARA MARY (1988, March). Oral reading cue strategies of better and poorer readers. *Reading Research and Instruction, 27*(3), 35–50. (EJ371811)

> Fourth grade readers reading low and high difficulty material show better readers tend to use context and poorer readers use graphic cues.

GREENE, BRENDA M. (1988). *A case study of the problem identification and resolution strategies used by basic writers as they read their texts and the texts of their peers with the intention of improving them.* Unpublished doctoral dissertation, New York University, New York, NY. (UMI No. AAC 88-12506)

> This study examines writers' identification of errors when readers read their own written text and text written by peers. It finds that writers identify more problems at the semantic level of discourse. Data generated from each participant are analyzed to determine (a) the degree to which writers miscue, (b) the kind of problem identification and resolution strategies writers use, and (c) whether writers' perceptions of their reading with the intention to improve texts approximates their performance.

HARP, BILL (1988, November). When you do whole language instruction, how will you keep track of reading and writing skills? (When the principal asks). *The Reading Teacher*, 42(2), 160–161. (EJ381763)

> Offers ways to evaluate reading and writing in a whole language classroom. Includes checklists, holistic scoring, and miscue analysis.

HARTLE-SCHUTTE, DAVID (1988). *Home environment characteristics of successful Navajo readers*. Unpublished doctoral dissertation, University of Arizona, Tucson. (UMI No. AAC 89-07403)

> Social conditions, linguistic differences, and limited materials can not be categorized as uniform social deficits. Successful literacy development is achieved in a variety of ways.

HYMAN, LETHIA (1988). *A comparative analysis of miscues in oral reading of English and Spanish by Spanish-speaking bilingual students*. Unpublished doctoral dissertation, University of Southern California, Los Angeles. (UMI No. AAC 05-65197)

> The psycholinguistic model is shown to cross language boundaries. Strategy transfer across languages appears to vary at an individual level. Language competence influences prediction and interpretation of text.

LERNER, ANDREW NATHAN (1988). *The effect of seating arrangement on oral reading fluency*. Unpublished doctoral dissertation, Hofstra University, Hempstead, NY. (UMI No. AAC 88-15589)

> In one-on-one reading situations, seating arrangement between teacher and student does not affect reading miscues, self-assigned grades on reading, time to read, or comprehension.

MALICKY, GRACE V., & NORMAN, CHARLES A. (1988, December). Reading processes subgroups in a clinical population. *Alberta Journal of Educational Research*, 34(4), 344–354.

> One hundred twenty-three first through ninth graders and special education students show some relation of mode of processing to reading level, but readers differ within and across all levels.

MARTIN-WAMBU, JUDITH (1988). *Case studies of nine community college good writers/poor readers*. Unpublished doctoral dissertation, Teachers College at Columbia University, New York, NY. (UMI No. AAC 89-06469)

> Miscue analysis is used in the study of students' preferences for self-expression in writing, positive feedback versus no reading feedback, and poor test taking abilities.

NORMAN, CHARLES A. (1988). The reading processes of adults in literacy programs. *Adult Literacy and Basic Education*, *12*(1), 14–26. (EJ379547)

> Study describes the reading process of 122 adults reading at various levels using miscue analysis and retellings.

O'BRIEN, DAVID GERARD (1988, September). The relation between oral reading miscue patterns and comprehension: A test of the relative explanatory power of psycholinguistic and interactive views of reading. *Journal of Psycholinguistic Research*, *17*(5), 379–401.

> For 30 average seventh graders, correlations between the oral reading and comprehension measures indicate a negative relation between oral reading and recall following the reading of familiar passages and a positive relation between oral reading and an inferential comprehension measure following the reading of unfamiliar passages. Results are discussed in terms of a comparison between psycholinguistic and interactive models of reading comprehension.

O'NEILL, IRMA JOSEFINA (1988). *The production of comprehensible reading texts in Spanish*. Unpublished doctoral dissertation, Teachers College at Columbia University, New York, NY. (UMI No. AAC 88-24409)

> Fourth and sixth graders' responses to text are incorporated in later versions that are found to be improved in comprehensibility and reading ease. This study suggests that instructional use of reader/text analysis and revision replace leveling by readability score.

PAZ, DARZELL STROTHER HOUSTON (1988). *Teacher's responses to ebonic miscues during reading instruction in first and second grades*. Unpublished doctoral dissertation, University of Maryland, College Park. (UMI No. AAC 88-18195)

> Although 10 voluntarily observed teachers' responses to students' dialect miscues do not vary, no correlation is found between professed

and actual responses. Reading ability is not found to be a significant factor, but race is.

PETERSON, BARBARA L. (1988). *Characteristics of texts that support beginning readers*. Unpublished doctoral dissertation, The Ohio State University, Columbus. (UMI No. AAC 88-20339)

> An analysis of texts used with at-risk first graders in the Ohio reading recovery program describes increasing complexity and suggests readers do not need controlled text to learn to read.

POLLOCK, MARY ANNE CURRY (1988). *Preservice teachers' correction responses to Appalachian English miscues after training in miscue analysis*. Unpublished doctoral dissertation, University of Kentucky, Lexington. (UMI No. AAC 89-03572)

> Study of using Appalachian dialect miscues in training Appalachian teachers shows teachers change behavior regarding meaning-changing miscues. Dialect awareness is recommended.

RHODES, LYNN KNEBEL, & DUDLEY-MARLING, CURT (1988). *Readers and writers with a difference: A holistic approach to teaching learning disabled and remedial students*. Portsmouth, NH: Heinemann. (ED 293 117)

> Provides an introduction for the learning disabled teacher to holistic reading and writing instruction. Includes teaching strategies and how to meet traditional assessment requirements from a holistic perspective.

SAMPSON, MICHAEL R., BRIGGS, L.D., & WHITE, JANE H. (1988, March). Student authorship and reading: The joy of literacy. *Reading Improvement, 25*(1), 82–84. (EJ371742, See also: ED 236 551)

> First grade students using student-authored (vs. basal) material employ more efficient strategies and understand more.

SAMWAY, KATHERINE DAVIES (1988). *The writing processes of nonnative English speaking children in the elementary grades*. Unpublished doctoral dissertation, University of Rochester, Rochester, NY. (UMI No. AAC 88-03327)

> ESOL children are shown to be successful in communicating ideas in writing. Teacher's expectations and meaning-centered instructional practices have substantial influence.

SIMONS, HERBERT D., & AMMON, PAUL R. (1988). Primerese miscues. In J.E. Readence & R.S. Baldwin (Eds.), *Dialogues in literacy research.* (Thirty-seventh Yearbook of the National Reading Conference, pp. 115–121). Berkeley, CA: University of California.

> Sixty first graders reading controlled basal text and more natural versions show the controlled text conflicts with the linguistic knowledge the readers possess.

SMITH, FRANK (1988). *Understanding reading: A psycholinguistic analysis of reading* (4th ed.). Hillsdale, NJ: Erlbaum.

> A view of the complexities of reading utilizing physiological, psychological, and social research.

TAYLOR, STEPHANIE B. (1988). *An analysis of comprehension during oral and silent reading in sixth grade students.* Unpublished doctoral dissertation, University of Southern California, Los Angeles. (UMI No. AAC 05-65228)

> Sixth graders reading two folktales silently and orally demonstrate no group difference in comprehension. Individual scores vary dramatically however. A trend is noted toward increased comprehension in silent reading.

THOMAS, FELTON AUGUSTUS (1988). *The efficacy of assisted reading as a strategy for facilitating the reading success of adult disabled readers.* Unpublished doctoral dissertation, Virginia Polytechnic Institute and State University, Blacksburg. (UMI No. AAC 89-11066)

> Four prison inmates read language experience texts and regular texts under a whole language approach. Findings include modest gains in comprehension and word recognition; differences in patterns of miscues respective to type of text; and growth of a positive attitude toward reading.

VAUGHT-ALEXANDER, KAREN ANN (1988). *Contexts which connect writers, readers, texts: A teacher-researcher observes high school freshmen.* Unpublished doctoral dissertation, Indiana University, Bloomington. (UMI No. AAC 89-14838)

> High school freshmen demonstrate development by showing strategies like older vs. younger writers. A flexible writing-reading curriculum fosters development.

VINEGRAD, M.D. (1988, November). Miscue analysis and computer-assisted learning. *Reading*, 22(3), 152–157. (EJ392001)

> Suggests that when miscue analysis is associated with remedial techniques, computer-assisted learning constitutes a viable method of remediation.

WILLICH, YVE, PRIOR, MARGOT, CUMMING, GEOFF, & SPANOS, TOM (1988, November). Are disabled readers delayed or different? An approach using an objective miscue analysis. *British Journal of Educational Psychology*, 58(3), 315–329. (EJ389326)

> Australian study of normal and disabled students. Discusses miscue analysis, theories of disability, and methodology.

WINSER, BILL (1988, November). Readers getting control of reading. *Australian Journal of Reading*, 11(4), 257–268. (EJ383663)

> Study of strategies readers use by analyzing their self reported responses during and after reading a passage.

WOODLEY, JOHN W. (1988). *Reading assessment from a whole language perspective*. (ED 296 309)

> Presents means of assessment that are alternative to standardized tests from print awareness task to situational responses to reading.

ZHANG, JIAN (1988, October). Reading miscues and 9 adult Chinese learners of English. *Journal of Reading*, 32(1), 34–41. (EJ377353)

> Looks at typical miscue patterns of adult Chinese ESL readers.

1989

ARGYLE, SUSAN B. (1989). Miscue analysis for classroom use. *Reading Horizons*, 29(2), 93–102. (EJ383689)

> Looks at using miscue analysis to document and focus on student strengths.

ARTOLA-GONZALEZ, T. (1989, July). Problemas metodológicos y críticas al "Miscue Analysis" (Methodological problems and critique of "Miscue Analysis"). *Revista de Psicología General y Aplicada*, 42(3), 299–305.

> Examines methodological problems related to Miscue Analysis Techniques (MAT) and offers possible solutions. MAT seems to be one of

the most promising instruments for the evaluation of reading processes and strategies.

BOCK, JOAN (1989, November). *Portraits of six developing readers in a whole language classroom.* Paper presented at the 39th Annual Meeting of the National Reading Conference, Austin, TX. (ED 318 988)

> Uses RMI to document six second grade children's changing perceptions of the reading process. Also looks at social interaction, individual independent reading time activities, and books selected.

CHANG, JI MEI (1989). *Psycholinguistic analysis of oral reading performance by proficient versus nonproficient Chinese elementary students.* Unpublished doctoral dissertation, University of Southern California, Los Angeles. (UMI No. AAC 05-66732)

> Use of miscue with Chinese students shows universal aspects with specific orthographic effects on word for word substitutions; a graphic and parsing division is noted. Repeated retelling improves nonproficient readers' text recall.

FULLER, LAURICE MARION (1989). *The relative effectiveness of a meaning emphasis approach and a phonics emphasis approach to reading beginning reading in English to second- or third-grade bilingual Spanish readers.* Unpublished doctoral dissertation, Boston University, Boston, MA. (UMI No. AAC 90-05507)

> A one-year study of eight transitional Spanish/English classes shows phonics awareness is similar regardless of instructional approach. Previous Spanish reading ability also correlates with better English comprehension.

GESPASS, SUZANNE R. (1989). *Control and use of pronouns in the writing of Native American children.* Unpublished doctoral dissertation, University of Arizona, Tucson. (UMI No. AAC 90-00129)

> Six Native American students demonstrate significant control of pronominal usage conforming early to the principle that pronouns may be used except where ambiguity would result. Conclusion suggests direct instruction could be counterproductive through unnatural emphasis on already controlled language use.

GOODMAN, KENNETH S. (1989, November). Whole-language research: Foundations and development. *Elementary School Journal*, 90(2), 207–221. (EJ404268)

> Summarizes key characteristics of whole language. Theoretical views of learners, teachers, language, and curriculum are explicated. The strong research base for whole language is considered and potential research is discussed.

GOODMAN, YETTA M. (1989, November). Roots of the whole-language movement. *Elementary School Journal*, 90(2), 113–127. (EJ404262)

> Gives a history of the whole language movement. Looks at the early use of the term "whole language." Explores influences from philosophy, psychology, linguistics, and education on development of whole language. Discusses influences from early educational movements in the United States, England, and New Zealand.

GOODMAN, YETTA M., & MAREK, ANN (1989). *Retrospective miscue analysis: Two papers* (Occasional Paper No. 19). Tucson, AZ: University of Arizona, Center for Research and Development, Program in Language and Literacy.

> Includes paper by Yetta Goodman on retrospective miscue analysis: history, procedures, and prospects, and a summary of Marek's dissertation—case studies of two adult readers.

GREENE, BRENDA M. (1989a). *The influence of miscues on basic writers' revision strategies.* (ED 305 665)

> Using think-aloud protocols, three writers read their own material. Most miscues are non–meaning loss substitutions showing writing miscues have little influence on revision.

GREENE, BRENDA M. (1989b). *Paths to empowerment: Problem identification and resolution strategies of basic writers.* (ED 307 620)

> Using their own writing, three students (Guyanese, Belizean, African-American) have their think-aloud protocols recorded as they read and revise. Perceptions correlate with what is done when composing and reading texts.

GREENE, BRENDA M. (1989c). *Reading with the intention to improve texts: A case study*. Unpublished; ERIC document only. (ED 305 619)

> A case study of a reader engaged in revising. Looks at miscues, problem identification strategies, problem resolution strategies, and perception of reading ability. The reader focuses on a semantic level in cohesiveness, clarity, and completeness. Beliefs and practices are found to be related.

JOHNS, JERRY L., & MAGLIARI, ANNE MARIE (1989, June). Informal reading inventories: Are the Betts Criteria the best criteria? *Reading Improvement*, 26(2), 124–132. (EJ398839)

> Criticizes the Betts Criteria on grounds that they do not consider quality of miscues.

KINDER, SANDRA JEANE (1989). *Literature study groups: Effects on readers' proficiency, concepts of the reading process, and attitudes*. Unpublished doctoral dissertation, University of Missouri, Columbia. (UMI No. AAC 90-19649)

> Increased proficiency or maintenance of proficiency with increasing difficulty characterizes the literature study experience. Students' perceptions increase with accuracy but vary in implementation. Students consider basal stories too short.

KLEIN, CYNTHIA (1989, December). Specific learning difficulties. *Adult Literacy & Basic Skills Unit Newsletter*, 32, 1–4. (ED 303 667)

> With a focus on adult dyslexia, miscue analysis is one of the diagnostic methods for developing a suggested learning support class for students.

KOZLESKI, ELIZABETH B. (1989, December). Improving oral reading performance through self-monitoring and strategy training. *Reading Improvement*, 26(4), 305–314. (EJ408390)

> Examines the effects of self-monitoring and task-specific strategy training on a poor reader's oral reading miscues. Finds that self-monitoring reduces oral reading errors but that the combination of both strategies yields no further reduction in miscues.

LEE, LIAN JU (1989). *Emergent literacy in Chinese: Print awareness of young children in Taiwan*. Unpublished doctoral dissertation, University of Arizona, Tucson. (UMI No. AAC 90-13150)

Beginning Chinese readers are found to draw on context clues, personal experience, and background knowledge and show evidence of construction of conceptual knowledge about print. No linear style of progression is noted.

MAGUIRE, MARY H. (1989). *Middle-grade French immersion children's perceptions and productions of English and French written narratives.* Unpublished doctoral dissertation, University of Arizona, Tucson. (UMI No. AAC 90-05724)

> Finds children's proficiency supports the hypothesis that a single across-language process accounts for their French and English writing. Teaching linguistic forms has negative effects on the written product and children's views of themselves. Verb form usage is examined.

MASCHOFF, JANET BRANDT (1989). *A post hoc psycholinguistic analysis of oral and silent reading miscues of second, fourth and sixth-graders.* Unpublished doctoral dissertation, Southern Illinois University, Edwardsville. (UMI No. AAC 89-23255)

> RMI and cloze procedures are used with 145 second, fourth, and sixth graders to show correlations between oral and silent reading miscues. Whereas syntactic acceptability correlations are found, only grade 2 scores show correlation for semantic acceptability and no correlation is found for grammatical function and meaning change.

MUDRE, LYNDA HAMILTON, & MCCORMICK, SANDRA (1989, Winter). Effects of meaning-focused cues on underachieving readers' context use, self-corrections, and literal comprehension. *Reading Research Quarterly, 24*(1), 89–113. (EJ385142)

> Looks at the effort to work with parents using miscue strategies; finds parents learn to be helpful in ways that change reading strategies.

OYETUNDE, TIMOTHY O., & UMOLU, JOANNE J. (1989, November). A comparison of reader strategies on two versions of a newspaper editorial. *Reading, 23*(3), 184–195. (EJ400412)

> Uses miscue analysis to look at reader strategies in newspaper editorials that are syntactically complex with high vocabulary and simple with low vocabulary.

PUMFREY, PETER DAVID, & FLETCHER, J. (1989, September). Differences in reading strategies among 7 to 8 year old children. *Journal of Research in Reading, 12*(2), 114–130. (EJ396476)

Increasing complexity of text is related to decreasing quality of miscues in high- and above-average readers.

SHAPIRO, JON, & RILEY, JAMES D. (1989, January). Over-reliance on data processing in reading: A technique for holistic assessment. *Clearing House, 62*(5), 211–215. (EJ391986)

> Divides readers into non-concept-aware (lacking background knowledge) and non-data-aware (lacking graphophonic and skills knowledge). Discusses how overreliance on data processing (graphophonics and skills) inhibits meaning gain. Adaptation of RMI is used.

SIMONS, HERBERT D., & AMMON, PAUL R. (1989, December). Child knowledge and primerese text: Mismatches and miscues. *Research in the Teaching of English, 23*(4), 380–398. (EJ402234)

> Considers the problems controlled text presents to children with respect to the knowledge of language they already have.

SINGH, JUDY (1989, January). Teacher behavior during oral reading by moderately mentally retarded children. *Journal of Reading, 32*(4), 298–304. (EJ381814)

> Finds instant correction is prevalent among the four teachers studied.

WALLACE, CATHERINE, & GOODMAN, YETTA M. (1989, September). Research Currents: Language and literacy development of multilingual learners. *Language Arts, 66*(5), 542–551. (EJ394981)

> Discusses current research and issues concerning multilingual learners and makes suggestions for school programs addressing bilingualism and multilingualism.

WASHINGTON, VALERIE M., & MILLER-JONES, DALTON (1989, July). Teacher interactions with nonstandard English speakers during reading instruction. *Contemporary Educational Psychology, 14*(3), 280–312.

> When confronted with dialect miscues, teachers' knowledge of features of black and nonstandard English speakers is related to appropriate behaviors supportive of reading.

PART 7

1990–1995

1990

AMMON, PAUL, SIMONS, HERBERT D., & ELSTER, CHARLES (1990). *Effects of controlled primerese language on the reading process* (Tech. Rep. No. 45). Berkeley, CA & Pittsburgh, PA: Center for the Study of Writing. (ED 334 542)

> Sixty first graders in high and low ability groups read either original basal texts or basal texts rewritten for more natural language. Readers of rewritten versions have more syntactically appropriate or meaning preserving miscues.

CAMPBELL, ROBIN (1990, November). Reading and the national curriculum: Responding to miscues. *Reading, 24*(3), 133–138. (EJ418081)

> Discusses the nonstatutory guidance sections of Great Britain's national curriculum that deal with teacher responses to students' oral reading miscues.

CARWILE, NANCY RAMSEY (1990). *The value of predictable books for adult beginning readers.* Unpublished doctoral dissertation, University of Virginia, Charlottesville. (UMI No. AAC 91-31561)

> It is found that 12 primer level adults all use semantic cues consistently though few use reliable decoding and spelling strategies. Students and instructors find the materials rewarding.

CHATTIWAT, WISA (1990). *A psycholinguistic study of the oral reading miscues of Thai college students reading in English and Thai.* Unpublished doctoral dissertation, University of Missouri, Columbia. (UMI No. AAC 91-19254)

> In comparing miscues of Thai students reading Thai and English the reading process is found to be similar with a greater number of omissions in reading Thai and more frequent substitutions in reading English.

COLL, JULIA, & OSUNA, ADELINA (1990, September). A comparison of reading miscue analysis between bilingual and monolingual South American third graders. *Hispania*, *73*(3), 807–815. (ED 309 621)

> Three Venezuelan third graders read a folktale in Spanish. Similar miscues are found in the bilingual and the two monolingual subjects.

HARTLE-SCHUTTE, DAVID (1990, April). *Beating the odds: Navajo children becoming literate.* Paper presented at the 19th Annual International Bilingual/Bicultural Education Conference, Tucson, AZ. (ED 336 219)

> A study of successful Navajo fifth grade readers reveals that child initiated activities and questioning and supportive adult responses within the home, not direct instruction in the school, are significant to the development of literacy.

KING, DOROTHY F., & GOODMAN, KENNETH S. (1990, October). Whole language: Cherishing learners and their language. *Language, Speech, and Hearing Services in Schools*, *21*(4), 221–227. (EJ420018)

> Explores and offers guidelines for working with cultural and linguistic differences.

KLUMB, KELLY (1990). *Patterns of children's reading and spelling substitution errors: "DO NAT DSTRB GNYS AT WRK."* Report prepared for the Lucerne Valley Unified School District, San Bernardino County, CA. (ED 323 515)

> Summary of knowledge on substitution errors in reading and spelling. (See Section 5 on miscue analysis and context).

LEROY, CAROL (1990). *Reading: A descriptive study of four Cree children.* Unpublished master's thesis, University of Alberta, Edmonton. (UMI No. AAC MM64883)

> Analysis is made of miscues, retellings, and responses to questions to discern how the children use text information and background knowledge. Consistent with how children view their involvement, each child reads at the level where his or her comprehension is adequate. There is a great deal of variation among the children in the types of cues used in oral reading, in the use of prior knowledge, and in tendencies to extend the text in personal ways.

MALIK, ALI A. (1990, March). A psycholinguistic analysis of the reading behavior of EFL-proficient readers using culturally familiar and culturally nonfamiliar expository texts. *American Educational Research Journal, 27*(1), 205–223.

> Examines 15 proficient English as a foreign language speakers, finding cultural schemata affect comprehension and strategies used. Nonfamiliar text is read relatively accurately but with little integration.

MILNE, LYNDA M. (1990). *Using metacognitive strategies to enhance reading comprehension for students with learning disabilities.* Unpublished master's thesis, Lakehead University, Thunder Bay, ON. (UMI No. AAC MM69154)

> An explicit focus on self-questioning is found to improve the reading comprehension of twenty learning disabled students as measured by miscue analysis and Gates-MacGinitie measures.

MIRAMONTES, OFELIA (1990). A comparative study of English oral reading skills in differently schooled groups of Hispanic students. *Journal of Reading Behavior, 22*(4), 373–394. (EJ418069)

> Using miscue analysis, this study finds mixed dominant students cannot be separated from single dominant readers. Suggests that instruction has not taken their abilities into account.

MOORE, CAROL (1990). *Increasing reading fluency for learning-disabled and remedial readers.* Educational Specialist Practicum, Nova University, Melbourne, FL. (ED 323 519)

> Twenty-four first grade retainees are placed and then followed in a holistic instructional program. Attitudes change and fluency increases. Analysis of miscues is used in evaluation.

NOSEWORTHY, RANDY PITTMAN (1990). *The effects of individualized reading program involving three grade four students experiencing difficulties in reading.* Unpublished master's thesis, Memorial University of Newfoundland, St. John's. (UMI No. AAC MM61781)

> RMI is used in the evaluation of three fourth grade problem readers who read self-selected trade books for 15 weeks. Parent involvement is included in this investigation.

PANTONG, BANG O. (1990). *Cross-linguistic influence in reading: Miscues and language transfer in an English text read by six Thai speakers*. Unpublished doctoral dissertation, University of Missouri, Columbia. (UMI No. AAC 91-00220)

> Evidence of language transfer is found on phonology, syntax, and semantic levels with some tonal, article, and prepositional problems arising.

PARKER, CONNIE MACDONALD (1990). *An investigation of unexpected spelling difficulties in successful readers and writers: A socio-psycholinguistic perspective*. Unpublished master's thesis, Mount Saint Vincent University, Halifax, NS. (UMI No. AAC MM62623)

> Among findings with grade 5 successful readers and writers, they have less conscious awareness of common patterns and orthographic knowledge, are more limited in ability to orchestrate a combination of strategies, have difficulty spelling while composing, and have less articulated awareness of strategy use.

RASINSKI, TIMOTHY V. (1990). Investigating measures of reading fluency. *Educational Research Quarterly, 14*(3), 37–44.

> Five measures of oral reading fluency are used with 77 third and 65 fifth graders. Findings suggest three distinct factors: reading rate, miscues, and phrasing.

RHODES, LYNN KNEBEL, & SHANKLIN, NANCY L. (1990, November). Miscue analysis in the classroom. *The Reading Teacher, 44*(3), 252–254. (EJ416393)

> Discusses the procedures for using the classroom reading miscue assessment, which was developed by Denver area coordinators/consultants applying whole language to help teachers efficiently gather miscue data.

RIGG, PAT, & KAZEMEK, FRANCIS E. (1990). Four inmates read. *Adult Literacy and Basic Education, 14*(1), 28–44. (EJ411386)

> The reading practices of four prison inmates are analyzed, showing very distinct approaches to reading. Standardized tests prove inadequate for their learning needs but miscue analysis is useful.

SERGENT, WALLACE KEITH, JR. (1990). *A study of the oral reading strategies of advanced and highly advanced second language readers of Chinese.* Unpublished doctoral dissertation, The Ohio State University, Columbus. (UMI No. AAC 90-22550)

> Graphic constraint appears to operate more strongly than contextual constraint though contextual constrained miscues are more often corrected. Developmental differences are noted in comparison with reading L2 in alphabetic orthography.

SHANKLIN, NANCY L. (1990, April). Improving the comprehension of at-risk readers: An ethnographic study of four Chapter 1 teachers, grades 4–6. *Journal of Reading, Writing, and Learning Disabilities International,* 6(2), 137–148. (EJ411823)

> Reports on four teachers' strategies for improving comprehension in their students: creating literate environments using whole texts; changing students' miscue patterns; and instructional use of predicting, story mapping, semantic mapping, and retelling.

WALLACE, CATHERINE (1990). Learning to read in a second language: A window on the language acquisition process. In M. Halliday, J. Gibbons, & H. Nicholas (Eds.), *Learning, keeping, and using language: Selected Papers of the Eighth World Congress of Applied Linguistics* (pp. 219–240). Philadelphia, PA: John Benjamin.

> An examination of a 19-year-old ESL reader emphasizes the importance of print as a stable medium for ESL learners to reflect upon syntactic, semantic, and pragmatic levels of language.

WUTHERICK, MARJORIE A. (1990, December). What should I do when they don't know the words: A review of the literature. *Ohio Reading Teacher,* 24(2), 32–40.

> Reviews literature that helps teachers make decisions about children's reading.

1991

ADAMS, ARLENE (1991, January). The oral reading errors of readers with learning disabilities: Variations produced within the instructional and frustrational ranges. *Remedial and Special Education (RASE), 12*(1), 48–55, 62. (ED 320 113)

> Looking at differences of miscues for 32 grade 2, 5, 8 and 11 learning disabled readers when reading instructional vs. frustration level materials finds that substitutions, omissions, insertions, and reversals are similar. Differences occur in syntactic and semantic acceptability.

ANDERSON, JACQUELINE CHERYL (1991). *Reading assessments and oral deaf/hard of hearing students: The 1982 Stanford Achievement Test, for use with hearing impaired students vs. the Reading Miscue Inventory.* Unpublished master's thesis, York University, North York, ON. (UMI No. AAC MM68693)

> Compares Stanford Achievement Test-Hearing Impaired and RMI with five hearing impaired students. Finds that SAT-HI consistently underestimates performance and fails to reflect authentic reading situations.

CHAPMAN, MARILYN LESLEY (1991). *Function and form in first grade writing.* Unpublished doctoral dissertation, University of Victoria, Victoria, BC. (UMI No. AAC NN6265)

> Six first grade children show changes in function to be due to their interests and preferences with a trend toward multifunctionalism. Increased use of written language conventions over time is noted.

DEAN, SYLVIA ESTELLE (1991). *A study of qualitative miscue analysis scoring systems for identification of instructional reading levels.* Unpublished doctoral dissertation, Portland State University, Portland, OR. (UMI No. AAC 92-13873)

> Frank May's poor reader scoring system, which is limited to only defaults and meaning denigrating miscues, is found comparable in assessment results to traditional IRI assessments.

FROESE, VICTOR (1991, December). *Aspects of reading in ESL and L1 students.* Paper presented at the 41st Annual Meeting of the National Reading Conference, Palm Springs, CA. (ED 343 104)

> Thirty 9–13 years olds (Cantonese, Punjabi, Vietnamese) and 30 native English speakers are compared. Results indicate non-English speakers handle inferential questions differently, differ in interpretation of story endings, and produce a higher number of miscues.

GUPTA, ABHA (1991). *Linguistic issues in the competence and performance of hearing-impaired children: The Gael Test.* Unpublished doctoral dissertation, University of Arizona, Tucson. (UMI No. AAC 92-00034)

> Examines students' test responses and suggests psycholinguistic processes explain various inconsistencies found in students' responses. Procedures for analysis are developed and presented in the study.

HARP, BILL (ED.). (1991). *Assessment and evaluation in whole language programs.* Norwood, MA: Christopher-Gordon. (ED 331 043)

> A collection of articles that discuss critical assessment questions regarding the use of whole language in schools.

HINNENKAMP, BARBARA (1991, January). Reading and writing with a special needs student: A case study. *Insights into Open Education, 23*(5), 1–6. (ED 326 846)

> Uses miscue analysis as part of a one year documentation of the growth of a 12-year-old moderately handicapped girl.

HUSS, REBECCA LOUISE (1991). *Among diverse worlds: An ethnographic study of young children becoming literate in English as a second language in a British multiethnic primary school classroom.* Unpublished doctoral dissertation, Georgia State University, Atlanta. (UMI No. AAC 92-20334)

> School, home, and religious school are all found to complement 5- and 6-year-old second language learners of English. Reading miscue analysis along with overall ethnographic data is used with a special focus on three Pakistani children.

ITTZÉS, KATA (1991, February). Lexical guessing in isolation and context. *Journal of Reading, 34*(5), 360–366.

> This study measures the extent secondary students' ability to guess meaning of unknown foreign words in isolation is related to guessing words in context.

REUTZEL, D. RAY, & FAWSON, PARKER (1991, June). Literature webbing predictable books: A prediction strategy that helps below-average, first-grade readers. *Reading Research and Instruction, 30*(4), 20–30. (EJ432442)

> Analysis of miscues shows the literature webbing strategy improves 22 below average first grade readers' comprehension significantly more than a directed listening/reading thinking activity by helping readers organize their predictions and attend to text structure.

TRAW, RICK CHARLES (1991). *A descriptive study of the development of metalinguistic awareness in developmentally delayed first-grade students in a holistic meaning-centered language program*. Unpublished doctoral dissertation, University of South Dakota, Vermillion. (UMI No. AAC 92-12699)

> This ethnographic study of a transitional first grade class documents significant metalinguistic development for word awareness, sound/symbol correspondence, some morphological structures, punctuation, and increasing syntactic and semantic complexity in writing. Movement away from the use of memory and illustrations, toward the use of print cues is also noted.

ULASEVICH, ALEC, LEATON, BROOKE, KRAMER, DAVID, HIECKE, ADOLF E., & O'CONNELL, DANIEL C. (1991). American and Japanese subjects' reports of pause occurrences and duration. *Language and Communication: An Interdisciplinary Journal, 11*(4), 299–307.

> Finds that semantic and linguistic cues appear to have substantial effects on the accuracy of readers' reporting of pauses.

WINSER, WILLIAM NELSON (1991). Metacognitive processes in reading. Unpublished doctoral dissertation, University of Wollongong, NSW, Australia.

> Forty readers grouped from grades 2, 4, 6, 8, and adults are asked to think aloud when correcting miscues while orally reading; they were interrupted five times during silent reading of a second text. While younger readers show similar awarenesses to older readers, less proficient readers are less flexible in using appropriate strategies for comprehension.

XIANLONG, FAN (1991, May). Using the process approach to reading in an EFL class. *Journal of Reading, 34*(8), 624–627.

> Results of one teacher's struggle to get students beyond word-for-word reading through working with the Goodman model.

YETMAN, SHEILA ANN (1991). *Grade three readers' inference strategies: The identification of a relationship to reading ability.* Unpublished master's thesis, Memorial University of Newfoundland, St. John's. (UMI No. AAC MM68255)

> Analyzes the verbalized thinking of 30 grade three children to identify nine inference strategies.

1992

ANDERSON, VALERIE KAREN (1992). *An instructional development project on the use of computer-assisted instruction for vocabulary in the college reading class.* Unpublished doctoral dissertation, Teachers College at Columbia University, New York, NY. (UMI No. AAC 92-18675)

> Using a psycholinguistic model of reading based on Goodman and Smith, this study examines teachers' learning and use of a commercial vocabulary development computer program.

BIERMAN, SANDRA BARRICK (1992). *Cognitive processing of adult and sixth-grade readers through written in-process responses.* Unpublished doctoral dissertation, East Texas State University, Commerce. (UMI No. AAC 92-22515)

> By analyzing 20 adult and 20 sixth graders' self-reflections on their reading it is found that summarizing, speculating, inquiring, evaluating, inferring, and confirming/disconfirming is present for both groups. A descriptive analysis of the predictions reveals the same types for both groups.

BOURASSA, EILEEN LEE (1992). *Accelerated reading: Impetus for change in first grade classroom instruction.* Unpublished doctoral dissertation, University of Northern Colorado, Greeley. (UMI No. AAC 92-35573)

> A qualitative study of teacher change through accelerated reading in-service work finds teachers change their concepts of reading, focus more on student needs rather than teacher inadequacies, and become active decision makers in their choice of which cueing systems to emphasize.

CHALMERS, LYNNE (1992, April). Going out on a limb: Teaching adolescent boys to be readers. *Insights into Open Education*, 24(7), 1–9. (ED 343 085)

> Looks at the miscues and activities of three learning disabled boys introduced to literature that interests them. Discusses the experience of the teacher and a colleague watching problem students become advocates of reading.

CHANG, JI MEI, HUNG, DAISY L., & TZENG, OVID J.L. (1992, January). Miscue analysis of Chinese children's reading behavior at the entry level. *Journal of Chinese Linguistics*, 20(1), 120–158.

> Thirty-two normal and school-labeled disabled elementary readers are compared. Analysis reveals both groups use various language cueing systems. Orthographic issues are discussed.

COSTA, RICIO (1992). *Biliteracy development: A case study.* Unpublished doctoral dissertation, University of Massachusetts, Amherst. (UMI No. AAC 92-19421)

> Reading miscue inventories are administered twice to a bilingual kindergartner in both English and Spanish. Reading strategies used are consistent and migrate across languages. The study suggests biliteracy development findings are congruent with language acquisition research.

COSTELLO, SARAH A. (1992a). *Collaborative retrospective miscue analysis with middle school students.* Unpublished doctoral dissertation, University of Arizona, Tucson. (UMI No. AAC 92-23547)

> In-depth case studies of the collaborative meetings of four seventh graders over a four month period. Students identify and discuss their own miscues. It is found that readers move toward a more positive and process view of themselves as readers. Shifts in strategies toward meaning construction are noted.

COSTELLO, SARAH A. (1992b). Retrospective miscue analysis: In the classroom. In K.S. Goodman, L.B. Bird, & Y.M. Goodman (Eds.), *The whole language catalog: Supplement on authentic assessment* (pp. 152–153). Santa Rosa, CA: American School Publishers.

> Discusses middle school students as they use the Goodman Model of Reading to reflect on their reading. Suggests Collaborative Retrospective

Miscue Analysis is an appropriate teaching strategy for classroom or for small groups of peers.

GARCIA, GEORGIA EARNEST (1992). *The literacy assessment of second-language learners*. Urbana, IL: Center for the Study of Reading. (ED 348 665)

> A review of formal and informal means of evaluation measures for second-language learners, including oral miscue analysis, though as an informal assessment, retellings, and use of tape recordings for evaluations.

GOODMAN, KENNETH S. (1992, September). Why whole language is today's agenda in education. *Language Arts*, 69(5), 354–363.

> Discusses the transactional view of writing, social/personal views of learning, teachers redefining themselves and their relationship to learners, and the curriculum of whole language.

GOODMAN, YETTA M., & GOODMAN, KENNETH S. (1992). Vygotsky in a whole-language perspective. In L. Moll (Ed.), *Vygotsky and education: Instructional implications of sociohistorical psychology* (pp. 223–250). New York: Cambridge University Press.

> Explores Vygotsky's notions about the role of context in the development of written language understanding and Vygotsky's influence on whole language by looking at the role of play, learning language and learning through language, the teacher's role, curriculum issues, and language empowerment.

JUNG, HESHIM (1992). *The relationship between adult second language readers' metacognitive awareness of reading and their reading processes in a second language*. Unpublished doctoral dissertation, University of Arizona, Tucson. (UMI No. AAC 92-23563)

> For six in-depth studies drawn from 139 surveys with ESL adults, text-bound tendencies when reading the second language relate to more linguistic perceptions. The more the subjects perceive differences between first and second languages, the greater the differences in readers' transactions with text.

LEENAM, WUTTI (1992). *The role of cultural schemata on oral reading of Thai college students reading English as a foreign language*. Unpublished doctoral dissertation, University of Missouri, Columbia. (UMI No. AAC 93-07428)

> For readers reading culturally familiar and unfamiliar text, this study finds more miscues, more low level miscues, and less grammatical acceptability associated with unfamiliar text.

LI, WEI (1992). *Chinese and English reading miscues of six Chinese graduate students*. Unpublished doctoral dissertation, University of Missouri, Columbia. (UMI No. AAC 93-27845)

> The roles of orthography and grammar systems in affecting the reading process in different languages seem to be limited to the degrees to which three language cueing systems (syntax, semantics, graphophonics) are used.

MARON, LINDA RAE (1992). *A comparison study of the effects of explicit versus implicit training of test taking skills for learning disabled fourth-grade students*. Unpublished doctoral dissertation, University of Wisconsin, Madison. (UMI No. AAC 92-31212)

> Pre- and posttest differences on miscues are noted though no differences are indicated between pre- and posttests using the Gates-MacGinitie test. A positive correlation between preprobe miscue and posttest Gates-MacGinitie is found.

NORTON, MARIAN, & FALK, IAN (1992). Adults and reading disability: A new field of inquiry. *International Journal of Disability, Development and Education, 39*(3), 185–196.

> Looks at the Australian development of literacy theory related to adults and presents two studies. The studies presented suggest that reading tests developed for use with children are of questionable value for use with adults.

OGLAN, GERALD RICHARD (1992). *Spelling growth: A transactive process*. Unpublished doctoral dissertation, University of South Carolina, Columbia. (UMI No. AAC 92-39075)

> Case studies of three grade 4 students' spellings and teachers' observations on spelling development. The range of strategies used is explored respective to writing experiences for different audiences.

POUW-BARTNICKI, ODETTE (1992). *Tutor-Tutee Interaction and their perceptions of the process of learning to read in a cross-age peer-tutored reading programme.* Unpublished master's thesis, York University, Toronto, ON.

> Grade 5 tutors working with second graders are found to use a variety of reading strategies. All relationships appear supportive and a relationship is found between what the tutors believe makes them good readers and their interactions with the second graders.

SAULAWA, DANJUMA, & NWEKE, WINIFRED (1992, November). *Application of language experience approach to reading-disabled special-education adolescents in a rural black school.* Paper presented at the Annual Meeting of the Mid-South Educational Research Association, Knoxville, TN. (ED 354 482)

> Case study of a 15-year-old finds language experience approach and miscue analysis play a role in the improvement in this student's reading.

SENIOR-CANELA, FERNANDO ARTURO (1992). *The effects of computer-based training with multiple theoretical perspectives on the analysis of cases of reading errors.* Unpublished doctoral dissertation, University of Illinois, Urbana-Champaign. (UMI No. AAC 92-36592)

> One hundred eleven college students are given examples of oral reading miscues and asked to interpret and suggest remediation. Their responses are categorized according to phonics, sight-word, or whole language perspectives.

SIMONS, HERBERT D. (1992, December). *The effect of repeated reading of predictable texts on word recognition and decoding: A descriptive study of six first grade students.* Paper presented at the 42nd Annual Meeting of the National Reading Conference, San Antonio, TX. (ED 353 543)

> Although miscues tend to be contextually appropriate, decoding skills are found to vary widely.

WHITMORE, KATHRYN FAYE (1992). *Inventing a classroom: An ethnographic study of a third grade, bilingual learning community.* Unpublished doctoral dissertation, University of Arizona, Tucson. (UMI No. AAC 93-10593)

> Miscue analysis is used in this whole language classroom for student evaluation and parent conferencing.

WORTLEY, BEATRICE (1992, July). *Literature and literacy: The 'real' book approach to children learning to read.* Paper presented at the 21st Annual Conference of the International Association of School Librarians, Belfast, Northern Ireland, United Kingdom. (ED 359 954)

> A historical review of the development of Britain's 'real' book approach to learning to read, tracing its roots from Kenneth S. Goodman's work in psycholinguistics to the contributions of Margaret Meeks, Liz Waterland, and others.

1993

ARCURI, GUY MATTHEW (1993). *Interpretation of the oral reading miscues of proficient and less proficient foreign language comprehenders based on the interactive model of reading: A study with third, fourth and fifth year high school Spanish students.* Unpublished doctoral dissertation, University of North Carolina, Chapel Hill. (UMI No. AAC 93-23981)

> Compares proficient and less proficient comprehenders, finding that the less proficient appear to use a bottom-up processing model.

BADON, LINDA CAIN (1993). *Comparison of word recognition and story retelling under the conditions of contextualized versus decontextualized reading events in at-risk poor readers.* Unpublished doctoral dissertation, The Louisiana State University and Agricultural and Mechanical College, Baton Rouge. (UMI No. AAC 94-05384)

> A context focus in instruction is found to be favored respective to decontextualized reading activities on seven measures that include: (1) fewer miscues, (2) with fewer miscues the rate of the rereading increases, (3) more story grammar components are included in retellings, (4) retellings include more episodes, (5) retelling length is longer, (6) retellings consist of fewer maze behaviors, and (7) more interepisodic relations are included.

CHINN, CLARK A., WAGGONER, MARTHA A., ANDERSON, RICHARD C., SCHOMMER, MARLENE, & WILKINSON, IAN A.G. (1993, June).

Situated actions during reading lessons: A microanalysis of oral reading error episodes. *American Educational Research Journal, 30*(2), 361–392.

> The context of reading errors is examined, finding multiple influences. Results of a microanalysis of 3,003 oral reading errors by 116 second and third graders supports the idea that the actions of students and teachers during error episodes are situated in social contexts, emerging in response to a dynamic interplay of factors that converge at particular moments. (See: ED 361 654)

CHUNG, IN-HO (1993, January). Comprehension of story reading by hearing impaired children using miscue analysis. *Japanese Journal of Special Education, 30*(4), 55–56.

> Looks at 35 hearing impaired children and 20 normal fourth, sixth and eighth graders using miscue analysis for Japanese.

CROWLEY, PAUL L. (1993). *Perceptions of the reading process and reading instruction held by selected children in five whole language classrooms.* Unpublished doctoral dissertation, University of Missouri, Columbia. (UMI No. AAC 94-12472)

> This study examines selected first- through fifth-graders' views of the reading process, their own reading behaviors, and their reading instruction in the context of a school in which the teachers attempt to implement whole language principles.

DAVENPORT, M. RUTH (1993). *Talking through the text: Selected sixth-grade students' metacognitive awareness of their learning and reading processes.* Unpublished doctoral dissertation, University of Missouri, Columbia. (UMI No. AAC 94-04958)

> In this study, miscue analysis of students' oral reading of a social studies text is examined as one of several data sources used to develop in-depth profiles of three participants as readers and learners.

EVANS, MARY A., & BARABALL, LESLEY (1993, March). *Parent child book reading and parent helping strategies.* Paper presented at the 60th Biennial Meeting of the Society for Research in Child Development, New Orleans, LA. (ED 362 258)

> Examines parents of 19 children, ages 5 to 7, their views, and how they interact with their children as the children read 4 storybooks for beginning readers. Finds that the parents have a bottom-up view of reading;

the parents suggest sounding out words but focus more on context clues with children who show poorer reading ability.

FERNANDEZ, EVELYN, & BAKER, SUSAN (1993). *Assessment portfolio, grades K–5, Two-way Spanish partial immersion program.* Arlington, VA: Arlington County Public Schools. (ED 364 079)
> Miscue analysis serves as one component in assessment portfolios.

HENK, WILLIAM A. (1993). New directions in reading assessment. *Reading and Writing Quarterly: Overcoming Learning Difficulties*, 9(1), 103–120.
> Presents the historical trends in reading theory. Looks at the new view of reading and the practices that it advocates.

HOLM, DANIEL THOMAS (1993). *The influences of a literature-discussion group: 'Remedial' readers and teacher-research.* Unpublished doctoral dissertation, University of Arizona, Tucson. (UMI No. AAC 94-21765)
> Used in evaluation of literature discussion participants, miscue analysis shows improvements for the readers.

LEMLEY, PATRICIA ARTHUR (1993). *Deaf readers and engagement in the story world: A study of strategies and stances.* Unpublished doctoral dissertation, The Ohio State University, Columbus. (UMI No. AAC 93-16188)
> Case studies of three readers between ages 12 and 14 include miscue analysis of readers' sign-alouds.

LESLIE, LAUREN (1993, January). A developmental-interactive approach to reading assessment. *Reading and Writing Quarterly: Overcoming Learning Difficulties*, 9(1), 5–30.
> Presents four developmental views of learning to read that follow an interactive model. Procedures relevant to each are described, such as oral reading miscues, reading rate, and comprehension in various contexts.

MALONE, MARILYN MAXWELL (1993). *Self-knowledge of oral reading pronunciation miscues among second-grade readers.* Unpublished doctoral dissertation, University of New Orleans, New Orleans, LA. (UMI No. AAC 94-31,698)

This descriptive study finds lower instruction level students have a higher awareness of their own miscues.

McWILLIAMS, JEAN ANNE (1993). *The influence of cultural schemata on the comprehension strategies of black and white students.* Unpublished doctoral dissertation, Temple University, Philadelphia, PA. (UMI No. AAC 93-32826)
> Compares 30 white and 30 black tenth grade students' reading of culturally familiar and unfamiliar passages. While strategy use is similar, whites perform better on culturally familiar than unfamiliar material and black students perform equally well on both.

PRICE, JANET, & SCHWABACHER, SARA (1993). *The multiple forms of evidence study: Assessing reading through student work samples, teacher observations, and tests.* NCREST Reprint Series. New York: Teachers College at Columbia University, National Center for Restructuring Education, Schools, and Teaching. (ED 372 366)
> Finds discrepancies between test results and what students do in the classroom, and suggests classroom based evaluation techniques like miscue analysis should be used.

YANISH, TAMI CHERYL (1993). *Exploring the comprehension monitoring of six learning disabled students.* Unpublished master's thesis, University of Alberta, Edmonton. (UMI No. AAC MM82101)
> Uses miscue analysis and students' comments about miscues to determine that readers are self-monitoring their comprehension in reading.

1994

CAMPBELL, ROBIN (1994, September). The teacher response to children's miscues of substitution. *Journal of Research in Reading,* 17(2), 147–154. (EJ492760)
> Longitudinal case study of teacher's responses to substitution miscues made by two beginning readers.

DAVIS, MARGARET BELL (1994). *An examination of the effect of meaning-focused prompts on student effort and achievement in oral reading.* Unpublished doctoral dissertation, University of Kentucky, Lexington. (UMI No. AAC 94-29,091)

> Studies how a teacher's efforts to focus students on self-correction behavior results in increased balance in cuing systems use and improved retellings.

GILLAM, RON, & MCFADDEN, TERESA U. (1994). Redefining assessment as a holistic discovery process. *Journal of Childhood Communication Disorders, 16*(1), 36–40. (EJ485025)

> Suggests and presents use of reading miscue analysis, holistic scoring, and dynamic assessment for portfolio evaluation.

MALONE, MARILYN M., & SPEAKER, RICHARD B., JR. (1994, April). *Analysis of second graders' self-knowledge of oral reading miscues.* Paper presented at the Annual Meeting of the American Educational Research Association, New Orleans, LA. (ED 375 379)

> Study of 41 second graders finds no significant linear relationship between self-knowledge of miscues and oral instructional reading level.

RUDDELL, ROBERT B., RUDDELL, MARTHA RAPP, & SINGER, HARRY (EDS.). (1994). *Theoretical models and processes of reading* (4th ed.). Newark, DE: International Reading Association.

> Collection of articles exploring the reading process, models of reading, and teaching and research issues. The fourth edition includes the most comprehensive Goodman model.

WEAVER, CONSTANCE (1994a). *Reading process and practice: From socio-psycholinguistics to whole language* (2nd ed.). Portsmouth, NH: Heinemann. (ED 367 962)

> Explores the influence of sociopsycholinguistics and how it informs whole language. Presents extensive examples of the use and implications of miscue analysis.

WEAVER, CONSTANCE (1994b). Reconceptualizing reading and dyslexia. *Journal of Childhood Communication Disorders, 16*(1), 23–35. (EJ485024)

> Challenges the notion that word perfect reading is a sign of proficient reading and if not met, then the reader is dyslexic.

1995

GOODMAN, YETTA M., & MAREK, ANN (EDS.). (1995). *Retrospective miscue analysis: Revaluing readers and reading.* Katonah, NY: Richard C. Owen.

> Case studies are presented of poor adult, good and poor middle school, and younger readers. Readers are able to express awareness of the reading process and benefit from meaning focused discussion.

MARTENS, PRISCA, GOODMAN, YETTA, & FLURKEY, ALAN (November, 1995). Miscue analysis for classroom teachers. *Primary Voices K–6, 3*(4).

> Articles by editors and other classroom teachers discuss the use of miscue analysis in classroom settings from kindergarten through fifth grade and in special education settings.

AUTHOR INDEX

186

Leyba, Rachel, 36
Li, Wei, 176
Lim, Hwa Ja Lee, 150
Lindberg, Margaret, 27, 56
Lindberg, Sharryl Ann, 150
Lipset, Corine B., 46
Lipson, Marjorie Youmans, 112
Lipton, Aaron, 20
Little, Larry J., 31
Liu, Stella S.F., 25
Llabre, Maria M., 144
Loeffler, Ruth Eddleman, 112
Long, Patricia C., 127, 144
Longnion, Bonnie Ownby, 113
Lopez, Sarah Jane Hudelson, 35
Love, Fannye Epps, 78, 102
Ludwig, Jay B., 25

M
Macaul, Sherry Lynn, 91
Machura, Shirley, 143
MacLean, Margaret, 78
MacMullin, M. Roderick, 91
Madden, Mable, 2
Maggs, Alex, 102
Magliari, Anne Marie, 162
Maguire, Mary H., 66, 163
Maher, Karen, & Christiansen, Janet, 93
Mahlios, Marc, 117, 132
Malicky, Grace V., 113, 155
Malik, Ali A., 167
Malone, Marilyn M., 180, 182
Mansfield, Susan, 136
Marek, Ann, 151, 183
Maring, Gerald H., 67
Marks, Nancy Louise, 128
Maron, Linda Rae, 176
Marsden, Fleur Sybil, 78
Martellock, Helen, 10, 16, 46
Martens, Prisca, 183
Martin, Elaine Russo, 113
Martinez, Rebecca Ann, 144
Martin-Wambu, Judith, 155
Maschoff, Janet Brandt, 163
Mason, Jana M., 46, 147
Mavrogenes, Nancy A., 57
McArthur, Janice Rae, 102
McCaleb, Joseph L., 56
McClellan, Jean Godsman, 128
McCormick, Sandra, 163
McCullough, Constance M., 2

McCullough, Michele Page, 103
McDaniel, Ruth Rogers, 120
McDonald, Barbara, 51
McEachern, William, 75
McFadden, Teresa U., 182
McGinley, William J., 154
McKenna, Michael C., 121
McKenzie, Moira Gwendoline, 31
McKinney, O. Davene, 26
McNaughton, Stuart, 67, 103
McWilliams, Jean Anne, 181
Meeker, Lorelei, 87
Menosky, Dorothy M., 15, 17, 46, 47
Meredith, Robert, 149
Merrett, Frank, 153
Meyer, Linda A., 144
Mikdadi, Mohammad Fakhri Ahmad, 136
Miller, Bonnie L., 36, 57
Miller, John W., 36, 47
Miller, Lamoine, 77
Miller, Lynne D., 121
Miller-Jones, Dalton, 164
Milne, Lynda M., 167
Miramontes, Ofelia, 136, 151, 167
Mitchell, Carol, 47
Mitchell, Katerine A., 67
Moir, Leo Hughes, 10
Monaner, Armando Humberto Baltra, 113
Monroe, Marion, 1, 2
Montoro, Catherine Buck, 47
Moore, Carol, 167
Moore, David W., 144
Moore, Sharon A., 144
Morgan, C.L., 3
Mosenthal, Peter, 48
Moss, R. Kay, 113, 122
Mott, Barbara W., 57
Mudd, Norma R., 137, 151
Mudre, Lynda Hamilton, 163
Murphy, Sharon M., 151
Mutter, Davida Warrington, 79

N
Nash, Marcia F., 127
Newman, Harold, 67, 114
Ney, James W., 36, 48, 58, 91
Ng, Seok M., 91
Nicholson, Tom, 79
Nickolaus, Charlene Willson, 103
Nicolich, Mark J., 109

SUBJECT INDEX

ADULT READERS

Wallace, Catherine (1990), 169
Ward, Annita Maria (1986), 147
Watson, Ken (1985, May), 140
Wilson, Marilyn (1983, March), 124
Wolfe, Vicki Trasoff (1981), 104
Zhang, Jian (1988, October), 159

AFRICAN-AMERICAN READERS
Bousquet, Robert J. (1978), 62
Cunningham, Patricia M. (1976–1977), 42
Johnson, Kenneth R. (1975, April), 35
Lamberg, Walter J., & McCaleb, Joseph L. (1977, April), 56
Liu, Stella S.F. (1973), 25
Paz, Darzell Strother Houston (1988), 156
Raisner, Barbara Koral (1978, October), 69
Sims, Rudine (1972), 21
Stice, Carole F. (1983, April), 122
Washington, Valerie M., & Miller-Jones, Dalton (1989, July), 164
Weaver, Constance (1983, February), 124

ALTERCUE CONTINUUM
Carey, Robert F. (1978), 62
Chatel, Regina Gryczewski (1986), 141
Page, William D. (1977, October), 58
Sadoski, Mark C. (1980), 92
Sadoski, Mark C., & Page, William D. (1984, October), 129

ALTERNATIVE MISCUE ANALYSIS
Aulls, Mark W. (1979, November), 73
Bean, Thomas William (1979, May), 73
Bromley, Karen D'Angelo, & Mahlios, Marc (1985, September), 132
Carter, M.J. (1983), 117
Centurion, Cesar Enrique (1985), 132
Chatel, Regina Gryczewski (1986), 141
Cokely, Dennis R. (1985), 132
Cunningham, James W. (1984, December), 126
Engels, Shirley Eunice (1981), 97
Goldsmith, Josephine Spivack, Nicolich, Mark J., & Haupt, Edward J. (1982), 109
Goodman, Yetta M. (1976b), 44
Griffin, Margaret, & Jongsma, Kathleen (1980, May), 89
Hoffman, James V. (1980, December), 89
Hood, Joyce (1978, December), 65
Kamil, Michael, & Pearson, P. David (1978, March), 66
Kuhns, Carolyn O., Moore, David W., & Moore, Sharon A. (1986, March), 144
Leslie, Lauren (1980, June), 90
Long, Patricia C. (1984) (1986), 127, 144
MacLean, Margaret (1979, November), 78
Malik, Ali A. (1990, March), 167
Page, William D. (1976, May), 49

Pumfrey, Peter David (1985), 137
Rhodes, Lynn Knebel, & Shanklin, Nancy L. (1990, November), 168
Rosenberg, Mimi (1986), 145
Sachs, Arlene (1984, May), 129
Sadoski, Mark C. (1981) (1985), 103, 138
Senior-Canela, Fernando Arturo (1992), 177
Southgate, V., Arnold, H., & Johnson, S. (1981), 104
Upshur, John A. (1972, March), 21
Woodley, John W. (1988), 159

AUSTRALIA
Anderson, Jonathan (1980, August) (1982, July), 84, 105
Cambourne, Brian (1977, August), 53
Driver, D.C., & Elkins, J. (1981, April), 97
Norton, Marian, & Falk, Ian (1992), 176
Pinson, Sharon Lesley (1982), 114
Pollock, John F., & Brown, Garth H. (1980, August), 92
Rousch, Peter Desmond, & Cambourne, Brian L. (1977, May) (1978), 59, 69

AUTHORSHIP. see Student authorship

BACKGROUND EXPERIENCE
Anderson, Dorothy Jean (1974), 28
Bettelheim, Bruno, & Zelan, Karen (1982), 106
Buck, Catherine (1973), 22
Cambourne, Brian (1977, August), 53
Crawford, Leslie W. (1982, April), 108
Dilena, Michael James (1979), 75
DuBois, Diane Marie (1977), 54
Goodman, Kenneth S. (1972, January), 19
Guzzetti, Barbara Jean (1982) (1984, September), 111, 126
Hocevar, Susan Page, & Hocevar, Dennis (1978), 65
Kita, Mary Jane (1980), 90
Lamberg, Walter J. (1975), 35
Lee, Lian Ju (1989), 162
Leenam, Wutti (1992), 175
Leroy, Carol (1990), 166
Lopez, Sarah Jane H. (1975)
Malik, Ali A. (1990, March), 167
McWilliams, Jean Anne (1993), 181
Mutter, Davida Warrington (1979), 79
Rousch, Peter Desmond (1972), 21
Stenroos, Carol J. (1975), 38
Swager, Christine Louise (1984), 129
Taft, Mary Lynn, & Leslie, Lauren (1985), 139

BASAL READERS
Ammon, Paul, Simons, Herbert D., & Elster, Charles (1990), 165
Goodman, Kenneth S. (1969d) (1986, March) (1987, September), 9, 142, 149
Gourley, Judith W. (1984), 126
Hodges, Marcella Jane V. (1986), 143

BILINGUAL READERS

BLIND READERS

CASE STUDIES

CHINESE READERS

CHUNKING

CLOZE

CODE-SWITCHING

COGNITIVE DEVELOPMENT

COGNITIVE STYLE

Scott, Edward, Annesley, Frederick R., Maher, Karen, & Christiansen, Janet (1980, August), 93

COHESION
Anderson, Jonathan (1982, July), 105
Australian Journal of Reading Editors (1985, March), 132
Freeman, David E. (1986) (1986, December), 142
Smith, Judith, & Elkins, John (1985), 138

COLLEGE READERS
Anderson, Valerie Karen (1992), 173
Brown, Susan Cohen (1980), 84
Chattiwat, Wisa (1990), 165
Curtis, A. Cheryl (1982), 108
Earle-Carlin, Susan E. (1984), 126
Henrichs, Margaret (1981, April) (1986), 100, 143
Hoffner, Dorothea R. (1974), 30
Leenam, Wutti (1992), 175
Longnion, Bonnie Ownby (1982), 113
Martin-Wambu, Judith (1988), 155
Mikdadi, Mohammad Fakhri Ahmad (1985), 136
Nieratka, Ernest Blair (1978), 68
Ohaver, Allan Roy (1971) (1972), 17, 20
Otto, Jean A. (1977, March), 58
Raisner, Barbara Koral (1978), 68
Shelton, Rosemary Riggen (1982), 115
Smith, Christine C. (1980), 93
Stice, Carole F. (1983, April), 122
Torres, Frank John (1980), 94
Wolfe, Vicki Trasoff (1981), 104

COMMUNICATION
Johnson, John R. (1983, August), 120

COMPREHENDING SCORES
Page, William D. (1977), 58
Sadoski, Mark C. (1985), 138

COMPREHENSION
Anderson, Gordon S. (1985, May), 131
Aspden, Kathryn Jane (1987), 147
Beebe, Mona Jane (1980) (1984, May), 84, 125
Chippendale, Ene Kaja Harm (1979), 74
Cram, Ruby Victoria (1980), 86
Dilena, Michael James (1979), 75
Dybdahl, Claudia S. (1982), 109
Eberwein, Lowell (1982, March), 109
Englert, Carol S., & Semmel, Melvyn I. (1981, December), 98
Goodman, Kenneth S. (1965, December) (1970b), 5, 13
Goodman, Kenneth S., & Buck, Catherine (1973, October), 24

COMPUTER-ASSISTED LEARNING

CONCEPTS OF READING

CONCEPTS OF STORY

CONTENT AREA READING

CONTEXT

CORRECTIONS

CRITICISM OF MISCUE ANALYSIS

CUE SYSTEMS. see also specific systems by name

CURRICULUM

Goodman, Kenneth S., & Page, William D. (1978), 64
Goodman, Kenneth S., Smith, E. Brooks, Meredith, Robert, & Goodman, Yetta M. (1987), 149
Goodman, Yetta M. (1982), 110
Goodman, Yetta M., & Watson, Dorothy J. (1977, November), 55
Guzzetti, Barbara Jean (1982), 111
Harste, Jerome C., & Carey, Robert F. (Eds.) (1979), 77
Hayes, Christopher G. (1980, March), 89
Hood, Joyce (1982), 112
Howard, C. (1985), 134
Jackson, Susan M. (1978), 65
Jurenka, Nancy Elizabeth Allen (1978), 66
Llabre, Maria M. (1986, March), 144
McArthur, Janice Rae (1981), 102
McClellan, Jean Godsman (1984), 128
Miller, Bonnie L. (1975), 36
Miller, John W., & Isakson, Richard L. (1976, April), 47
Milne, Lynda M. (1990), 167
Mutter, Davida Warrington (1979), 79
Nieratka, Suzanne (1973), 26
O'Brien, David Gerard (1984) (1988, September), 128, 156
Page, William D. (1975, December) (1976, May) (1979), 37, 49, 79
Pollock, John F. (1985), 137
Prentice, Walter C., & Peterson, Joe (1977, December), 59
Whitmore, Kathryn Faye (1992), 177

DEAF READERS

Anderson, Jacqueline Cheryl (1991), 170
Chung, In-Ho (1993, January), 179
Cokely, Dennis R. (1985) (1986, December), 132, 141
Ewoldt, Carolyn (1977) (1978, December) (1981a) (1981b) (1981c) (1981d) (1982) (1982, September) (1983, May) (1987, March), 54, 63, 98, 109, 118, 149
Ewoldt, Carolyn, & Garner, D. (1979, December), 76
Ewoldt, Carolyn, Frick, Charlene, Lewis, Leslie, & Walker, Elizabeth (1981), 98
Gupta, Abha (1991), 171
Knell, Susan Marcia (1981), 102
Lemley, Patricia Arthur (1993), 180
Yurkowski, Peter, & Ewoldt, Carolyn (1986, July), 147

DETERMINERS

Goodman, Kenneth S. (1983b), 119

DIAGNOSIS

Allen, Edward D. (1976, December), 39
Anderson, Gordon S. (1984, April), 124
Au, Kathryn Hu-Pei (1977, October), 53
D'Angelo, Karen (1980, March), 86
Dean, Sylvia Estelle (1991), 170
Feeley, Joan T. (1979, March), 76

DISCOURSE GRAMMAR
Deyes, Tony (1987, March), 149

DISSERTATIONS
Akural, Kathryn Rider (1979), 72
Allen, P. David (1969), 8
Allouche, Edith Kroo (1977), 52
Altwerger, Bess I. (1982), 105
Anderson, Dorothy Jean (1974), 28
Anderson, Valerie Karen (1992), 173
Andrews, Nancy Cunningham (1976), 40
Angel, Carolyn Lindberg (1981), 95
Antes, Carole A. (1984), 124
Arcuri, Guy Matthew (1993), 178
Arellano-Osuna, Adelina E. (1988), 153
Aslanian-Nemagerdi, Yeghia (1986), 140
Aspden, Kathryn Jane (1987), 147
Auteri, Violette T. (1979), 73
Badon, Linda Cain (1993), 178
Barber, Wilfred Clifton (1982), 106
Barket, B. (1983), 116
Barksdale, Mary Alice (1988), 153
Barrera, Rosalinda B. (1978), 62
Bean, Thomas William (1976), 40
Benitez, Diana (1984), 125
Bianchi, Anne M. (1980), 84
Bierman, Sandra Barrick (1992), 173
Bisagna-Villafane, Joanne (1985), 131
Blair, H. Lynn (1977), 53
Board, Peter Emile (1982), 106
Botthof, Richard Nels (1980), 84
Bourassa, Eileen Lee (1992), 173
Brady, Mary Ella (1979), 74
Brazee, Phyllis Ellen (1976), 41
Brophy, Nancy Ellen (1987), 148
Brown, Dorothy Lloyd (1984), 125
Brown, Susan Cohen (1980), 84
Bunney, Karen Sue (1987), 148
Burk, Barbara June (1981), 96
Burke, Carolyn L. (1969), 8
Button, Linda Jean (1980), 85
Carder, Mary Elizabeth (1974), 29
Carey, Robert F. (1978), 62
Carlson, Kenneth L. (1970), 12
Carwile, Nancy Ramsey (1990), 165
Cashen, Carol Joan (1980), 85
Cavuto, George John (1982), 107
Centurion, Cesar Enrique (1985), 132
Chang, Ji Mei (1989), 160
Chang, Ye Ling (1987), 148
Chapman, Marilyn Lesley (1991), 170
Chatel, Regina Gryczewski (1986), 141

Gonzalez, Teresa Artola (1983), 119
Goodman, Yetta M. (1967), 6
Greene, Barbara H. (1974), 30
Greene, Brenda M. (1988), 154
Gupta, Abha (1991), 171
Gutknecht, Bruce Arthur (1971), 16
Guzzetti, Barbara Jean (1982), 111
Hahn, Lois Blackburn (1985), 134
Hartle-Schutte, David (1988), 155
Hatt, Clifford Van (1981), 99
Haussler, Myna Matlin (1982), 111
Hayden, John Blair (1974), 30
Henrichs, Margaret (1986), 143
Hittleman, Daniel R. (1971), 16
Hobson, Charles David (1981), 100
Hodes, Phyllis (1976), 45
Hodges, Marcella Jane V. (1986), 143
Hoge, Glenda Sharon (1983), 120
Hollander, Sheila K. (1973), 24
Holm, Daniel Thomas (1993), 180
Honeycutt, Charles Allen (1982), 111
Howard, C. (1985), 134
Hughes, Delora Joyce M. (1985), 134
Hughes, Margaret Ann (1977), 56
Hurtado, Rosemary (1985), 134
Huss, Rebecca Louise (1991), 171
Hyman, Lethia (1988), 155
Jackson, Evelyn Weichert (1975), 35
Jackson, Sheila M. (1975), 35
Jackson, Susan M. (1978), 65
Jensen, Louise J. (1972), 20
Johnson, Rhonda S. (1987), 150
Jones, Ruth Ellen (1981), 102
Jung, Heshim (1992), 175
Jurenka, Nancy Elizabeth Allen (1978), 66
Kalmbach, James Robert (1980), 90
Kaplan, Elaine M. (1973), 25
Kelly, Nancy Jean (1985), 135
Kinder, Sandra Jeane (1989), 162
King, Dorothy F. (1980), 90
Kirk, Barbara VanDyke (1984), 127
Kita, Mary Jane (1980), 90
Kligman, Philip Simon (1983), 120
Knell, Susan Marcia (1981), 102
Koblitz, Courtland William, Jr. (1985), 135
Kolczynski, Richard Gerald (1973), 25
Lagbara, Maya Snowton (1985), 135
Lamm, Jill Simpson (1982), 112
Lasko, Theodore William (1985), 135
Laws, William Ernest (1979), 78
Lee, Lian Ju (1989), 162
Leenam, Wutti (1992), 175

Tchaconas, Terry Nicholas (1985), 139
Terdal, Marjorie S. (1985), 139
Thomas, Felton Augustus (1988), 158
Thomas, Keith John (1975), 38
Thomas, Sharon Kay (1980), 93
Thornton, Mervin F. (1973), 27
Tien, Su O. Lin (1983), 123
Torres, Frank John (1980), 94
Tortelli, James Peter (1974), 32
Traw, Rick Charles (1991), 172
Tumarkin, Sandra Rita (1980), 94
Turner, Gladys H. (1980), 94
Umansky, Barron Marsha (1984), 130
Vaught-Alexander, Karen Ann (1988), 158
Vogel, Susan Ann (1972), 21
Vorhaus, Renee Pool (1976), 51
Ward, Annita Maria (1986), 147
Watson, Dorothy J. (1973b), 28
Webeler, Mary Elizabeth (1984), 130
Weed, Floy Baughman (1980), 95
Weidler, Sarah Darlington (1985), 140
Whitmer, Joan Elizabeth A. (1978), 72
Whitmore, Kathryn Faye (1992), 177
Willekens, Mary Guerra (1979), 82
Winser, William Nelson (1991), 172
Wofford, Barbara Ann (1975), 39
Wolf, Anne Elizabeth (1978), 72
Wolfe, Vicki Trasoff (1981), 104
Wood, Martha Windham (1976), 52
Woodley, John (1983), 124
Young, Kelvin K.K. (1973), 28
Zamora, Norma Ibanez (1981), 104
Zinck, R. Ann (1977), 61

EARLY STUDIES

Artley, A. Sterl (1943, February), 2
Davidson, Helen P. (1934), 2
Freud, Sigmund (1965), 4
Iredell, Harriet (1898, December), 1
Madden, Mable, & Pratt, Margorie (1941, April), 2
McCullough, Constance M. (1943, April), 2
Monroe, Marion (1928, October) (1932), 1, 2
Morgan, C.L., & Bailey, Wilbert L. (1943, December), 3
Payne, Cassie Spencer (1930, October), 1
Reed, H.B. (1938, September), 2
Seibert, Louise C. (1945, April), 3
Thorndike, Edward L. (1917, June), 1
Weber, Rose Marie (1968, Fall), 7

EDUCATION. see Instruction; Special education; Teacher education

ENGLAND
Pumfrey, Peter David (1985), 137
Southgate, V., Arnold, H., & Johnson, S. (1981), 104
Wortley, Beatrice (1992, July), 178

ENGLISH AS A SECOND LANGUAGE (ESL)
Aslanian-Nemagerdi, Yeghia (1986), 140
Baldauf, Richard B., Jr., & Propst, Ivan K. (1979, October), 73
Buck, Catherine (1973), 22
Centurion, Cesar Enrique (1985), 132
Clarke, Mark A. (1980, June), 86
Crawford, Leslie W. (1982, April), 108
Devine, Joanne Mary (1980), 87
Dulay, Heidi C., & Burt, Marina K. (1974), 29
Earle-Carlin, Susan E. (1984), 126
Ellinger, Romona J. (1985), 133
Ellis, Rod (1980, July), 87
Folman, Shoshana (1977), 55
Freeman, David E. (1986), 142
Froese, Victor (1991, December), 170
Huss, Rebecca Louise (1991), 171
Jung, Heshim (1992), 175
Lamberg, Walter J. (1979, April), 77
Lim, Hwa Ja Lee (1987), 150
Malik, Ali A. (1990, March), 167
Miramontes, Ofelia (1987), 151
Mott, Barbara W. (1977), 57
Pantong, Bang O. (1990), 168
Parker, Margaret, & Barroso, Juan VIII (1986, September), 144
Renault, Louise Helen (1985), 137
Rigg, Pat (1977), 59
Samway, Katherine Davies (1988), 157
Shannon, Albert J. (1983, September), 122
Sherman, Nancy Jo (1982), 115
Stone, Ruth J. (1985), 139
Stone, Ruth J., & Kinzer, Charles K. (1985, December), 139
Terdal, Marjorie S. (1985), 139
Twyford, C.W., Diehl, William, & Feathers, Karen (Eds.) (1981), 104
Upshur, John A. (1972, March), 21
Wallace, Catherine (1990), 169
Wilson, Marilyn (1983, March), 124
Zhang, Jian (1988, October), 159

ENGLISH FOR SPECIAL PURPOSES (ESP)
Deyes, Tony (1987, March), 149

ERROR ANALYSIS

Anderson, Richard C., Wilkinson, Ian, Mason, Jana M., Shirey, Larry, & Wilson, Paul T. (1987), 147

Dulay, Heidi C., & Burt, Marina K. (1974), 29

Lipton, Aaron (1972, May), 20

ESL. see English as a Second Language

ESP. see English for Special Purposes

ETHNOGRAPHY

Huss, Rebecca Louise (1991), 171

McClellan, Jean Godsman (1984), 128

Shanklin, Nancy L. (1990, April), 169

Traw, Rick Charles (1991), 172

Whitmore, Kathryn Faye (1992), 177

EVALUATION. see also Assessment; Tests

Bousquet, Robert J. (1978), 62

Burke, Suzanne M., Pflaum, Susanna W., & Knafle, June D. (1982, January), 107

Cunningham, Patricia M. (1977, October), 53

DeFord, Diane E., Meeker, Lorelei, & Nieratka, Ernest B. (1980, March), 87

Donald, D.R. (1979, July), 75

Ewoldt, Carolyn (1982, September) (1987, March), 109, 149

Glenn, Hugh W. (1975), 33

Goodman, Yetta M. (1972, October), 19

Goodman, Yetta M., & Burke, Carolyn L. (1972), 19

Harp, Bill (1988, November), 155

Hittleman, Daniel R. (1980), 89

Hoffman, James V., & Baker, Christopher J. (1985), 134

Kibby, Michael W. (1979, January), 77

Llabre, Maria M. (1986, March), 144

Miller, John W. (1975), 36

Mitchell, Carol (1976, August), 47

Nieratka, Ernest B. (1973a), 26

Page, William D. (1973) (1975a) (1976a), 26, 36, 48

Prentice, Walter C., & Peterson, Joe (1977, December), 59

Price, Janet, & Schwabacher, Sara (1993), 181

Rothstein, Evelyn (1976, August), 50

Rousch, Peter Desmond (1976c), 50

Sadoski, Mark C., & Lee, Sharon (1986, March), 145

Shannon, Albert J. (1983, September), 122

Shapiro, Jon, & Riley, James D. (1989, January), 164

EYE-VOICE SPAN

Rode, Sara S. (1974–1975), 32

FRENCH READERS

Allen, Edward D. (1976, December), 39

Dank, Marion E., & McEachern, William (1979, March), 75
Honeycutt, Charles Allen (1982), 111
Maguire, Mary H. (1989), 163

GENDER
Burke, Elizabeth (1976, November), 42
Robison, Sybil Lewis (1971), 17
Schamroth, Marilyn Vine (1982), 114

GIFTED READERS
Stenroos, Carol J. (1975), 38

GOODMAN TAXONOMY
Allen, P. David (1976d), 40
Allen, P. David, & Watson, Dorothy J. (Eds.) (1976), 40
Burke, Carolyn L. (1976a), 42
Gollasch, Frederick V. (Ed.) (1982), 118
Goodman, Kenneth S. (1969a) (1976a), 8, 43

GRADE LEVEL
Bean, Thomas William (1978, June), 62
Beebe, Mona J. (1976a), 41
Bierman, Sandra Barrick (1992), 173
Brophy, Nancy Ellen (1987), 148
Brown, Dorothy Lloyd (1984), 125
Christie, James F. (1981, July), 96
McArthur, Janice Rae (1981), 102
McDaniel, Ruth Rogers (1983), 120
Otto, Jean A. (1978, November), 68

GRAPHOPHONIC CUES
Adkins, Treana, & Niles, Jerome (1985, December), 131
Allington, Richard L., & Strange, Michael (1977), 52
Allouche, Edith Kroo (1977), 52
Barket, B. (1983), 116
Gollasch, Frederick V. (1980), 88
Harris, Anne Gilleland (1976), 45
Kaplan, Elaine M. (1973), 25
Menosky, Dorothy M. (1976b), 47

GREEK READERS
Tchaconas, Terry Nicholas (1985), 139

HANDICAPPED READERS
Adams, Arlene (1986) (1991, January), 140, 169
Board, Peter E. (1974), 28
Brophy, Nancy Ellen (1987), 148
Brown, Virginia (1975, December), 33
Bunney, Karen Sue (1987), 148

HEBREW READERS

HISPANIC STUDENTS

Hurtado, Rosemary (1985), 134
Hyman, Lethia (1988), 155
Jurenka, Nancy Elizabeth Allen (1978), 66
Kirk, Barbara VanDyke (1984), 127
Lamberg, Walter J. (1975), 35
Miramontes, Ofelia (1985) (1987) (1987, December) (1990), 136, 151, 167
Ney, James W. (1977), 58
Renault, Louise Helen (1985), 137
Rivera-Viera, Diana T. (1986), 145
Rosenberg, Mimi (1986), 145
Silva, Aurelia Davila De (1979), 81
Stephens, Deborah Anne (1986), 146
Whitmer, Joan Elizabeth A. (1978), 72
Willekens, Mary Guerra (1979), 82
Williams, Linda K. (1979), 83
Young, Freda McKinney (1972), 22
Zamora, Norma Ibanez (1981), 104

HUMOR
Cheek, Dallas Henderson (1983, July), 117

ILLUSTRATIONS
Beveridge, Michael, & Griffiths, Valerie (1987, February), 148
Botthof, Richard Nels (1980), 84
Curtis, William J. (1968), 7
Knell, Susan Marcia (1981), 102

IMAGERY
Sadoski, Mark C. (1983, Fall), 121

IMMERSION
Dank, Marion E., & McEachern, William (1979, March), 75
Maguire, Mary H. (1989), 163
Williams, Linda K. (1979), 83

INFORMAL READING INVENTORIES
Bean, Thomas William (1979, May), 73
Gonzales, Phillip C., & Elijah, David (1978, December), 64
Hoffman, James V. (1980, December), 89
Johns, Jerry L., & Magliari, Anne Marie (1989, June), 162
McKenna, Michael C. (1983, March), 121
Page, William D., & Barr, Rebecca C. (1975), 37
Paterra, Mary Elizabeth (1976), 49
Smith, Laura A., & Weaver, Constance (1978), 70
Weaver, Constance, & Smith, Laura (1979, December), 82

INSERTIONS
D'Angelo, Karen, & Mahlios, Marc (1983, April), 117
D'Angelo, Karen, & Wilson, Robert M. (1979, February), 75

INSTRUCTION

Allen, Edward D. (1976, December), 39

Allen, P. David (1976b), 39

Anastasiow, Nicholas J., Hanes, Madlyn Levine, & Hanes, Michael L. (1982), 105

Anderson, Richard C., Wilkinson, Ian, Mason, Jana M., Shirey, Larry, & Wilson, Paul T. (1987), 147

Argyle, Susan B. (1989), 159

Armstrong, Mavie Elizabeth (1977), 52

Au, Kathryn Hu-Pei (1976) (1977, October), 40, 53

Baghban, Marcia (1982, January), 106

Board, Peter Emile (1982), 106

Buck, Catherine (1973), 22

Cooper, Charles R., & Petrosky, Anthony R. (1976, December), 42

Costello, Sarah A. (1992b), 174

Crawford, Leslie W. (1982, April), 108

Crowley, Paul L. (1993), 179

Cunningham, Patricia M. (1977, October), 53

Curtis, A. Cheryl (1982), 108

Dank, Marion E. (1976) (1977, June), 43, 54

Dasch, Anne Louis (1986), 142

DeLawter, Jayne A. (1975), 33

Denner, Peter R., McGinley, William J., & Brown, Elizabeth (1988), 154

Dokes, Marion A. (1987), 149

Elliott, Cynthia Margot (1979), 76

Ewoldt, Carolyn (1976), 43

Ewoldt, Carolyn, & Garner, D. (1979, December), 76

Ewoldt, Carolyn, Frick, Charlene, Lewis, Leslie, & Walker, Elizabeth (1981), 98

Froese, Victor (1977, March), 55

Fuller, Laurice Marion (1989), 160

Gates, Vicki (1973), 23

Glenn, Hugh W. (1975), 33

Glenn, June, & Glenn, Hugh W. (1978), 64

Goodman, Kenneth S. (1969, October) (1971a) (1972, March) (1973b), 9, 15, 19, 23

Goodman, Kenneth S. (Ed.) (1973c), 23

Goodman, Kenneth S., & Goodman, Yetta M. (1981) (1983, May), 91, 119

Goodman, Kenneth S., & Menosky, Dorothy (1971), 15

Goodman, Kenneth S., & Niles, Olive S. (Eds.) (1970), 13

Goodman, Kenneth S., & Page, William D. (1978), 64

Goodman, Kenneth S., Smith, E. Brooks, Meredith, Robert, & Goodman, Yetta M. (1987), 149

Goodman, Yetta M. (1970, February), 14

Goodman, Yetta M., & Burke, Carolyn L. (1969), 10

Goodman, Yetta M., & Watson, Dorothy J. (1977, November), 55

Hahn, Lois Blackburn (1985), 134

Hart, M. Murlee (1978, November), 65

Hatt, Clifford Van (1981), 99

Henk, William A. (1993), 180

Hoge, Sharon (1983, October), 120

Jensen, Louise J. (1972), 20

218

Haussler, Myna Matlin (1982), 111
Kita, Mary Jane (1980), 90
Lazarus, Peggy (1985, March), 136
Lee, Lian Ju (1989), 162
Marsden, Fleur Sybil (1979), 78
McClellan, Jean Godsman (1984), 128
Miller, Bonnie L. (1975), 36
Ward, Annita Marie (1986), 147

LANGUAGE EXPERIENCE
Ewoldt, Carolyn (1976), 43
Goodman, Kenneth S. (1971a), 15
Ramig, Christopher J., & Hall, Mary Anne (1980, March), 92
Saulawa, Danjuma, & Nweke, Winifred (1992, November), 177

LINGUISTICS. see also Psycholinguistics
Goodman, Kenneth S. (1964, April) (1968, April) (1969, April) (1974, November), 4, 7, 9, 29
Goodman, Yetta M., & Burke, Carolyn L. (1969), 10
Shafer, Robert Eugene (Ed.) (1979), 80

LISTENING
Hutson, Barbara A., & Niles, Jerome A. (1981, June), 101
Kirk, Barbara VanDyke (1984), 127
Weaver, Wendell W. (1962), 4

LITERACY
Goodman, Kenneth S. (1985, February), 133

LITERARY ENGAGEMENT
Holm, Daniel Thomas (1993), 180
Lemley, Patricia Arthur (1993), 180
Vipond, Douglas, Hunt, Russell A., & Wheeler, Lynwood C. (1987, March), 152

LITERATURE
Kinder, Sandra Jeane (1989), 162
Moir, Leo Hughes (1969), 10
Watson, Dorothy J. (1973b), 28

LONGITUDINAL STUDIES
Andrews, Nancy Cunningham (1976), 40
Brophy, Nancy Ellen (1987), 148
Brown, Dorothy Lloyd (1984), 125
Campbell, Robin (1994, September), 181
Goodman, Yetta M. (1967) (1971), 6, 16
Goodman, Yetta M., & Marek, Ann T. (Eds.) (1995), 183
Haussler, Myna Matlin (1982), 111

221

Goodman, Kenneth S. (1967a) (1968) (1969a) (1969c) (1970d) (1970, Spring) (1971b), 5, 6, 7, 8, 9, 13, 15
Goodman, Kenneth S., & Fleming, James T. (Eds.) (1969), 9
Goodman, Kenneth S., & Goodman, Yetta M. (1977, August) (1981, June), 55, 99
Pikulski, John J. (1976, April), 49
Shafer, Robert E. (1977, March), 60
Smith, Frank (1988), 158
Smith, Frank (Ed.) (1973a), 27
Smith, Frank, & Goodman, Kenneth S. (1971), 17
Weaver, Constance, & Smith, Laura (1979, December), 82

READABILITY
Baldwin, R. Scott (1977, April), 53
Hittleman, Daniel R. (1973, May), 24
Kibby, Michael W. (1979, January), 77
Lindberg, Margaret Ann (1977), 56
Moir, Leo Hughes (1969), 10
Smith, Laura A. (1976b), 51

READER SELECTED MISCUES
Hoge, Glenda Sharon (1983), 120
Watson, Dorothy J. (1978, December), 71

READERS. see specific types

READINESS
Crawford, Leslie W. (1982, April), 108
Wangberg, Elaine G., & Thompson, Bruce (1982, June), 116

READING AND WRITING. see also Concepts of reading; specific types of reading
Armstrong, Mavie Elizabeth (1977), 52
Currie, Paula S. (1986), 141
Denner, Peter R., McGinley, William J., & Brown, Elizabeth (1988), 154
Dybdahl, Claudia S. (1982), 109
Goodman, Kenneth S., & Goodman, Yetta M. (1983, May), 119
Greene, Brenda M. (1989c), 162
Harp, Bill (1988, November), 155
Hinnenkamp, Barbara (1991, January), 171
Horning, Alice S. (1987, March), 150
Kita, Mary Jane (1980), 90
Koblitz, Courtland William, Jr. (1985), 135
Lasko, Theodore William (1985), 135
Maguire, Mary Helen (1978), 66
Martin-Wambu, Judith (1988), 155
McKenzie, Moira Gwendoline (1974), 31
Ney, James W. (1975) (1980, August), 36, 91
Page, William D. (1974, September), 31
Rhodes, Lynn Knebel, & Dudley-Marling, Curt (1988), 157
Schneebeck, Judith H. (1987), 152

Stolworthy, Doriann Lenadine (1986)
Terdal, Marjorie S. (1985), 139
Vaught-Alexander, Karen Ann (1988), 158

READING DEVELOPMENT
Auteri, Violette T. (1979), 73
Beebe, Mona Jane (1976a), 41
Burke, Elizabeth (1976, November), 42
Dank, Marion E. (1977, June), 54
Goodman, Kenneth S. (1985), 133
Goodman, Kenneth S., & Goodman, Yetta M. (1979), 76
Goodman, Yetta M. (1971) (1976a), 16, 44
Goodman, Yetta M., Haussler, Myna, & Strickland, Dorothy (Eds.) (1982), 110
Rousch, Peter Desmond, & Cambourne, Brian L. (1978), 69

READING MISCUE INVENTORY (RMI)
Anderson, Gordon S. (1984, April), 124
Anderson, Jacqueline Cheryl (1991), 170
Anderson, Jonathan (1980, August), 84
Angel, Carolyn Lindberg (1981), 95
Artola-Gonzalez, T. (1989, July), 159
Blair, H. Lynn (1977), 53
Bock, Joan (1989, November), 160
Brady, Mary Ella (1979), 74
Brody, Deborah P. (1973), 22
Brophy, Nancy Ellen (1987), 148
Brown, Susan Cohen (1980), 84
Brown, Virginia (1975, December), 33
Cashen, Carol Joan (1980), 85
Costa, Ricio (1992), 174
Cuthbertson, Beverly J. (1979), 74
Dasch, Anne Louise (1986), 142
Dewitz, Peter (1977), 54
Dokes, Marion A. (1987), 149
Ewoldt, Carolyn (1982, September), 109
Feeley, Joan T. (1979, March), 76
Goodman, Yetta M., & Burke, Carolyn L. (1972), 19
Goodman, Yetta M., Watson, Dorothy J., & Burke, Carolyn L. (1987), 150
Hodes, Phyllis (1977, May), 56
Hood, Joyce (1975–1976), 34
Kalmbach, James Robert (1980), 90
Kolczynski, Richard Gerald (1973) (1986, June), 25, 143
Lazarus, Peggy (1985, March), 136
Lindberg, Sharryl Ann (1987), 150
Little, Larry J. (1974), 31
Long, Patricia C. (1986), 144
Maschoff, Janet Brandt (1989), 163
Miller, John W. (1975), 36
Paterra, Mary Elizabeth (1976), 49
Rivera-Viera, Diana T. (1978) (1986), 69, 145

Sadoski, Mark C. (1980), 92
Smith, Mabel Glover (1978b), 70
Weed, Floy Baughman (1980), 95
Williamson, Leon E., & Young, Freda (1974, July), 32
Wolf, Anne Elizabeth (1978), 72

READING PROCESS

Allen, JoBeth (1983), 116
Angel, Carolyn Lindberg (1981), 95
Beebe, Mona Jane (1984, May), 125
Beveridge, Michael, & Griffiths, Valerie (1987, February), 148
Bierman, Sandra Barrick (1992), 173
Burke, Carolyn L. (1972) (1975), 18, 33
Burke, Carolyn L., & Goodman, Kenneth S. (1970, January), 12
Busch, Robert F., & Jenkins, Patricia W. (1982, September), 107
Cambourne, Brian (1976–1977), 42
Carey, Robert F. (1983, September), 116
Chattiwat, Wisa (1990), 165
Cooper, Charles R., & Petrosky, Anthony R. (1976, December), 42
Dank, Marion E., & McEachern, William (1979, March), 75
Ewoldt, Carolyn (1978, December) (1981b) (1981d), 53, 98
Gollasch, Frederick V. (Ed.) (1982), 118
Goodman, Kenneth S. (1966) (1967a) (1968) (1970a) (1970, Spring) (1971b)
    (1972) (1972, January) (1972, March) (1972, December) (1973a) (1974,
    November) (1976–1977) (1976b) (1979, September), 6, 7, 12, 13, 15,
    18, 19, 23, 29, 44, 76
Goodman, Kenneth S., & Burke, Carolyn L. (1968, March) (1973, April), 7, 24
Goodman, Kenneth S., & Goodman, Yetta M. (1977, August) (1978, August),
    55, 64
Goodman, Kenneth S., & Niles, Olive S. (Eds.) (1970), 13
Goodman, Yetta M., & Goodman, Kenneth S. (1992), 175
Greene, Barbara H., & Watson, Marianne (1976), 45
Hayes, Christopher G. (1980, March), 89
Henrichs, Margaret (1986), 143
Kolczynski, Richard Gerald (1978), 66
Loeffler, Ruth Eddleman (1982), 112
Malicky, Grace V., & Norman, Charles A. (1988, December), 155
McDaniel, Ruth Rogers (1983), 120
Mosenthal, Peter (1976–1977), 48
Murphy, Sharon M. (1987), 151
Nicholson, Tom, Pearson, P. David, & Dykstra, Robert (1979, December), 79
Norman, Charles A. (1988), 156
Otto, Jean (1977) (1977, March) (1978, November), 58, 68
Page, William D. (1970b) (1975a), 14, 36
Rivera-Viera, Diana T. (1978), 69
Ruddell, Robert B., Ruddell, Martha Rapp, & Singer, Harry (Eds.) (1994),
    182
Sherman, Nancy Jo (1982), 115
Smith, Frank (1988), 158
Sowell, Virginia, & Sledge, Andrea (1986, December), 146
Swan, Desmond (Ed.) (1982), 115
Thomas, Keith J. (1975) (1978), 38, 71

Twyford, C.W., Diehl, William, & Feathers, Karen (Eds.) (1981), 104
Watson, Dorothy J., & Stansell, John C. (1980, March), 95
Weaver, Constance (1994a), 182

READING PROFICIENCY

Allen, Edward D. (1976, December), 39
Anastasiow, Nicholas J., Hanes, Madlyn Levine, & Hanes, Michael L. (1982), 105
Andrews, Nancy Cunningham (1976), 40
Cooper, Charles R., & Petrosky, Anthony R. (1976, December), 42
Dybdahl, Claudia S. (1982), 109
Goodman, Kenneth S. (1968), 7
Goodman, Kenneth S., & Burke, Carolyn L. (1973, April), 24
Goodman, Yetta M. (1976a), 44
Henrichs, Margaret (1986), 143
Sahu, Shantilata, & Pattnaik, Susmita (1987, January), 152
Silva, Fatima Sampaio (1977), 60

READING PURPOSE

Chatel, Regina Gryczewski (1986), 141
Deyes, Tony (1987, March), 149
Montaner, Armando Humberto Baltra (1982), 113
Tanner, Michael Lowell (1979), 82
Thornton, Mervin F. (1973), 27

READING RATE

Bunney, Karen Sue (1987), 148
Cokely, Dennis R. (1986, December), 141
Keith, Claire, Carnine, Douglas, Carnine, Linda, & Maggs, Alex (1981, March), 102
Smith, Christine C. (1980), 93
Thomas, Keith J. (1978), 71

READING RECOVERY

Peterson, Barbara L. (1988), 157

READING STRATEGIES

Aslanian-Nemagerdi, Yeghia (1986), 140
Au, Kathryn Hu-Pei (1976), 40
Bean, Thomas William (1976) (1978, June), 40, 62
Costello, Sarah A. (1992a), 174
Ellinger, Romona J. (1985), 133
Ellis, Rod (1980, July), 87
Goodman, Kenneth S., & Menosky, Dorothy (1971, March), 15
Goodman, Yetta M. (1976c), 44
Guzzetti, Barbara Jean (1982) (1984, September), 111, 126
Hayden, John Blair (1974), 30
Hollander, Sheila K. (1973), 24
Hood, Joyce E., & Kendall, Janet R. (1975), 34
Kozleski, Elizabeth B. (1989, December), 162

Kuhns, Carolyn O., Moore, David W., & Moore, Sharon A. (1986, March), 144
Lemley, Patricia Arthur (1993), 180
Milne, Lynda M. (1990), 167
Mudd, Norma R. (1987, June), 151
Ng, Seok M. (1980, August), 91
Oyetunde, Timothy O., & Umolu, Joanne J. (1989, November), 163
Pinson, Sharon Lesley (1982), 114
Pumfrey, Peter David, & Fletcher, J. (1989, September), 163
Reutzel, D. Ray, & Fawson, Parker (1991, June), 171
Schlieper, Anne (1977, December), 60
Sergent, Wallace Keith, Jr. (1990), 168
Stolworthy, Dorian Lenadine (1986), 146
Tchaconas, Terry Nicholas (1985), 139
Wangberg, Elaine G., & Thompson, Bruce (1980, November), 94
Watson, Dorothy J. (1973a), 27
Weidler, Sarah Darlington (1985), 140
Winser, William Nelson (1988, November) (1991), 159, 172
Wolfe, Vicki Trasoff (1981), 104
Young, Kelvin K.K. (1978, March), 72

READING STYLE
Stuart-Hamilton, Ian (1984, September), 129

READING THEORY
Akural, Kathryn Rider (1979), 72
Burke, Carolyn L. (1976a), (1976b), 42
Goodman, Kenneth S. (1969a), 8
Kling, Martin, Davis, Frederick B., & Geyer, John J. (1971), 16
O'Brien, David Gerard (1988, September), 156
Page, William D. (1974, September), 31
Powers, William (1983), 121
Willich, Yve, Prior, Margot, Cumming, Geoff, & Spanos, Tom (1988, November), 159

READING-WRITING RELATIONSHIPS
Goodman, Kenneth S., & Goodman, Yetta M. (1983, May), 119

REASONING
Thorndike, Edward L. (1917, June), 1

REDUNDANCY
Shannon, Claude E. (1951), 3
Weaver Wendell W. (1962), 4

REFLECTIVE-IMPULSIVE READERS
Hood, Joyce E., & Kendall, Janet R. (1975), 34
Hood, Joyce E., Kendall, Janet R., & Roettger, Doris M. (1973, February), 25
Ney, James W. (1980, August), 91
Readence, John Edward (1975), 37
Waltz, Pennie Alice (1977), 61

Carey, Robert F. (1983, September), 116
Donald, D.R. (1980, September), 87
Goodman, Yetta M., Allen, Paul David, Burke, Carolyn L., & Martellock, Helen (1969, April), 10
Martin, Elaine Russo (1982, December), 113
McKenna, Michael C. (1983, March), 121
Meyer, Linda A. (1986, November), 144
Niles, Jerome A. (1985), 137
Pikulski, John J. (1976, April), 49
Rupley, William H. (1977, February), 59
Shafer, Robert E. (1977, March), 60
Shuman, R. Baird (1984), 129
Wade, Barrie, & Dewhirst, Wendy (1983, February), 123
Weaver, Constance (1994a), 182
Weber, Rose Marie (1968, Fall), 7
Wixson, Karen L. (1979, June), 83

REVISION
Currie, Paula S. (1986), 141
Dybdahl, Claudia S. (1982), 109
Greene, Brenda M. (1988) (1989a) (1989c), 154, 161, 162
Hittleman, Daniel R. (1971), 16
Hittleman, Daniel R., & Robinson, H. Alan (1973) (1975, December), 24, 34
Mansfield, Susan (1985), 136
O'Brien, David Gerard (1984), 128
O'Neill, Irma Josefina (1988), 156
Samway, Katherine Davies (1988), 157

RISK TAKING
Dulay, Heidi C., & Burt, Marina K. (1974), 29
Dybdahl, Claudia S. (1982), 109
Goodman, Kenneth S. (1967a), 6
Levin, Harry, & Kaplan, Eleanor L. (1970), 14
Marks, Nancy Louise (1984), 128

RMI. see Reading Miscue Inventory

SCHEMA THEORY
Goodman, Kenneth S., & Goodman, Yetta M. (1981, June), 99
Leenam, Wutti (1992), 175
Rigg, Pat (1986), 145
Swager, Christine Louise (1984), 129

SECOND LANGUAGE. see also English as a Second Language (ESL)
Garcia, Georgia Earnest (1992), 175
Zuck, Louis V., & Goodman, Yetta M. (1971), 18

SECONDARY READERS
Arcuri, Guy Matthew (1993), 178
Cashen, Carol Joan (1980), 85

Dagostino, Lorraine (1981), 96
Driver, D.C., & Elkins, J. (1981, April), 97
Folman, Shoshana (1977), 55
Hayden, John Blair (1974), 30
Hittleman, Daniel R. (1977, May), 55
Hoge, Glenda Sharon (1983), 120
Kelly, Nancy Jean (1985), 135
Mavrogenes, Nancy A. (1977, May), 57
Miller, Bonnie L. (1977b), 57
Mutter, Davida Warrington (1979), 79
Otto, Jean A. (1978, November), 68
Tanner, Michael Lowell (1979), 82

SELF-MONITORING
Hoge, Glenda Sharon (1983), 120
Kozleski, Elizabeth B. (1989, December), 162
Malone, Marilyn M., & Speaker, Richard B., Jr. (1994, April), 182
Malone, Marilyn Maxwell (1993), 180
Yanish, Tami Cheryl (1993), 181

SEMANTIC ACCEPTABILITY
Carey, Robert F. (1978), 62
Keith, Claire, Carnine, Douglas, Carnine, Linda, & Maggs, Alex (1981, March), 102
Page, William D. (1976b), 48
Thomas, Keith John (1975), 38

SEMANTIC CUES
Altwerger, Bess I. (1982), 105
Beardsley, Gillian (1982, September), 106
Burke, Elizabeth (1976, November), 42
Feathers, Karen M. (1985), 133
Keith, Claire, Carnine, Douglas, Carnine, Linda, & Maggs, Alex (1981, March), 102
Ohaver, Allan Roy (1971), 17
Page, William D. (1976b) (1976c), 48
Rousch, Peter Desmond (1972) (1976b), 21, 50
Wangberg, Elaine G., & Thompson, Bruce (1982, June), 116
Weaver, Wendell W. (1962), 4
Yurkowski, Peter, & Ewoldt, Carolyn (1986, July), 147

SENTENCE COMBINING
Lamm, Jill Simpson (1982), 112
Ney, James W. (1976), 48

SHORT CIRCUITS
Clarke, Mark A. (1980, June), 86
Goodman, Kenneth S., & Goodman, Yetta M. (1978, August), 64

SILENT READING

SLIPS OF THE TONGUE

SPANISH READERS

SPECIAL EDUCATION

SPEED READING

SPELLING. see also Invented spelling
Clemens, Lynda Pritchard (1985), 132
Klein, Cynthia (1989, December), 162
Klumb, Kelly (1990), 166
McKenzie, Moira Gwendoline (1974), 31
Oglan, Gerald Richard (1992), 176
Parker, Connie MacDonald (1990), 168
Robison, Sybil Lewis (1971), 17
Salem, Lynn L. (1986), 145
Scibior, Olga S. (1987), 152
Tovey, Duane R. (1976, March), 51

STAFF DEVELOPMENT
Goodman, Yetta M. (1973), 24

STATISTICS
Hood, Joyce (1975–1976), 34
Murphy, Sharon M. (1987), 151

STORY CONCEPTS
Corliss, J. (1984), 126

STRATEGIES. see also Reading strategies; Writing strategies
Aslanian-Nemagerdi, Yeghia (1986), 140
Cambourne, Brian (1977, August), 53
Coles, Richard E. (1981), 96
Cooper, Charles R., & Petrosky, Anthony R. (1976, December), 42
DeSanti, Roger Joseph (1976), 43
Elliott, Cynthia Margot (1979), 76
Ellis, Rod (1980, July), 87
Goodman, Yetta M. (1976c), 44
Greene, Brenda M. (1988), 154
Kibby, Michael W. (1979, January), 77
Leslie, Lauren, & Osol, Pat (1978, December), 66
Malicky, Grace, & Norman, Charles A. (1982, May), 113
Mudd, Norma R. (1987, June), 151
Raisner, Barbara Koral (1978, October), 69
Ramig, Christopher J., & Hall, Mary Anne (1980, March), 92
Stockdale, Betsy S., & Crump, W. Donald (1981, September), 104
Stolworthy, Dorian Lenadine (1986), 146
Tanner, Michael Lowell (1979), 82
Wangberg, Elaine, & Thompson, Bruce (1980, November), 94
Watson, Dorothy J. (1973a), 27
Wilson, Marilyn (1983, March), 124
Yetman, Sheila Ann (1991), 173

STRATEGY LESSONS
Dokes, Marion A. (1987), 149
Goodman, Yetta M. (1970, February) (1975), 14, 34
Hoge, Sharon (1983, October), 120

Johns, Jerry L. (1975), 35
Love, Fannye Epps (1979) (1981, December), 78, 102
Smith, Brenda Vogel (1974), 32
Watson, Dorothy J. (1973a), 27

STRUCTURAL LEVELS
McKenzie, Moira Gwendoline (1974), 31
Sims, Rudine (1976a), 50

STUDENT AUTHORSHIP
Froese, Victor (1983, November), 118
Hodges, Marcella Jane V. (1986), 143
Sampson, Michael R., Briggs, L.D., & White, Jane H. (1988, March), 157
Thomas, Sharon Kay (1980), 93

STUDENTS. see Teacher-student interactions

STYLE
Mansfield, Susan (1985), 136
Moir, Leo Hughes (1969), 10

SUBSTITUTIONS
Allen, P. David (1969), 8
Allington, Richard L., & Strange, Michael (1977), 52
Beebe, Mona Jane (1976b) (1980), 41, 84
Carnine, Linda, Carnine, Douglas, & Gersten, Russell (1984, Spring), 125
Coomber, James Elwood (1971), 15
Cusumano, Joe Dennis (1986), 142
Englert, Carol S., & Semmel, Melvyn I. (1981, December), 98
Klumb, Kelly (1990), 166
Little, Larry J. (1974), 31
MacMullin, M. Roderick (1980), 91

SYNTACTIC CUES
Barket, B. (1983), 116
Burke, Carolyn L. (1969), 8
Christie, James F. (1978, June), 63
Clay, Marie M. (1968), 6
Ewoldt, Carolyn (1983, May), 118
Goodman, Kenneth S., & Burke, Carolyn L. (1969), 9
Johnson, Rhonda S. (1987), 150
Keith, Claire, Carnine, Douglas, Carnine, Linda, & Maggs, Alex (1981, March), 102
Kozachuck, Jean Karabin (1969), 10
Montoro, Catherine Buck (1976), 47
Nurss, Joanne R. (1969, March), 11
Ohaver, Allan Roy (1971) (1972), 17, 20
Rode, Sara S. (1974–1975), 32
Rousch, Peter Desmond (1976a), 50
Smith, Laura A. (1978), 70

Vogel, Susan Ann (1972) (1975), 21, 39
Weaver, Constance (1978, March), 71
Weaver, Wendell W. (1962), 4
Weber, Rose Marie (1970), 14

TEACHER EDUCATION
Allen, P. David (1972), 18
Allington, Richard L. (1978, November), 62
Burke, Carolyn L. (1973), 22
DeLawter, Jayne A. (1973), 23
Geissal, Mary A., & Knafle, June D. (1978, November), 63
Goodman, Yetta M. (1972) (1973), 19, 24
Hoffman, James V., & Baker, Christopher J. (1985), 134
Hoffman, James V., Gardner, C.H., & Clements, Richard O. (1980), 90
Long, Patricia C. (1984), 127
Ludwig, Jay B., & Stalker, James C. (1973), 25
Nieratka, Ernest B. (1973b), 26
Page, William D. (Ed.) (1975b), 37
Page, William D., & Carlson, Kenneth L. (1975), 37
Prosak, Leslie Ann (1980), 92
Scales, Alice M. (1977), 60
Terry, Pamela R. (1982, April), 115

TEACHER RESPONSE
Campbell, Robin (1994, September), 181
Chinn, Clark A., Wagoner, Martha A., Anderson, Richard C., Schommer, Marlene, & Wilkinson, Ian A.G. (1993, June), 178
Esselman, Birdlene (1978), 63
McNaughton, Stuart (1981, December), 103

TEACHERS
Davey, Beth, & Theofield, Mary (1983, June), 117
Goodman, Kenneth S. (1968, April), 7
Greene, Barbara H., & Watson, Marianne (1976, February), 45
Hodges, Richard, & Rudorf, E. Hugh (Eds.) (1972), 20
Knafle, June D., & Geissal, Mary Ann (1979, November), 77
Shanklin, Nancy L. (1990, April), 169
Steinruck, Yvonne Siu (1976), 51
Watson, Ken (1985, May), 140

TEACHER-STUDENT INTERACTIONS
Allington, Richard L. (1978, November), 62
Antes, Carole A. (1984), 124
Brady, Mary Ella (1979), 74
Campbell, Robin (1988) (1990, November), 154, 165
Cavuto, George John (1982), 107
Chinn, Clark A., Wagoner, Martha A., Anderson, Richard C., Schommer, Marlene, & Wilkinson, Ian A.G. (1993, June), 178
Cortez, Jesus (1980), 86
Cox, J. (1982), 107
Davey, Beth, & Theofield, Mary (1983, June), 117

TESTS. see also Assessment; Evaluation

TEXT ANALYSIS

THAI READERS
Chattiwat, Wisa (1990), 165
Leenam, Wutti (1992), 175
Pantong, Bang O. (1990), 168

THEORY. see also Reading theory; Schema theory
Baghban, Marcia (1982, January), 106

THESES
Anderson, Jacqueline Cheryl (1991), 170
Armstrong, Mavie Elizabeth (1977), 52
Beebe, Mona Jane (1976b), 41
Young, Freda McKinney (1972), 22

THINK-ALOUD PROTOCOL
Bierman, Sandra Barrick (1992), 173
Davenport, M. Ruth (1993), 179
Greene, Brenda M. (1989a), 161
Winser, William Nelson (1991), 172

THOUGHT PROCESSES
Swain, Emeliza (1953), 3

UNDERACHIEVING READERS
Davey, Beth (1971), 15
Mudre, Lynda Hamilton, & McCormick, Sandra (1989, Winter), 163
Piper, Carol Jean (1975), 37
Smith, Judith, & Elkins, John (1985), 138

VERBAL LEARNING
Chomsky, Noam (1959, January), 3

VYGOTSKY
Bock, Joan (1989, November), 160
Chinn, Clark A., Wagoner, Martha A., Anderson, R.C., Schommer, Marlene, & Wilkinson, Ian A.G. (1993), 178
Goodman, Yetta M., & Goodman, Kenneth S. (1992), 175
Johnson, John R. (1983, August), 120
Williamson, Leon E., Allen, Sue, & McDonald, Barbara (1976), 51

WEST-INDIAN READERS
Amorose, Henry Charles (1978), 62

WHOLE LANGUAGE
Bock, Joan (1989, November), 160
Goodman, Kenneth S. (1987, September) (1989, November) (1992, September), 149, 161, 175
Goodman, Kenneth S., & Goodman, Yetta M. (1981), 99

Goodman, Yetta M. (1989, November), 161
Goodman, Yetta M., & Goodman, Kenneth S. (1992), 175
Harp, Bill (1988, November), 155
Harp, Bill (Ed.) (1991), 171
Henrichs, Margaret (1981, April), 100
King, Dorothy F., & Goodman, Kenneth S. (1990, October), 166
Lim, Hwa Ja Lee (1987), 150
Moore, Carol (1990), 167
Thomas, Felton Augustus (1988), 158
Woodley, John W. (1988), 159

WORDS. see also Pronouns

Anderson, Valerie Karen (1992), 173
Biemiller, Andrew (1979, December), 73
Board, Peter E. (1974), 28
Brandt, Dorey (1976), 41
Brody, Deborah P. (1973), 22
Burke, Carolyn L. (1965), 5
Corliss, J. (1984), 126
Cox, J. (1982), 107
Davidson, Helen P. (1934), 2
Ehrlich, Susan F. (1981, June), 97
Ewoldt, Carolyn (1982), 109
Froese, Victor (1977, March), 55
Gonzales, Phillip C., & Elijah, David (1978, December), 64
Goodman, Kenneth S. (1965, October) (1967b) (1969b) (1983a), 5, 6, 8, 119
Goodman, Kenneth S., & Bird, Lois B. (1982), 110
Goodman, Kenneth S., & Gollasch, Frederick V. (1980) (1981), 88, 99
Hoffner, Dorothea R. (1974), 30
Hughes, Margaret Ann (1977), 56
Irwin, Joan M. (1969), 10
Kaufman, Maurice (1976, October), 46
Kot, Carol A. (1972), 20
Kozachuck, Jean Karabin (1969), 10
Leroy, Carol (1990), 166
MacMullin, M. Roderick (1980), 91
Maguire, Mary H. (1978), 66
McDaniel, Ruth Rogers (1983), 120
McKinney, O. Davene (1973), 26
Miller, John W. (1975, June), 36
Milne, Lynda M. (1990), 167
Mott, Barbara W. (1977), 57
Noseworthy, Randy Pittman (1990), 167
Nurss, Joanne R. (1969, March), 11
Page, William D. (1970a) (1971) (1976d), 14, 17, 49
Parker, Connie MacDonald (1990), 168
Payne, Cassie Spencer (1930, October), 1
Pinson, Sharon Lesley (1982), 114
Pouw-Bartnicki, Odette (1992), 176
Seibert, Louise C. (1945, April), 3
Sherman, Barry W. (1979, November), 81
Taylor, Barbara M., & Nosbush, Linda (1983, December), 123

Waltz, Pennie Alice (1977), 61
Weber, Rose Marie (1970, Spring), 15
Williams, Linda K. (1979), 83
Worsnop, Chris M. (1980), 95
Yanish, Tami Cheryl (1993), 181
Yetman, Sheila Ann (1991), 173

WRITING. see also Reading and writing
Ney, James W. (1977) (1980, August), 58, 91
Ney, James W., & Leyba, Rachel (1975), 36
Salem, Lynn L. (1986), 145
Samway, Katherine Davies (1988), 157
Schneebeck, Judith H. (1987), 152
Stansell, John C. (1981, February), 104
Stansell, John C., & Moss, R. Kay (1983), 122
Stolworthy, Dorian Lenadine (1986), 146
Vaught-Alexander, Karen Ann (1988), 158

WRITING DEVELOPMENT
Goodman, Yetta M. (1982, May), 110

WRITING STRATEGIES
Chapman, Marilyn Lesley (1991), 170
Currie, Paula S. (1986), 141
Denner, Peter R., McGinley, William J., & Brown, Elizabeth (1988), 154
Ewald, Helen Rothschild (1980), 87
Froese, Victor (1983, November), 118
Gespass, Suzanne R. (1989), 160
Greene, Brenda M. (1989a) (1989b) (1989c), 161, 162
Horning, Alice S. (1987, March), 150
Maguire, Mary H. (1989), 163
Mansfield, Susan (1985), 136
Martin-Wambu, Judith (1988), 155
Oglan, Gerald Richard (1992), 176

WRITING SYSTEMS
Koblitz, Courtland William, Jr. (1985), 135

WRITTEN LANGUAGE
Allen, P. David (1972), 18

YIDDISH READERS
Hodes, Phyllis (1976) (1977, May) (1981), 45, 56, 100